TURNER'S PAPERS

TURNER'S PAPERS

A Study of the Manufacture, Selection and Use of his Drawing Papers 1787-1820

PETER BOWER

TATE GALLERY

EXHIBITION AND CATALOGUE SUPPORTED BY VOLKSWAGEN

cover/jacket
'Distant View of London from Nunhead? with the sun breaking through stormy clouds', 1796–7
from the *Wilson* Sketchbook (detail) cat.no.16

ISBN 1 85437 049 9 paper
ISBN 1 85437 051 0 cloth

Published by order of the Trustees 1990
on the occasion of the exhibition at the
Tate Gallery: 10 October 1990 – 13 January 1991

Designer: Caroline Johnston
Photomicrography: Marcus Leith
Published by Tate Gallery Publications, Millbank, London SW1P 4RG

Printed on Parilux matt cream 150gsm and typeset in Baskerville.
Printed in Great Britain by Balding + Mansell plc, Wisbech, Cambs

Contents

Foreword

In 1988 Volkswagen offered to support two scholarships at the Tate Gallery to further Turner research. The first scholarship was awarded for one year to Peter Bower, a paper historian, and this publication presents the results of his research.

Mr Bower has used his scholarship to study the way Turner selected his paper to accord with his work and has discovered that the choice of material was always informed and deliberate, indeed that the paper was an integral part of the work and never merely a surface carrying an image. Turner himself, later in life, was to acknowledge his life-long concern with materials.

The accompanying exhibition gives a broad look at the subject and charts the developing relationship between the artist's techniques and the grounds on which he worked during the first half of his working life. Although based mainly on works in the Turner Bequest a few loans are also included. I should like to give special thanks to the private collector who so generously lent us 'Egglestone Abbey'. The display relies on photographic and textual explanation and we are grateful to Philip Miles for his solution to the presentation. I should also like to thank Peter Bower himself for the time and enthusiasm he has devoted to this project.

We are above all most grateful to Volkswagen and in particular, to John Meszaros, for having the imagination and generosity to support this unusual and fascinating project expanding, as it does, our knowledge of Turner's working methods. We look forward to our further collaborations in the future.

Nicholas Serota *Director*

Sponsor's Foreword

It gives Volkswagen enormous pleasure to be associated with 'Turner's Papers' – the exhibition and the catalogue. These represent the results of research by Peter Bower, the first of the Turner Scholars supported by Volkswagen.

The Turner Scholarships are offered by the Tate Gallery in association with Volkswagen for important new research related to the works in the Turner Bequest and are open to students from the United Kingdom proposing original topics in the areas covered by the Bequest.

The Turner Bequest comprises the works left to the nation by J. M. W. Turner and contains almost 300 oil paintings and nearly 30,000 watercolours and drawings, many of which have never been properly catalogued.

Peter Bower, the first scholar, is a paper historian and has been studying the manufacture, selection and use by Turner of paper for his drawings during the period 1787–1820. His findings will, I am sure, enhance our knowledge and understanding of Turner's work. Volkswagen offer him congratulations for his painstaking analysis and for the enterprise of his research results.

Volkswagen is also supporting research by other Turner Scholars who will in turn exhibit the results of their work at the Clore Gallery during the next two years.

Our thanks go to the Tate Gallery for all their help and encouragement.

John Meszaros
V.A.G. (UK) Ltd
Marketing Manager

Acknowledgments

It has been a great privilege to research into Turner's use of paper. Having the opportunity to explore one man's work on paper in such detail, particularly one of the most innovative and technically complex artists of all time, has been a fascinating challenge.

I should like to thank Nicholas Serota, the Director, and all those members of The Tate Gallery staff, from many different departments, who have made my stay at the Tate a happy and educational experience and who have been unfailingly helpful in furthering my understanding of Turner and his works during both the research and the preparation of this exhibition.

A great many people have very generously helped with encouragement, advice, practical help, information and criticism, throughout this research. I would like to thank Gwen Campbell, Julia Clarkson, Tom Collings, Henry Cooke Ltd, Michael Grey, John Hazell, Luke Herrmann, Lorraine Johnson, Clio Jones, Michael Kitson, Bruno Navarre, Eric Shanes, Peter Staples, David Wallace-Hadrill, Stuart Welch, Alan Witt and Whatman Ltd., and my colleagues in the British Association of Paper Historians, in particular Robin Clarke, Colin Cohen and Richard Hills.

I would also like to express my appreciation for the kindness and patience shown by the staff of many institutions: the British Library, Kent County Archives, the National Paper Museum at the Greater Manchester Museum of Science and Industry, Manchester, the Print room of the British Museum, the Patent Office, the Science Museum Library, the Whitworth Art Gallery, Manchester, and also Tony Woolrich who generously made available his transcriptions of the unpublished *Journals of Joshua Gilpin.*

My particular thanks must go to Marcus Leith for his photomicrography, to Andrew Wilton for his advice and encouragement and to my fellow Turner Scholar, Cecilia Powell for her unfailing kindness in answering so many questions relating to Turner, his life and working habits. I must also thank Andrew Wilton, Cecilia Powell and Conal Shields for their comments, advice and information during the writing of this catalogue. Any errors of fact or interpretation are of course my own.

But my greatest thanks go to my wife, Sally, for her patience while having to live in the late eighteenth and early nineteenth centuries amongst all the demands of the twentieth century.

Peter Bower

Introduction

First of all, respect your paper![1]

On being asked, late in life, for his advice on painting, Turner brought a lifetime of experience, years of both conscious and absorbed understanding to his deceptively simple reply. This exhibition attempts an introduction to the depths of that knowledge and experience and shows something of its complex evolution. With one or two exceptions, such as this remark, there is very little direct evidence of Turner's actual thoughts or feelings about paper in general, or the particular papers that he used, other than the papers themselves, where his actual use of individual papers is perhaps the most eloquent testimony that we could have.[2]

Any work of art on paper is in a very real sense an intimate object, meant to be seen close to. The actual interplay of the surface and the marks made on it is an integral, often crucial part of the actual visual effect of the work, though the importance of this does, to some extent, depend on the concerns and intentions of the artist. Subtle qualities of texture, tone and the actual three dimensional nature of any mark made on the surface are often ignored when examining a picture, though, in a purely physical sense, they are the work.

Given Turner's success in changing the very nature and range of watercolour and in increasing its stature as a means of expression, we need to know as much as possible about how the physical aspects of such changes were achieved: how he matched all his materials so vividly to his vision of the work in hand. We need to understand those qualities and characteristics of paper that were quite literally the ground for his success.

This exhibition surveys Turner's paper usage during the first half of his working life: charting the constantly developing relationship between his often very imaginative techniques and the grounds he worked on. It documents part of his complex responses to the rapid changes and increasing sophistication of the design and production of papers for artists. Turner's working life covered a period of great change in papermaking history: developments in new raw materials and production methods, and increasing competition from the newly developed papermaking machine, forced the handmade mills into an increased specialisation in order to survive. The production of papers specifically for drawing began sometime in the 1770s but was not to become a major part of the handmade paper industry until the early years of the nineteenth century.[3] Until this time 'drawing' papers, which included papers for watercolour as well as those for pencil, chalk and ink, were quite simply those papers which artists found they could work on, regardless of the use for which papermills had made them.

The research into Turner's use of paper during the first half of his career has consisted of a sheet-by-sheet analysis of specific details of the papers: watermarks, dates, wire profiles, colour and tone, sheet size, surface finishes, sizing, surface strength, bulk, density, opacity and fibre used, to discover some of the criteria that governed Turner's choice of papers, and to throw more light on the nature of both creative processes and his working methods. The first stage of the research consisted of an examination of watermarks, dates and paper sizes, which led to a much clearer identification of both individual papers, and types of papers used. This greatly facilitated the second stage of the research: the examination of the papers in respect of both actual historical papermaking practices and Turner's working methods. The main areas looked into at this stage were: the use the paper was originally designed for and the use Turner actually put it to; whether or not the paper was prepared in any way before use; and the relationship between the marks made and the surface of the sheet. The prime importance being what the paper itself has actually contributed to both the execution and expression of the various marks made.

As we delve further into Turner's complex development, and the growth of his aspirations and capabilities, his experience and understanding, it becomes increasingly obvious that very definite and particular choices of paper were being made. What might appear at first sight to be a fairly limited range of papers actually exhibit a great range of qualities and characteristics. He explored surfaces, exploited sizings and strengths, experimented with tones and colours, always learning. The paper is always an integral part of the work, from the slightest, speediest pencil sketch, to the most highly finished watercolour. It is never merely a ground to carry an image, perhaps not as obviously so as with his contemporary Girtin's use of heavy cartridge paper, but still as an effective and demanding presence.[4] Sometimes in the grey washed sheets, where the colour has been scratched away or scored off to give the original white as a highlight or detail, it is quite literally part of the work (see cat.no.32).

It takes a subtle and knowledgeable eye, an educated and experienced sensibility, not merely to make some of the choices that he made, but also to develop those choices, acting on the potential of that particular paper, especially with some of the sheets prepared with colour. Washing the surface of a sheet of paper can have the effect of slightly raising a 'nap' on the surface as well as very slightly increasing the surface strength of the sheet, by the addition of a further coating to supplement the gelatine already present. This is particularly effective if the colour wash is allowed to dry right out before the paper is worked on, which would be the case with the grey washed sheets taken with him on his first continental tour in 1802, and must also have been the case with many of the prepared papers taken to William Dickie for binding up into sketchbooks (see cat.no.38).

He had a sure understanding of the behavioural characteristics of many papers, particularly those that only reveal their real and vivid potential during use, such as surface strengths, tone and texture, and the degree and depth of sizing. He matched all his materials, techniques and subject matter, with a fine discrimination. But such skills are not completely instinctive. Whilst he did have an almost intuitive feel for his materials, he also learnt from his mistakes. In the two early unfinished watercolours on two different papers, from Stourhead (cat.nos.19 and 20) the paper of both has been overworked in certain areas of the sheet and left unfinished. These two works are both very good examples of the development of his understanding, where perhaps his intention was not quite matched by his actual technical prowess on the day. He had not quite realised the effect on the surface of the paper of the vigorous scrubbing he gave it in trying to achieve a particular effect of sunrise.

Before I began my research into Turner's use of paper for watercolours and drawings I had found it difficult to understand quite how he had achieved some of his effects, on papers that I knew, from earlier examinations, would, in many cases, not have been able to take some of the very vigorous handling techniques, of washing, scrubbing, and scraping, without considerably more break-up in the surfaces than appeared in the works that I had seen. I felt that it was a distinct possibility that some of the papers had been at least resized, and possibly resurfaced, before use. The research has shown that, with most of the works, this is in fact unlikely to have been the case; though there are one or two possible exceptions, where gelatine size has perhaps been used as part of a masking-out medium, (possibly developed from printmaking techniques) or may well have been added to the colour used to wash some of the prepared sheets. One possible indication of this is the way the rather coarse ground pigment has broken up on the surface of some of the early Whatman papers prepared for the first Swiss tour. The high surface strength exhibited in many of these sheets does not come from preparations given to the sheets by Turner, but actually derives from the fact that they were made as writing papers rather than as drawing papers.

Whilst the complete analysis of any particular artist's use of paper is ultimately a desirable goal, we must reconcile ourselves to only ever achieving a certain measure of comprehensiveness. Despite the lack of documentary evidence as to his sources of supply, or to his actual thoughts on particular papers, what we do have are the papers themselves and his complex pattern of use and experiment: papers that he worked on throughout his career; those he used once; those that he worked on only occasionally. We can also compare the papers he used with those papers that were available to him, but which he never used. The nature of the marks he made, whether with chalk, pencil, pen and ink, or watercolour and bodycolour, in relationship to the surface, can give us real criteria to judge what conditioned his choice of paper for particular purposes. The internal evidence shows a deep and growing understanding of the place of the ground in his images, of what would work for him in very precise ways.

This is not to say that Turner was engaged in a particularly conscious research programme into the capabilities of various surfaces under the varying demands placed on them by certain uses. Quite simply he was an artist, working in his own way, deeply involved in his own concerns, of which paper and its potentials were only a small part. The collection of all such data on the physical nature of works is not an end in itself but is important in terms of our increased understanding of this most technically complex artist.

It would be of inestimable value if those working in all the different fields concerned with works of art on paper, would actually record and publish the watermarks existing in those works. In the case of those works, by Turner, outside the Turner Bequest, one occasionally faces the situation where the existence of any watermarks in a particular collection of Turners is not acknowledged at all, even denied, and yet watermarks are clearly visible in some of them, with the naked eye, under no special conditions. Watermarks in themselves often cannot tell us much, but in conjunction with the condition, size, texture and sizing of the sheet can be most informative. Given the differing nature of particular papers, and the varying conditions under which they can be viewed, it is not surprising when some marks are missed, particularly when pictures are framed up or backed. It would generally be most helpful if such records could be made. The works outside the Turner Bequest are after all, for the most part, the 'finished' works, those that Turner sold. It would be of great interest to discover the nature of that usage, and whether the incidence of particular papers, or makers, or types of surface and sizing, is similar to that found in the Turner Bequest, or whether it differs, and if so, how?

The bulk of the works in the Turner Bequest did not go for sale, and the details of these papers may not accurately reflect Turner's preferences for those works that left his studio. Just under half the works in this exhibition were executed on papers designed for writing on, just under a quarter on papers designed for drawing, with printing and wrapping papers making up about another quarter, leaving a few sheets whose original purpose is still uncertain. This proportion reflects the designed use of the papers in the Turner Bequest, up to 1820.

1 The advice given to Mary Lloyd and recollected by her in 'A Memoir of J.M.W. Turner, R.A. by 'M.L.', reproduced in *Turner Studies* Vol. 4 No.1 p.22 and 23, also included 'Keep your corners quiet' and 'Centre your Interest.'

2 There are few annotations in Turner's hand, amongst the works in the Turner Bequest, that relate to paper. Cat.nos.54 and 55 deal with two such annotations, relating to possible origins for particular papers. Another annotation is the simple description 'Demy' on a drawing TB LXXX H, connected with the first Swiss tour. It is possible that Turner wrote this paper's size on it because Demy was a size which varied tremendously, from mill to mill, maker to maker, and in some cases was almost indistinguishable from the size called Medium. Much depends on the use the paper was intended for. Writing Demy was made approximately $19\frac{1}{2} \times 15\frac{1}{4}$in. Printing Demy varied from $19\frac{1}{4} \times 21\frac{1}{4}$in to $17 \times 22\frac{1}{2}$in, (sometimes called Medium). Drawing Demy was made in sizes from $15\frac{1}{2} \times 20$ up to 18×23 (also known as Medium) and Wrapping Demy around 18×24. It would appear that from its size, and by its surface, TB LXXX H was a writing paper.

3 One area of the making of artists' papers which had already seen considerable progress in the eighteenth century was the development of fine printing papers for engravings. This had come about in response to demands from printers such as Basire and the needs of The Society of Antiquaries, who desired both particular characteristics and quality in their printing papers. Throughout the earlier part of the century most plates had been printed on French made papers, particularly those of the Auvergne, where the whiteness and soft strength of the sheet had given a very fine definition to the engraved mark. The various wars with France during the eighteenth century, when supplies of these French-made papers became impossible to obtain, coupled with the gradual development of an English Fine Paper industry, had led to an increased demand for home-produced papers.

4 Cartridge paper, as its name implies, was originally developed for wrapping powder and shot, but its hard sized strength and rugged surface soon led to it being used as a general wrapping paper. Artists were attracted to both its strength and versatility and its warm off-white or pale buff tones.

Catalogue

Unless otherwise stated, all works are by J.M.W. Turner.

Where it has been possible, the original sheet size and folding arrangement of sketchbooks has been indicated. Where several sketchbooks, with different measurements, have been given the same paper size descriptions, the differences in measurement are the result of different folding and trimming patterns. Similarly, sketchbooks with the same measurements but described as having come from different paper sizes, are also the result of trimming and folding patterns.

Where possible, the original designed use of the paper has been indicated.

Quotations from contemporary accounts are given in their original spelling and punctuation.

All measurements are given in millimetres, followed by inches, height before width. It must be stressed, however, that a better understanding of the scale and proportions of particular papers can be achieved using the traditional measures. All the English hand-made papers used by Turner, during this period, were made in inches, and, for the most part, the continental papers were also made in traditional measurements.

Paper and its Making (cat.nos.1–7)

The paper that Turner worked on, with few exceptions, mostly later in his career, was all made by hand: laborious and demanding work, patiently forming sheet after sheet, building ream upon ream. Some of the individual quality and character of hand-made paper derives from this long and arduous process, for at every stage the maker is directly and physically involved, with the materials, processing and design of the paper. The maker shows in the rich, warm and infinitely variable tones, weights, texture, and performance of each individual sheet.

THE RAW MATERIALS AND THEIR PREPARATION

The basis of all paper is cellulose fibre, derived from plants. In the western European tradition of papermaking such cellulose was rarely derived directly from the plant, but indirectly, from the waste of our culture, from materials past their useful life such as old rags, ropes, sailcloth and sacking. Whatever the precise raw materials used, all paper is made by breaking down vegetable matter into individual cellulose fibres and washing out the non cellulose matter present. These fibres are then held in solution in water and rearranged into thin flat sheets. In making handmade paper, a sieve-like mould is dipped into this solution and pulled out, allowing the excess water to drain through the wire, leaving the pulp on the surface of the mould.[1]

Most of the papers used by Turner, early in his career, were made from linen rag fibre, with some hemp from ropes and sailcloth. But no industry works in isolation and the invention of Arkwright's Cotton Gin, in 1793, led to the wide availability in England of cotton clothing and materials, which, as rags, would eventually filter through to papermakers a few years later. Both linen and hemp are very versatile fibres, capable of being developed into many kinds of paper. Cotton proved to be less versatile, despite its general availability, and indeed was to cause considerable problems to both papermakers and users of paper in the first quarter of the nineteenth century.[2]

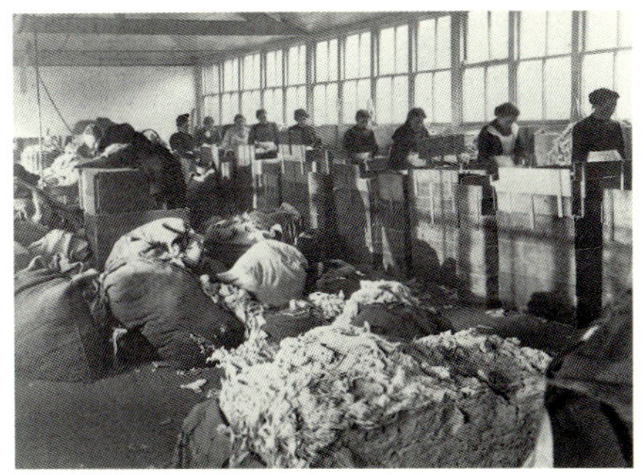

fig.1 The Rag Room, Springfield Mill, 1906, *Whatman Ltd*

The rags were sorted by women, who possibly had one of the worst jobs ever invented. The rags arrived in all sorts of conditions. They had to be sorted and checked for colour and quality, and unwanted buttons, fasteners and other rubbish removed. Leaving just one button in a batch of rags could mean blighting a whole batch of paper. As the rags were beaten, the button would be crushed to a fine powder, producing thousands of tiny particles that would disfigure every sheet.[3]

The rags were often filthy and needed considerable washing. It could be very unpleasant working with them: they often stank and handling them produced a very fine dust that could settle on the lungs, giving rise to serious illness. Sometimes the rags would actually carry infectious diseases. After the rags were sorted and 'dusted', to remove any loose dirt, they would be cut into small squares, by pulling the cloth towards one, against the blade of a very sharp knife fitted into a wooden bench top.

In the late eighteenth century, rags were generally sorted into five categories, from 'superfine', the best and cleanest linen for writing papers, down to the coarsest bagging, coloured rags and old ropes, all mixed up and unsorted, used in wrapping papers. Gradually the coding of rags became more and more complex, partly owing to the increasingly particular papers that the mills were making. By the middle of the nineteenth century some rag merchants were sorting their wares into as many as fifty categories.

Before the introduction of the beater, rags were fermented to facilitate the breaking down of the fibre. Rees describes the process thus:

> The rags being sorted, are put into a large stone vat, . . . water is poured on them to the top during ten days, and eight or ten times every day without stirring them. They are afterwards left to rest, the same number of days, and sometimes more or less, without pouring water on them. Then being turned over, the centre is brought to the surface, to facilitate the fermentation; and after being turned again, they are still left fifteen or twenty days in fermentation, so that the rotting may last five or six weeks; the term is not fixed, but when the heat becomes so great, that the hand, thrust in, cannot endure it above some seconds, it is judged that it is time to stop it. . . . When champignons grow on the heaps of rags, it is reckoned to be a sign of their being well rotted.[4]

Much of the rich and beautiful variety of white and off-white tones found in European papers over the centuries had come from the different degrees of fermentation given to different qualities of rags. When the hollander beater superseded stampers for pulp preparation, the fermentation process began to die out. The mills found that boiling the rags under pressure softened them sufficiently for beating.

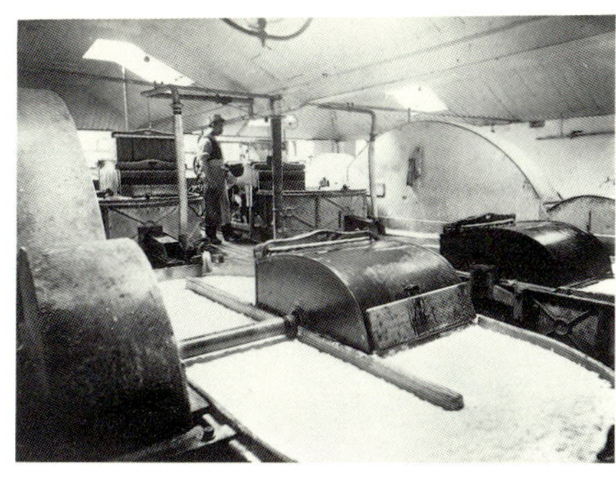

fig.2 The Beater Floor, Springfield Mill, 1906, *Whatman Ltd*

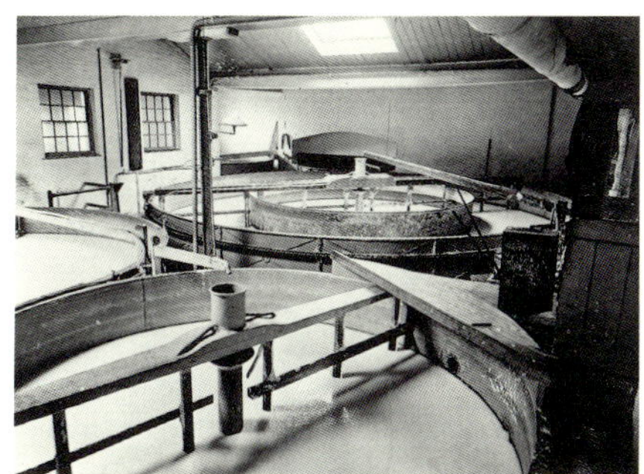

fig.3 Stuff Chests, Springfield Mill, 1906, *Whatman Ltd*

BEATING

The Hollander beater consists of an oval trough, divided in the middle by a wall, and having a heavy roll placed midway down one side of the trough. The rags are loaded into the trough and water is added. The roll, which has a series of bars all around it, is powered[5] and rotates. As the roll 'travels' it passes over a barred bed plate positioned underneath it, pushing the fibrous material around the trough. The quality, behavioural characteristics, and durability of the finished paper, depend to a great extent on the treatment of the fibres during the beating process.

Rag fibres, after boiling and washing, are still largely bits of woven fabric, and require a fairly drastic and long breaking treatment. The breaker, a form of Hollander with a different arrangement of bars, crushes and grinds the rags so that the original weave of the fabric is lost. Some preliminary beating can be done in the breaker but there is a danger of over-breaking the fibres. If they are shortened too much there will be a loss of strength in the finished sheet. For the finest papers the fibre should be left as long as possible, so that the strength and appearance of the fibre can be developed as much as possible in the beating.[6]

The object of beating is not just to separate the individual fibres, but to develop their potential, so that they will take up water and, by the gradual break-up of their outer layers, increase in surface area and flexibility. The great range of qualities that different papers possess derives from the structure of cellulose. Most of the cellulose present in the fibre is linked, via complex chemical changes, into long chain-like structures which are aligned fairly regularly, giving the fibre great stability and tensile strength. The flexibility of the fibre comes from the varying amounts of amorphous cellulose also present, which help in the absorbtion of water and the swelling of the fibre during beating.

Whilst part of the strength, and some of the final character of any paper, comes from the actual entangling of the fibres during the formation of the sheet, the main cause of coherence and strength is chemical rather than mechanical, and takes effect as the paper dries. As the fibres shrink they give up the water taken up during beating: more and more of the fibres are brought into actual contact with each other, and where they touch, a process known as hydrogen bonding, takes place. The greater the area of contact between fibres, the greater the amount of bonding that can occur. The greater the bonding, the stronger the sheet will be.[7]

The fibres are formed of extremely fine strands, bundled together in fibrils. In the early stages of beating the fibres become more flexible and the fibrils loosen. As the beater roll is lowered, getting closer and closer to the bed plate, the fibres are caught, crushed, bruised and cut. Some fibrils break away, some begin to break up, and they all hydrate, taking up more and more water. This increasing fibrillation leads to what is known as a 'wet' pulp, that feels somewhat greasy to the touch. Wet pulp has the advantage of draining more slowly on the mould giving the vatman more time to form the sheet.

Rag beating can never be reduced to a set of rules, times or techniques. The rags vary in condition, the papers to be made need different properties, temperature and humidity vary, and each beater has its own idiosyncracies, such as the age and condition of the bars on the roll and the bedplate, and the alignment of the roll in its bearings. Making pulp demands a fine personal judgement and much skill in handling the equipment. The traditional beaterman's method of testing the condition of the pulp as it is being beaten is to dip one's hand into the pulp, remove a small amount and gently squeeze it through the fingers. The amount of slipperiness, or greasiness, will tell you how well the fibre has taken up water during the beat, and also give a sense of the length of the fibres. Repeating this simple act throughout the course of the beat tells one, almost without conscious effort, of the progressive shortening of the fibre and its changing state. It is also possible to listen to the beating as it takes place. By placing a metal bar on the end of the plate, putting one's thumb over the end of the rod, and one's ear to the thumb, you can amplify the sound of the beater roll, and hear every roll bar as it passes over the bed plate.

The skill in beating comes from years of working with the same equipment and knowing its nature and limitations. It is fascinating that Turner, in many cases, continues to use papers from the same mill, regardless of changes in ownership. This could partly be because his suppliers continued to buy in from their usual sources, but has more to do with the continuity of experience amongst the actual workforce of the mill, which would have remained, regardless of any changes in ownership. Turner would not have continued to use papers that did not satisfy the demands he made of them.[8] (see cat.no.8 and the introduction to the Italian Tour of 1819–1820)

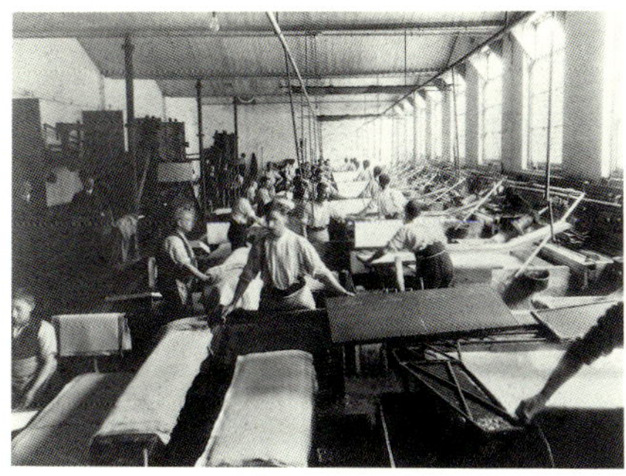

fig.4 The Vat Room, Springfield Mill, 1906, *Whatman Ltd*

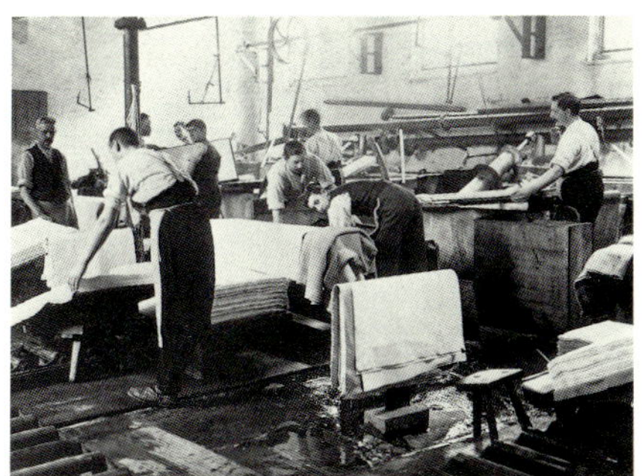

fig.5 The Vat Crew, Springfield Mill, 1906, *Whatman Ltd*

THE VAT ROOM

The vatman forms the paper, sheet by sheet, using a mould and deckle (see cat.nos. 1 and 2). A practised vatman makes forming the a sheet look deceptively easy, but his craft takes years to master. The crew have to cope with the heat of the vat, the constant dampness and the strain of continually stooping. For the vatman in particular, great practice and endurance are necessary to learn and then maintain the monotonous repetition of movements that ensure that the sheets produced are consistent, not just in their weight, but in their actual formation, so that the finished papers in any one batch all match the original specification, and all behave in the same way when in use.

To form a sheet, the vatman takes up more pulp than is needed and by shaking the mould away from him, 'throws' the excess pulp off the far side of the mould, sending a wave running across its surface. The mould is then shaken sideways, sending another wave to 'close' the sheet, interlocking the fibres and orientating them in every direction. This helps to increase the strength of the sheet. The dipping of the mould and the 'shake' form one action, and it has to be done fast: the excess water begins to drain through the wire mould cover as soon as the mould has broken the surface of the vat. The thickness of the sheet is determined by the consistency of the pulp in the vat, the depth of the deckle and above all, the skill of the vatman. Even today, there is no machine that can duplicate the 'shake' of a good vatman. It is not just a question of the even and consistent formation of the sheets,

> The dipper should be attentive, in distributing the matter on the mould, to reinforce the corner the coucher is to take hold of, in raising and extending the sheets; for without this precaution he would break a great many.[9]

The vatman removes the deckle and slides the mould up onto the 'ass', a curved bar protuding from the far left corner of the vat, where the mould rests for a moment or two before being taken up by the next member of the vat's crew, the 'coucher'. The vatman then places the deckle on a second mould and makes another sheet.[10]

The job of the 'coucher' (the name comes from the French *coucher* to lay down) is to transfer the newly formed sheet from the mould onto a wet woven blanket, known as a 'felt'. He lifts the mould from the ass where it has been draining, and carefully places its bottom edge along the edge of the felt, and with an even rolling motion, presses the mould down onto the felt and off again, leaving the wet sheet behind. The coucher passes the mould back to the vatman, lays down another felt on top of the sheet that he has just couched, takes up the mould and sheet that the vatman has just formed, and couches it, building a pile of felts and paper, known as a 'post'. When the post is complete, it is rolled away to the press and the crew begin another post.

Some of the faults that occur during formation and couching, such as 'tears', differences in thickness across areas of the sheet, wild look-through, air bubbles, folded corners and edges, can be very useful in determining whether or not two individual pieces of paper were ever once part of the same sheet. One can often follow the fault across the cut or torn edges, or through the pages of a bound book. In most instances none of them would particularly detract from the actual working surface of the sheet. Those that were really bad would never leave the mill, but be repulped.[11]

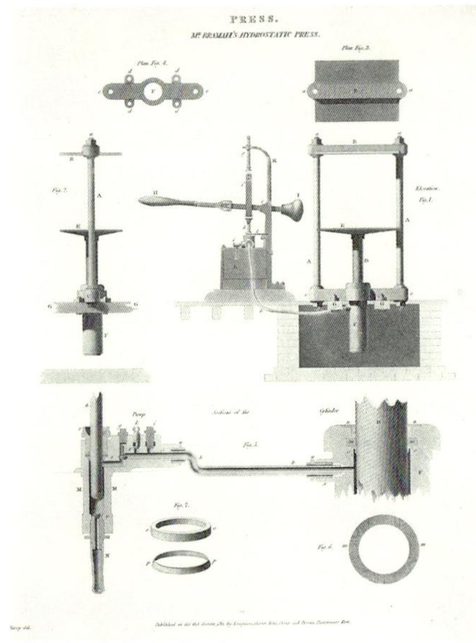

fig.6 Mr Bramah's Hydrostatic Press, Engraving

The functions of pressing are to remove as much water from the sheets as possible before drying, and to help compact the fibres, in order to increase the amount of hydrogen bonding that can take place, to ensure a strong sheet. The felts play a very important part in this process:

> The stuff of which the felts are made should be sufficiently strong, in order that it may be stretched exactly on the sheets, without falling into folds, and at the same time sufficiently pliant to yield in any direction, without injury to the wet paper. As the felts have to resist the reiterated efforts of the press, it appears necessary that the warp be made strong, of combed wool and well twisted. On the other hand, as they have to imbibe a certain quantity of water, and to retain it, it is necessary that the woof be of carded wool, and drawn out into a slack thread.[12]

At the beginning of the nineteenth century presses were undergoing considerable changes. The capstan and screw presses (see cat.nos. 3 and 5) were gradually beginning to be replaced by Joseph Bramah's newly invented 'Hydrostatic' (or hydraulic) press.[13] The greatly increased power of the new presses placed even more importance on the making of the felts. The strong and particular weave ensured that the textures they produced in the wet paper would be the same on each side of the sheet, and also that the wet paper did not distort during pressing. As the sheets were pressed, the excess water flowed out through the felts, and as the pressure was released at the end of the pressing, the felts acted, to some extent, like a sponge, taking up even more water from the paper.

When pressed, the post of paper is returned to the vat crew and the 'layer' separates out the felts and paper, returning the felts to the coucher for re-use, and building a 'pack' of still wet paper. Though the sheets are strong enough to be handled at this stage, they still contain some 50–60% water, and the layer must take great care not to damage the corners of the sheets as he removes them from the felts. If a 'rough' finish is required on the paper, it will be taken up to the drying loft at this point: The 'rough' texture coming simply from the wet felts in the press. Alternatively the pack may be 'pack pressed', with less pressure than before. By pressing the damp sheets against each other some of the texture left by the felts will be removed. The more this process is repeated, the smoother the sheet will become. Pressing sequences varied, depending on the type of paper being made.

Over the last years of the eighteenth century, and the early years of the nineteenth, complex pack pressing and parting sequences were developed to arrive at very definite finishes on the sheets. These involved pressing the papers over and over again, separating each sheet from the others and changing the position of the sheets in the pack (parting) to lessen the risk of any small blemish marking the sheets. It is important to realise that many of these practical improvements, which had such a direct and vital effect on the actual behaviour of the sheet during use, were never patented, rarely described and then usually only in manuscript notes and mill notebooks. Refinements like these, based on experience and a thorough practical understanding of the nature and possibilities of the materials being worked with, were passed on from papermaker to papermaker, often with no explanation of why such a particular sequence of actions was being done: it was merely the way a particular paper was made.

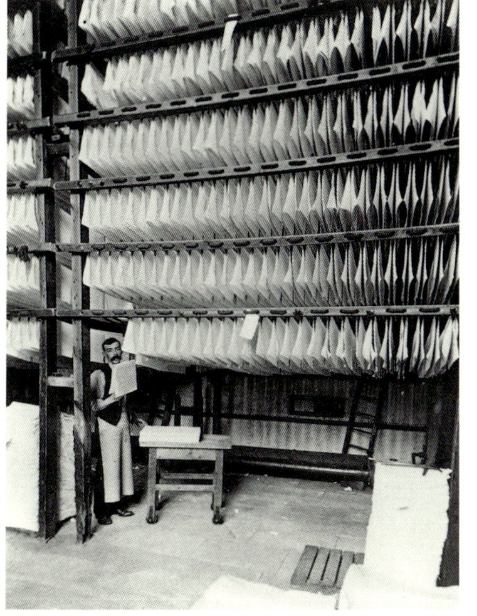

fig.7 Drying Paper over Ropes, Springfield Mill, 1906, *Whatman Ltd*

THE DRYING LOFT

The chief method of drying paper at this date was to hang the paper over ropes. Between four and ten sheets at a time, depending on their size and weight, were peeled from the pack. These groups of papers, known as 'spurs', were hung carefully over horsehair or cowhair ropes using a T shaped wooden cross. The paper was dried in spurs as opposed to single sheets because in the moist state they adhere slightly to each other, which helps to regulate the cockling of the sheets as they dry. When the paper is dry, the spurs are stripped, the sheets are separated, and left to stand in tall stacks gradually getting flatter under their own weight. Each sheet dried by this method has a 'back', (see cat.nos.25, 26 and 27), a ridge in the centre of the sheet where it has hung over the rope. This is partly removed by the standing process and partly by later pressing and finishing.

The drying and curing of handmade paper is a very lengthy process. The actual drying times vary, depending on the weight, bulk and size of the sheets, the season of the year, the surrounding humidity and temperature, and the air-flow in the drying loft, which is controlled by louvre boards running the length of the walls. In winter, and for certain papers, heat is sometimes used.

> The principal care in drying the paper, consists in gradually admitting the external air, and in preventing the cords from imbibing moisture; for this reason the lattices or luffer boards should be constructed with great exactness, and the cords may be prevented from imbibing the water by covering them with wax.[14]

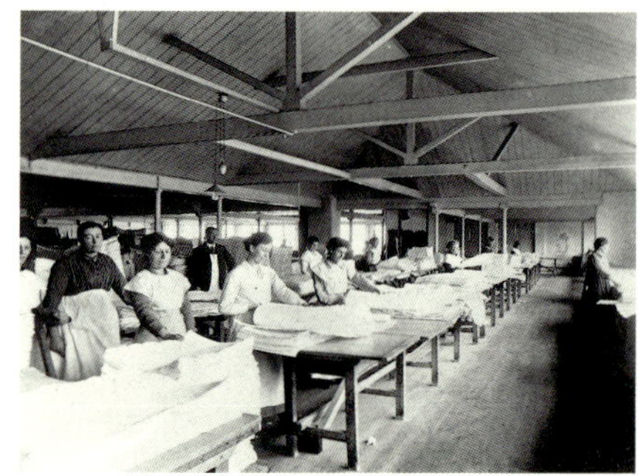

fig.8 Sorting Paper, Springfield Mill, 1906, *Whatman Ltd*

Paper should always be dried slowly if it is to give of its best when worked on. The tensions produced in the sheet, as it shrinks on drying, as it gives up the water in and around the fibres, must have the time to resolve out to the edges of the sheet. The more these tensions resolve, the more stable the sheet will be when dry. Some of the very vigorous techniques of washing colour out, and the scrubbing and scraping used by Turner, would quite simply not work on many quick dried modern papers. It is only the great stability and internal and surface strengths of air-dried, tub-sized paper that allowed Turner to develop such techniques.

After drying the sheets are matured in a cool place. The stacks of paper sit under light pressure and are 'exchanged' regularly: the sheets are turned and re-stacked in a different order from time to time, so that air gets through to all surfaces of all the sheets and moulds cannot take hold on them. This dry pressing helps to remove the last traces of cockling. At this stage, also, the papers are sorted and graded, those to be sized in particular ways are separated out, bad sheets are put to one side, and the worst are sent back for repulping.

SIZING

At this stage of the process the paper is still 'waterleaf', that is to say, unsized. Without some measure of sizing, paints and inks would bleed across the surface of the sheet, giving a furred edge to the mark. The process in use at the beginning of Turner's career was 'tub sizing', where the surface of the sheet was coated with various

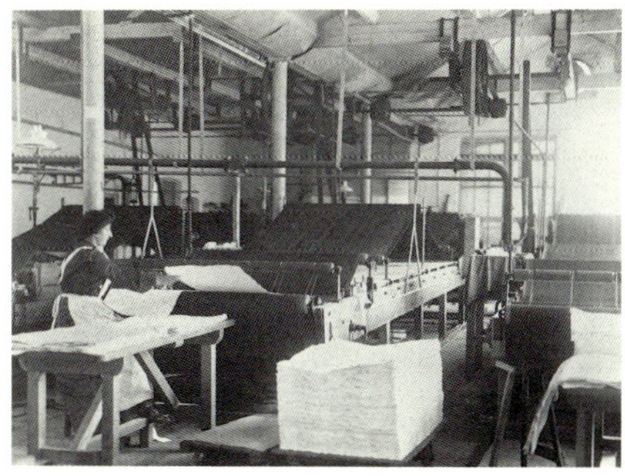

fig.9 Dry End, Size Bath, Springfield Mill, 1906, *Whatman Ltd*

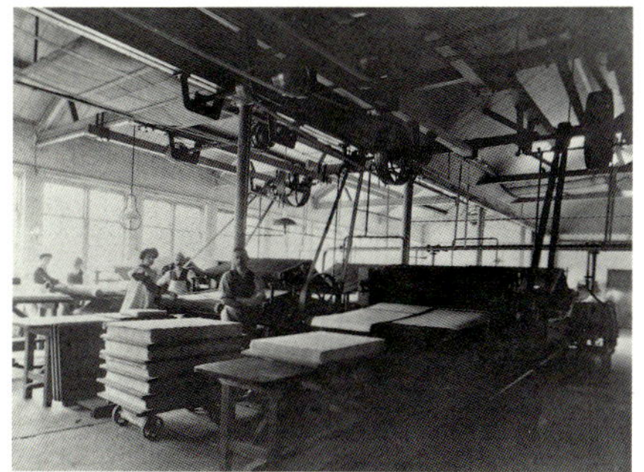

fig.10 Wet End, Size Bath, Springfield Mill, 1906, *Whatman Ltd*

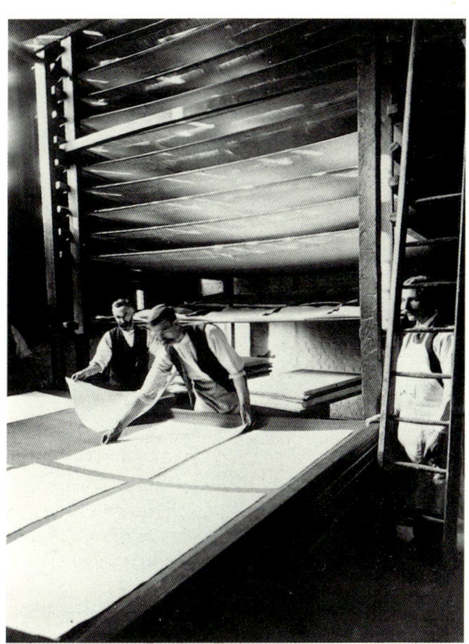

fig.11 Drying paper flat, Springfield Mill, 1906, *Whatman Ltd*

forms of gelatine derived from animals. The importance of this for Turner's work cannot be stressed enough. Without the great increase in surface strength that all gelatine sizing gives to the paper, he would not have been able to work his surfaces to quite the degree he did.[15]

After the sheets have dried, they are left to cure for a month or so before the size is applied. The gelatine was usually mixed with a small proportion of potash alum and water. The alum helped the size bite the surface of the sheet and helped to harden it as it dried. Rees describes the process thus:

> The size for paper is made of the shreds and parings got from tanners, curriers, and parchment makers. . . . The workman takes a handful of the sheets, smoothed and rendered as supple as possible, in his left hand, dips them into the vessel, and holds them separate with his right hand, that they may equally imbibe the size. After holding them above the vessel for a space of time, he siezes on the other side with his right hand, and again dips them into the vessel. When he has finished ten or a dozen of these handfuls, they are submitted to the action of the press . . . and a piece of thin board or felt is placed between every handful of sheets, as they are laid on the table of the press.[16]

Towards the end of the eighteenth century great advances were made in terms of the finishing and sizing of papers, with many mills experimenting with the development of their own processes. Whatman appears to have developed a method of sizing a whole post of paper at once (see cat.no.12).

Drying gelatine-sized papers takes great care, as the gelatine, when newly applied, is very sensitive to the environment. It was discovered that cool misty mornings in October and early November, with their very particular temperature and humidity, were admirably suited to gelatine sizing: neither too cold to chill the size, nor too hot to lead to mould growth. The paper is hung in a cold loft and the temperature is allowed to rise slowly. The temperature must not drop during the forty-eight hours or so that it takes to dry newly sized paper in a heated loft. The paper should then have another twenty-four hours with the louvre boards open to give a good air flow. It should finally be left to stand in a cool place for a few days.[17]

FINISHING

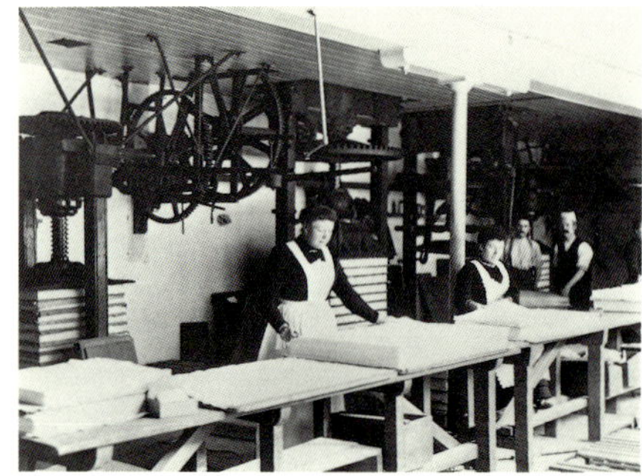

fig.12 Quality Control and Curing, Springfield Mill, 1906, *Whatman Ltd*

Traditionally the word 'finishing' refers to those processes which affect or alter the surface of the dry sheet of paper. Paper has no intrinsic surface or texture of its own; when it is wet it will pick up texture from the wire of the mould, from the weave of the felts, or indeed, anything it comes into contact with. The following factors all affect the finish of the sheet: the furnish used in the beater, the beating treatment, the formation of the sheet, sizing, pressing, drying and curing. But the most important factor of all was the use the paper was intended for, which determines all the details of the process.

After sizing, the paper was sorted again and the worst sheets removed, either to be repulped, or to be sold cheaper, before the paper was placed in a dry press (see cat.no.5) and 'squeezed with a most immense force, to render the paper flat and give it a good surface.' Rees considered that

> The processes for improving the general texture and appearance of the paper, by the more skilful use and application of sizing and hot-pressing, have certainly made important advances, even in the course of the last twenty years,[18]

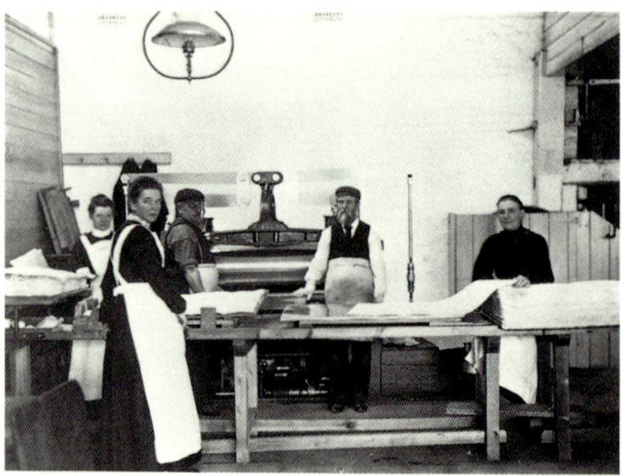

fig.13 Glazing Rollers, Springfield Mill, 1906, *Whatman Ltd*

The names 'Rough', 'Not' and 'HP' were just beginning to be used to describe what we have come to know as the traditional finishes of handmade paper. 'Rough' describes the finish produced on the paper surface by the first wet press in the vat room. 'Not', (meaning 'not hot-pressed') a surface often used for drawing and printmaking, is the natural finish of the paper when it is pressed against itself when it is still wet. The mills developed their own ways of achieving these surfaces, using different pressing sequences and different amounts of pressure. A 'not' surface from one mill might look like a 'rough' from another, 'HP' or the hot-pressing referred to by Rees above, was originally produced by a screw press using heated and burnished metal plates between the sheets.[19]

When one looks at the range of finishes possible, and then compares them with those that Turner liked to work on, it immediately becomes apparent that variations of relatively smooth 'Not' finishes, and slightly rough 'HP' finishes, where the process has still left some nap on the surface of the sheet, were his preferred finishes. These are basically finishes that were designed for writing papers.

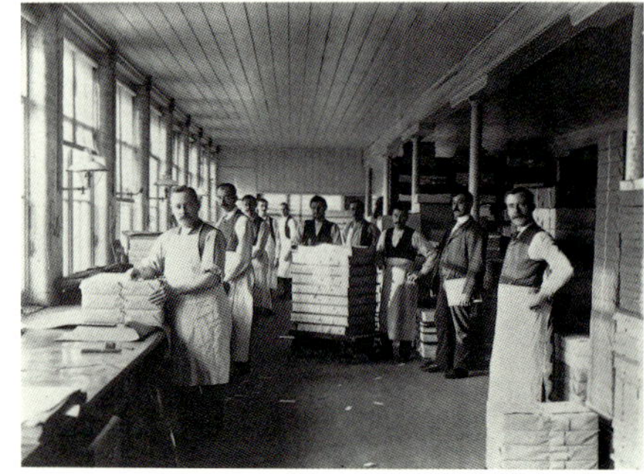

fig.14 The Packing Department, Springfield Mill, 1906, *Whatman Ltd*

QUALITY CONTROL

The labour intensive nature of making paper by hand allowed the makers great control at every stage of the process. But at this period of papermaking history the concept of quality control, and the sheet by sheet checking of the sheets before they left the mill, was perhaps a rarity: something only for those mills that prided themselves on making the 'finest' papers. In such mills great care was taken with every batch of paper as it went through each stage of manufacture. Other mills were not so careful. It is fascinating to examine such a large body of paper as this, one man's choice over such a long period of time, and see how the quality varies from year to year in the products of the same mill. We can see the formation faults and quirks which the mills let go by, either through carelessness, or for economic reasons: they needed to get their paper sold. Many of the deficiencies were in fact only superficial and had little bearing on the actual behaviour of the sheet during use.

The problems of the papermakers often came from the difficulty in obtaining consistent supplies of raw materials. The real skill in many mills was achieving a measure of consistency, not just within a particular batch of paper, but from batch to batch. Variation is inherent in the hand-made paper process. Even the best mills were not free from such problems and customers were not slow to complain:

> A letter from Longmans stating that the 12 reams of plate Imperial you sent last are not so good as what they had had from you before and that they cannot possibly use it. They desire to know what you would have done with it.[20]

The continuing problems of consistency were to be solved with a combination of changes in the raw materials used, the increased dependence on the more plentiful cotton,[21] and a better grounding in the basic science of papermaking; what actually goes on inside the sheet, as it is being made, and afterwards, when it is being used.

1 The same basic process also operates on a paper machine: the pulp solution is distributed evenly onto a moving wire mesh, and the water drains away, leaving the pulp as a thin, flat, continuous sheet on the wire.

2 Cotton in itself was not really the problem. It was to be the combination of really inferior cotton rags and the overuse of Campbell's chlorine-based bleaching powder, by papermakers trying to turn low grade waste into 'fine' papers that led to many very inferior papers being made. (see cat.no.53 for such an example). The problem was made worse when the bad cotton and over bleaching were combined with too high a proportion of china clay, (sometimes as high as 30%) initially added as a cheap filler to bulk up the fibre, but increasingly used as another whitening agent and as an aid to ink retention in printing papers.

See Murray, 1824, for a discussion of some of the effects of these processes.

By the 1820s the problem was so bad that many people were losing confidence in some papers and their makers. Enterprising makers, who did not use such methods, started to market their products differently, making a feature of their paper's purity. One such sheet can be found in the Bequest, amongst the miscellaneous works from 1830–1841: the various small torn-down drawings TB CCCXLIV 23, 34–37, 39, 43–46, 99–103, 105–107, can be reconstructed into a white wove Imperial sheet, watermarked: T EDMONDS 1825 / NOT BLEACHD

3 The worst example of such pollution in the Bequest comes in another reconstructed sheet from TB CCCXLIV: made up from nos.21, 22, 54, 55, 116–123, 137–142, 348, 349, TB XLVI is a rare example of such process dirt caused by a crushed button in Whatman paper.

4 Rees, 1819, entry on 'Paper'.

5 For most of European papermaking history the mills had been water powered but, by the latter part of the eighteenth century, Boulton and Watt & Co were supplying steam engines to paper mills. William Balston's newly built Springfield Mill was supplied by them with a 36 horse power steam engine, at a cost of £1698. The water used both for the new steam engine and in the making of the paper came from an 'abundant supply of spring water of remarkable purity . . . believed to come from a very great depth, and in the 150 years since (the mill was built) has never failed, even in the driest summers.' Balston, 1954, pp.39, 40.

6 See the letter from Catharine Balston to her husband quoted in cat.no.40 for an indication of the importance attached to fibre length.

7 During this bonding process, oxygen atoms, in fibres next to each other, are chemically linked to each other, via the hydrogen atoms in the water still remaining in the sheet. All paper contains water, even after it is 'dry'. If it did not, all you would have in your hands would be a brittle collection of dusty fibres.

8 For example, besides the papers watermarked SMITH & ALLNUTT, made at Ivy Mill, Maidstone, and taken on the Italian Tour of 1819–1820 and listed later in this catalogue, Turner had been using papers from that Mill from as early as 1795. It can be found in the Bequest under various watermarks:

E & P / 1794	TB XXIV, XXV, XXVI
E & P / 1796	TB XXXV, LXIII
EDMEADS & PINE	TB LXX L
IVY MILL / 1811	TB CXXXI, CXXXVI
IVY MILL / 1812	TB CXXXI, CXXXII
PINE SMITH & ALLNUTT / 1813	TB CXLVI

Outside the Bequest, 'A Gothic arch in a garden at Salisbury', (Wilton 206), in the Lloyd Bequest at the British Museum, is also on an Ivy Mill paper, watermarked E & P.

9 Rees, 1819. Entry on 'paper'.

10 Moulds are usually made in pairs to speed up the production process. It is often possible to distinguish which sheets in a particular batch of paper were made on which particular mould. However well made, the wire profiles and the watermarks will exhibit subtle differences. A good example of such a batch of paper made on an easily distinguishable pair of moulds is discussed in cat.no.24. This pair of moulds consists of:

Mould 1: Watermarked J WHATMAN. The letter H has one of its uprights broken. The date 1794 was added later above the name, but the broken letter was not repaired.

Mould 2: Watermarked J WHATMAN. Has a small letter M and a slightly leaning N. As with the above mould, the date 1794 was added later, above the name.

Both the undated watermarks can be found in TB XXV and TB XXVI. The rest of the sketchbooks in the group of sketchbooks and loose paper, discussed in cat.no.24, contain the dated versions of the mark.

11 For examples of such faults in the Bequest, see TB XXXIV 89, TB XCI 39, 40 and TB XL.

12 Rees, 1819, Entry on 'Paper'.

13 Joseph Bramah, Patent no.2045, 1795 and Patent no.2840, 25th April 1805.

14 Rees, 1819, Entry on 'Paper'.

15 For the different forms of gelatine used see cat.no.12.

16 Rees, 1819, Entry on 'Paper'.

17 One of the differences between the papers used by Turner and his contemporaries and the watercolour papers available today is that modern hand-made or mould-made papers are very rarely sized using gelatine. Modern artists' papers are internally sized, using chemicals to coat each individual fibre without inhibiting hydrogen bonding. Such chemical sizes are either added to the pulp at the beating stage, or in the vat. The great advantage of this method is that it speeds up production dramatically. The paper does not have to be pressed and dried twice, nor does it need curing before it is sized. The big disadvantage is a loss of quality: unlike gelatine sizing, internal sizing gives no increase in the surface strength or durability of the sheet.

18 Rees, 1819, Entry on 'Paper'.

19 The 'HP' finish is nowadays approximated by the use of glazing rolls. The very slightly damp 'Not' paper is placed between polished metal sheets to produce a 'book' of several sheets, which is then passed through rollers, which are so arranged as to give a small amount of slippage between the metal and the paper. As the 'book' passes through the glazer, the metal polishes the surface of the paper, producing a controllable amount of glaze, from quite subtle to a very high finish, depending on the use of the paper.

20 Catharine Balston to William Balston, 8th December 1813, The Whatman and Balston Archives, Kent County Archives. U2161 / Z1 / 2.

21 Much later in the century the continuing shortage of raw materials, which effected both the hand-made and machine-made paper industries, was to be solved by the introduction of wood based pulps. But before this, many mills were already recycling. Mills have always used their own mill 'broke' (paper that, for whatever reason, was not up to the quality necessary), but some were obviously recycling post consumer waste in quite a large way. When Richard Barnard of Eyehorne Mill, Kent, put his mill on the market he offered, besides the mill and its equipment, several tons of raw materials, including five tons of rags and three tons of 'paper shavings'. Barnard papers can be found in the Bequest in some sketchbooks, in use during the 1820s: TB CCXI, TB CCXIII, TB CCXXVI, TB CCXXXVIII and TB CCXXXIX.

Watermarks

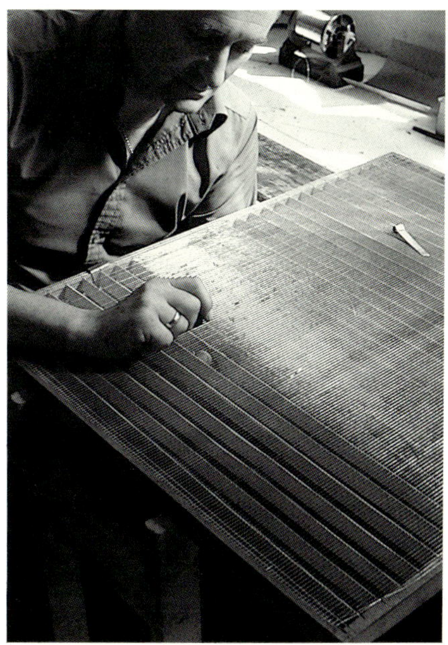

fig.15 Sewing down a laid wire mould cover

One of the most distinctive characteristics of European paper since the earliest days has been its ability to carry an image and information inside the sheet and not just on its surface.[1]

The term watermark is somewhat misleading since water plays no particular part in the production of the image in the sheet. The French word *filigrane* and an earlier English term, wiremark, are more accurate descriptions, for the marks we find in these papers are created by wire, bent and shaped into letters and images. In England, until the late eighteenth century, they were always known simply as papermarks.

To make the simple wiremarks found in the papers in the Bequest, a line drawing was made on a sheet of paper, and a thin wire laid down on this pattern. The completed mark was then sewn down onto the surface of the mould. Watermarking a sheet of hand-made paper takes place during the actual formation of the sheet. As the pulp forms in an even thickness on the surface of the mould, any alteration of that surface will produce a difference in the amount of pulp at that point in the sheet. The pulp will lie thinner over the wires of the mark. When the sheet is pressed, it will appear to be completely flat, but will be less dense where the mark is. If it is held up to the light, the light will shine through more easily at those points and the image will show.

The majority of the papers in the Bequest are wove, rather than laid, (see cat.nos.1 and 2). In wove papers the watermark usually consists of a maker's name or initials and a date, and the mark is usually placed in one corner of the bottom edge of the sheet. In laid papers the Watermark is usually centred in one half of the sheet, and usually consists of an image, which by the eighteenth century would generally be an indication of the paper size: eg, Posthorn (Post or Large Post), Fleur-de-lys (Demy, Medium etc), Britannia (Foolscap, Double Foolscap), etc. In such cases the watermark is accompanied by a countermark, situated in the centre of the other half of the sheet, which consists of the maker's name or initials and often a date. Cat.no.46 is an example of a wove paper bearing a water mark (Fleur-de-lys) and a countermark (IV), each centred in the half sheet. Wove papers marked like this usually date from the early years of wove paper production (see cat.no.2).

The more one looks at watermarks from a particular period the more it becomes possible to recognise the 'hands' of particular makers, even when faced with only a part of a mark. Individual mouldmakers had their own styles, even within the rather formal fashion for an outline Roman capital that evolved in English watermarking. The subtle contrasts between individual letterforms from different makers begins to become apparent. If one examines the several different variants of the J WHATMAN mark in Turner's papers, a pattern begins to emerge. The lettering style of the watermarks change as the actual design and composition of the papers change: a useful aid when attempting to date papers with only traces or parts of marks in them.

The Whatman marks are especially interesting in that, to the unwary, they disguise great differences between the actual papers. In this exhibition are many different papers bearing the Whatman mark, but which come from three different mills and four different companies. All the papers marked J WHATMAN, and in one case JW,[2] were made by James Whatman the younger, working Turkey Mill, Kent. Those papers bearing the Whatman mark and a date between 1794 and 1805 were all made by the partnership of William Balston and the two brothers, Finch and Thomas Robert Hollingworth.[3] After 1805 and the dissolution of the partnership, the Hollingworths remained at Turkey Mill, and watermarked their papers J WHATMAN / TURKEY MILL (occasionally, MILLS) and a date. William Balston built himself a new mill, Springfield, on the other side of Maidstone, watermarking his papers J WHATMAN and the date.[4] His new mill was not in fact ready until 1807, so he took a short lease on Hollingbourne Mill, the third mill to produce Whatman paper.

Whilst watermarks are always of interest, one must not place too much reliance on their evidence alone when trying to date or identify the origin of a particular sheet of paper. Both names and dates can be misleading. Watermarks were often copied by other mills (see cat.no.37), moulds changed hands (see cat.no.18), dates on the surface of the mould were sometimes not changed for years.[3]

But when faced with part of a torn, or cut down, sheet, or the pages of a sketchbook, which contain marks or parts of marks, the size and style of the actual lettering and its location in relation to the edge of the sheet, where the deckle is still present, can give us the original size of the paper, and can help in the reconstruction of torn down sheets (see cat.no.45). With sketchbooks, the orientation of the mark, horizontally or vertically, in relation to the spine and the dimensions of the page size can tell us how the papers in the book were folded, and thus help in determining the original size of the sheet.

Knowing the original size of the sheet is helpful in determining the designed use of the paper, because many papers were only made in particular sizes for particular uses. The surprisingly large number of Post and Large Post papers used by Turner was the first indication I had that Turner had a real preference for working on writing papers. They occur too often in the Bequest, both in sketchbooks that he had had made up rather than bought from stock, and as loose sheets, for this to be a matter of chance. This realisation was further reinforced by the number of Double Foolscap sheets also found. Post, Large Post and Double Foolscap were made as writing papers or as printing papers. The nature of the surfaces and the degree of sizing present in the papers that Turner worked on, indicate that his papers were made as 'writings'.[5]

1 The earliest examples of wiremarks come from late 13th century Italy, and the papermakers of the town of Fabriano. The earliest watermarks were all pictorial: images of animals, birds, suns, moons, stars, human figures, pots, hands, waterwheels, abstract patterns, coats of arms, and the letter P for paper, as might be expected in the work of craftsmen who, for the most part, were illiterate. Various theories have been advanced as to the nature of these early marks. Were they trade marks, indications of paper qualities and sizes, symbols of magical and religious significance, or just a convenient way of identifying a particular pair of moulds amongst many? The answer probably lies in an amalgam of all these reasons. Gradually the initials of the maker began to be added to the mould. Particular makers gained reputations for quality and their marks passed into general use amongst other makers. By the end of the eighteenth century watermarks were quite simply trademarks.

2 Cat.no.19, TB XLIV f. Another mark in the exhibition, Cat.no.10, with its part mark of a Crown, was also made by James Whatman the younger.

The only dated mark ever found for James Whatman the younger is in an Antiquarian sheet, used for a watercolour in the Victoria and Albert Museum: *The Rowing match at Richmond* by Robert Cleveley. This sheet is watermarked J WHATMAN / TURKEY MILL / 1792. see Balston, 1957, p.160.

I was most intrigued therefore to find on the margin of a backing mount, for TB CXXI S, 'Quarter-deck of the *Victory*', the paper of which appeared to be a Whatman, a note reading 'paper-mark 1793'. Finberg had catalogued this note and said it was 'not in Turner's handwriting.' In a raking light, traces of a watermark could be seen along the top half of the right hand edge of the sheet. This area was X-rayed and the watermark was found to be 1794 / J WHATMAN.

3 In the period 1794–1805, the dates on the moulds at Turkey Mill were changed irregularly. The only dates in Whatman marks for this period that can be found in the Bequest are 1794, 1797, 1801, 1804 and 1805. This accords with the dates one finds in Whatman papers outside the Bequest, though 1798 does occur occasionally.

4 During his first years at Springfield, Balston also watermarked his papers JW, WB, W BALSTON, J WHATMAN & W BALSTON, J WHATMAN & W BALSTON & CO, BALSTON & CO, SM (Springfield Mill), all with the relevant dates. This early attempt to establish his own identity failed and the Whatman mark continues in fine paper to this day, despite a brief interlude this century when no artists' papers were being produced at this highly successful mill.

5 Turner also drew and painted occasionally on printing papers. see cat.nos.14, 38 and 49.

1 Laid papermaking mould and deckle

Oak, pine, copper and brass

Two sheet mould: outside dimensions: 426 × 1072 ($16\frac{3}{4} \times 42\frac{1}{4}$)
Chain lines: 32 mm ($1\frac{1}{4}$ in) apart

Laid line frequency: 8 per cm (10 per in)[1]

Deckle: outside dimensions:
457 × 1078 (18 × 43)

Watermarked: (once in each sheet) Fleur de lys, on a shield, crowned, plus a GJ monogram.
Countermarked: G JONES / 1809[2]

The mould carries the makers name on a small brass plate reading DONKIN & DAVIS[3]

Peter Bower

1A Detail of Watermark and reversed monogram

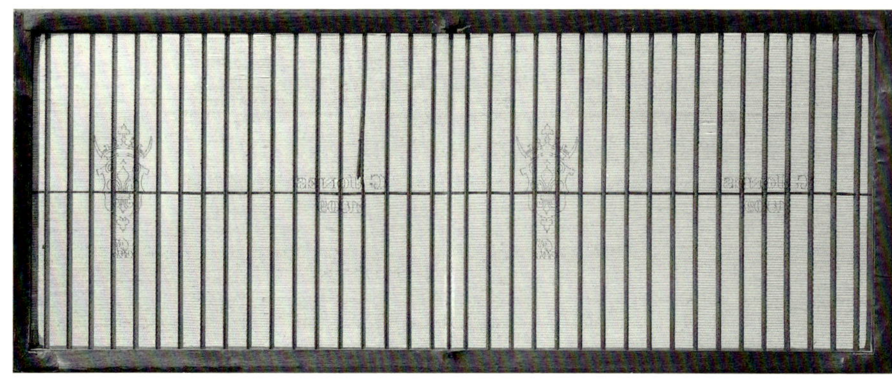

1

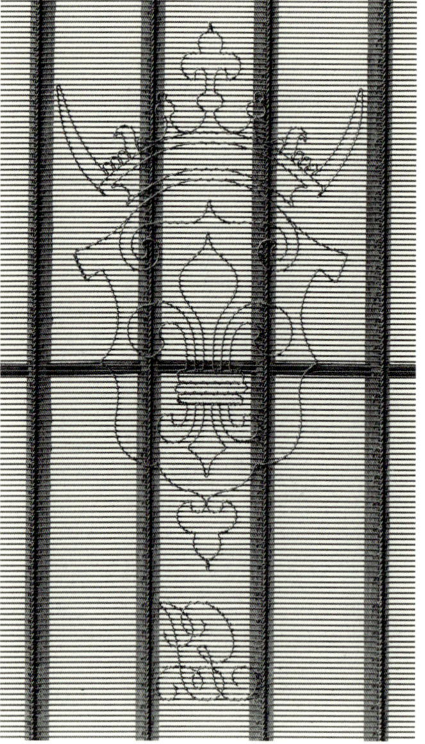

1A

This mould was designed to produce two sheets at a time, each 393 × 510 ($15\frac{1}{2} \times 20\frac{1}{8}$), when wet, a size of paper known as Post. This is a single faced mould, where the laid wire is sewn down directly onto the struts. A single faced laid mould such as this produces a sheet, which when held up to the light would have darker shadows either side of the chain lines. Around 1800, probably as a development borrowed from the design of the newer Wove moulds (see cat.no.2), double faced laid moulds were introduced. In these moulds the laid wire was supported on the struts by a second set of wires, to hold the actual papermaking surface away from the wooden struts, allowing the water to drain away more easily during the formation of the sheet. This stopped the build-up of pulp either side of the chain lines, which had led to the creation of the shadow marks. There is a strengthening bar running the full width of the mould, through the struts, which are $1\frac{1}{4}$ in apart. One rib is damaged and the centre bar of the deckle is missing.

1 Because the paper shrinks during drying, the chain line measurements and laid line frequency of an actual sheet formed on this mould would probably be nearer 1 in, for the chains, and 25 per inch for the laid lines.

2 Griffith Jones worked Nash Mill, Hertfordshire, from 1796 until 1811, at first in partnership with Ann Blackwell, who had run the mill on her own since the death of her husband William in 1777.

3 Bryan Donkin had started his career as an apprentice to the Dartford mouldmaker John Hall, and though he continued to be involved in the making of moulds for handmade papermaking, his most important contribution to papermaking lies in his development of the first practical papermaking machine, in partnership with the London based stationers and mill owners, the Fourdrinier brothers. (cat.nos.55 and 56)

2 Wove papermaking mould and deckle *c.*1811

Oak, pine, copper and brass

Two sheet mould: outside dimensions: 480 × 1196 × 50 (19⅛ × 47¼ × 2)

Deckle: outside dimensions: 504 × 1221 (19⅞ × 48¼)

Watermarked: (once in each sheet) 1811

Both the mould and the deckle are stamped with the maker's mark WE. (This mould maker has so far not been identified).

Peter Bower

2A Detail of the underside of the mould, showing the supporting wires under the wove surface.

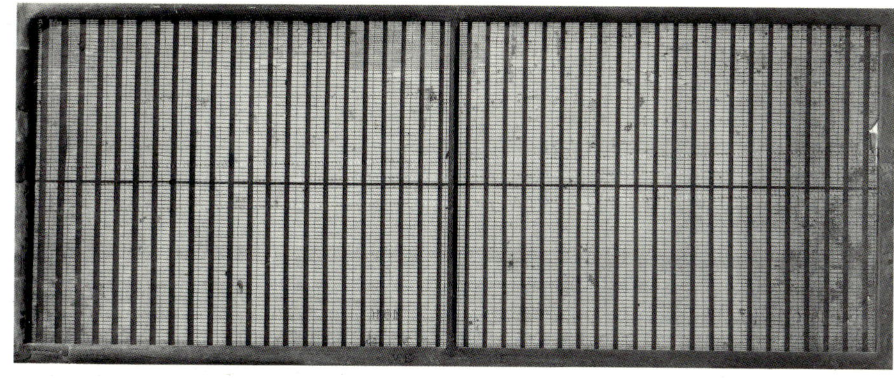

2

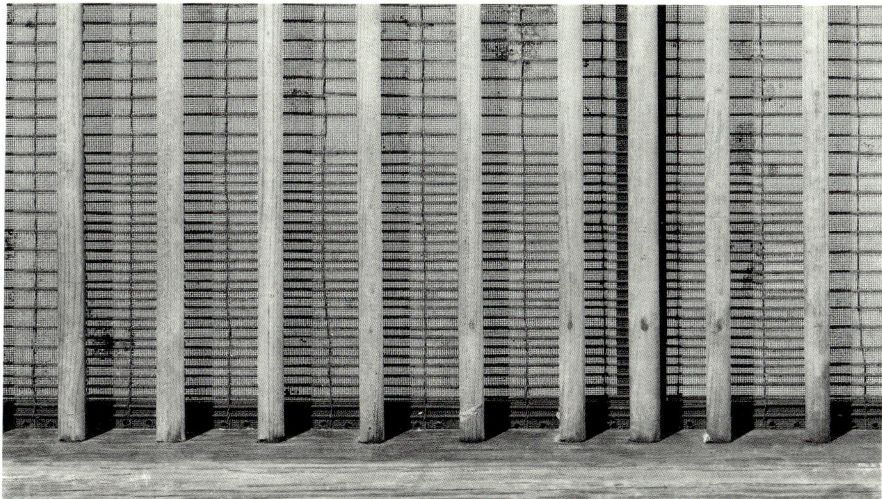

2A

This mould was designed to produce two sheets at a time, each 447 × 475 (17⅝ × 22⅝), when wet, producing a size of paper variously known as Demy or Medium, depending on the mill that was making it and the use the paper was intended for. The woven wire mould cover is supported by a grid of wires resting on the support ribs of the mould and is further strengthened, on the side nearest the vatman, by extra wires in the supporting grid. Moulds with such supporting wires became known as double faced moulds, and were introduced around 1800, to stop 'shadows' appearing in the sheet, where pulp built up during the formation of the sheet, on either side of the ribs. A strengthening bar runs the full width of the mould, through the ribs, helping to keep the whole mould rigid.

One of the most far reaching developments of the eighteenth century was the development of the wove mould surface. The fine detail of its actual genesis is still something of a mystery, but the first wove papers were made for the printer John Baskerville by James Whatman at Turkey Mill, Kent, and first used in the printing of his 'Virgil', of 1757. The importance of wove paper is not merely an aesthetic one, resulting from the smooth even surface, unmarked by the laid and chain lines of a laid mould. It also lies in the effects it has during the formation of the sheet. A wove mould, owing to the finer gaps between the wires, drains slower than most laid moulds, allowing the vatman a little more time to form and close the sheet. The generally better formation gives a subtle increase in internal stability and strength to the sheet, which has a beneficial effect on the behaviour of the paper when it is in use.

According to the younger James Whatman, in conversation with the American papermaker Joshua Gilpin, who visited England in the 1790s, the earliest wove paper made by his father dated from 1756, though it was not until 1778 that it came 'into repute'.[1] But as early as 1767 Thomas Gainsborough, had been greatly excited by the first wove papers he had come across. He wrote to Christopher Anstey, the publisher of the *New Bath Guide* for that year, asking him to obtain for him some wove paper, but Anstey sent him laid paper, Gainsborough wrote again:

> I had set my heart on some of it . . . . I wish sir, that one of my landscapes, such as I could make upon that paper, would prove a sufficient inducement for you to make still further enquiries . . . . upon my honour I would give a guinea a quire for a dozen quires of it.[2]

An Imperial wove paper sold, at this point, for some three shillings a quire in London.

Though artists were amongst the first to appreciate the new paper, it was to be printers who would ensure its continued success. The combination of the wove mould and improvements in sizing and finishing techniques in the specialist production of 'drawing' papers brought many papermakers, such as Whatman in England and Canson et Montgolfier in France, great renown in the nineteenth century. So much so that both 'Whatman' and 'Canson' became synonymous with fine paper, and are still, to some extent, used as generic terms in England and France for fine drawing papers.[3]

It was not however the approval of the fine artist that led to the real success and continued production of wove drawing papers over such a long period. The painter, whether amateur or professional, could never use enough paper to keep a mill in business. Turner, for instance, despite his prolific output, probably used, in over sixty years of working, an amount of paper equivalent to a day or a day and a half's production from the Whatman Mill in 1794. It was to be the rapidly increasing numbers of technical draughtsmen working in a variety of fields: engineers, surveyors, map makers, architects etc, who provided the bulk of the demand for these new strong, durable and above all, workable surfaces.

1 *The Journal of Joshua Gilpin*. Vol. VII 17th March 1796. Pennyslvania State Archives. From an unpublished transcription by A.P. Woolrich.
2 Balston, 1957, p.40.
3 Occasionally leading to some inaccuracies in the details of the cataloguing of some works of art. For instance I have come across anomalies such as a particular work being described as on 'Whatman watermarked MLC', MLC being the initials of the late nineteenth century French paper company Montgolfier, Luquet et Cie.

UNKNOWN ENGRAVER

3 A Paper Mill, with the Men at Work 1752

Engraving
Plate size: 181 × 250 ($7\frac{1}{8}$ × 11)
White laid
Chain lines: 24 mm (1 in) apart, variable.
Laid line frequency: 10 per cm, (25 per in)
Shadows present
Watermarked: Crown / GR

Peter Bower

This print is a plate from 'The Method of Making Paper', published in *The Universal Magazine* of 1752. The publisher of the magazine, John Hinton, has taken most of the text from the 1741 edition of Ephraim Chambers' *Cyclopaedia*. Unlike later encyclopaedia references to paper, such as Rees, of 1819, the text which accompanies this plate is not particularly accurate but does contain some useful information.

The mid-eighteenth century saw the real beginnings of a fine paper industry in this country. There had been earlier mills producing good papers, but by the time this work appeared the number of mills was increasing and so was the scale of their output. At the beginning of the century most mills had been small one or two-vat mills, but by the end of the century mills of three, four, five and even more vats were becoming commoner. By the 1750s, *The Universal Magazine* could announce proudly that

> The English manufacture is daily growing in reputation . . . and there's great hopes, from the improvement lately made in this business, that we shall soon make as good paper at home as any part of Europe can produce.[1]

This print is based on an earlier plate originally engraved for a text by Gilles Filleau des Billettes, which is now lost. Five of the plates in this series were re-engraved, on a smaller scale, for the *Universal Magazine*. The text itself is an edited translation of Lalande.[2]

The text describes the detail of the plate thus:

- A the wheel which turns the engine.
- B the cover of the engine, which hinders the water and stuff from being thrown out of the trough, by the velocity of the engine.
- C the spindle of the engine.
- D a lever, whereby the engine is either raised, or depressed, as occasion requires.
- a hammers for pounding the rags.
- E a roll for drawing up the penstock, or sluice.
- F the water wheel, which turns the engine, hammers, etc.
- G a windlass, for pressing the paper.
- H a lever, one end of which goes to the nut of the press, and to the other is fastened a rope, going round the windlass.
- I the press.
- K the maker at work at the vat.
- L the chimney, which carries off the smoke from the fire under the vat.
- M a mould, on which the paper is made.
- N the couch-man at work.
- O the mould, containing a sheet of paper, couching upon a felt.
- P a pile of paper and felts, before it is pressed.
- Q the layer at work.
- R a sheet of paper which he is laying smooth on the heap.

The terminology used to describe this somewhat stylised illustration has undergone some changes. The 'engine' is, more often than not, now known as a

3

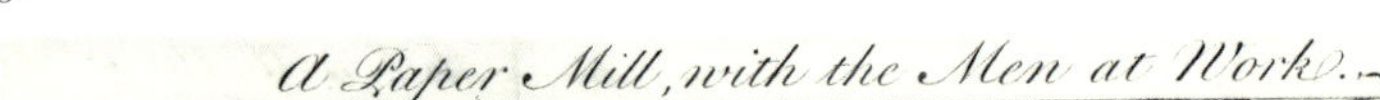

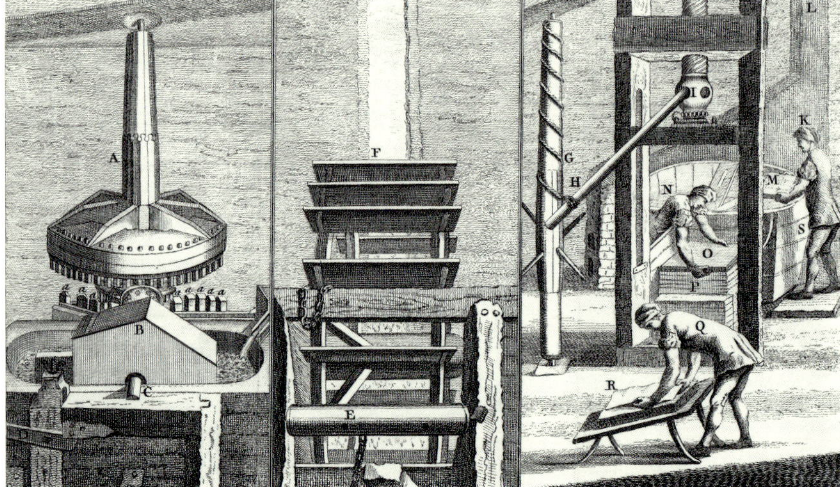

Hollander, the 'hammers' as stampers, the windlass, as a capstan press, or more occasionally as a 'Sampson'. In the main body of the text, the author also uses the old terms 'form' and 'cover' for the mould and deckle.

It is also slightly unusual to find both stampers and a Hollander depicted together. The invention of the Hollander beater, or rag engine, in the late 17th century,[3] was to have a very dramatic influence on the quantity and quality of pulp production. The output of one Hollander beater was equivalent to that of eight sets of stampers. It could also break down much tougher rags, without too much prior fermentation, which helped in the production of white papers. Too much fermentation could lead to the rags being 'burnt', giving them a yellow or, in the worst cases, buff colour.[4] Perhaps most importantly it allowed the controlled variation of fibre length and condition, within the same stock, in the beater.[5]

This innovation would pave the way for an increasing sophistication in the design of papers for specific uses; different papers for engraving, drawing, writing, or printing, as papermakers realised that they could develop different potentials of strength and flexibility in the same fibre as it was beaten. The papermaker was no longer dependant on the finishing techniques of sizing, pressing and glazing to differentiate particular papers. The combination of the new beating techniques and further developments in finishing and sizing would lead, during the eighteenth century, to the very fine papers produced by the Whatmans and many other makers.

1 *The Universal Magazine*, 1752, reproduced from *The Art of Making paper*, 1978, eds Colin Cohen and Geoffrey Wakeman, p.6.

2 J.J. Le Francais de la Lande, *L'Art de Faire le Papier*, 1761.

3 Most probably invented at The Salamander Mill, in the Zaanland, Holland, (hence the name) around 1673.

4 The yellowish tone of the paper that this engraving was printed on, is just such an example of the over fermention of the rags, prior to pulping.

5 The fibres travelling closest to the central wall of the beater trough pass under the roll many more times than those travelling the outside of the trough. The fibres in the centre will thus be better hydrated and also shorter.

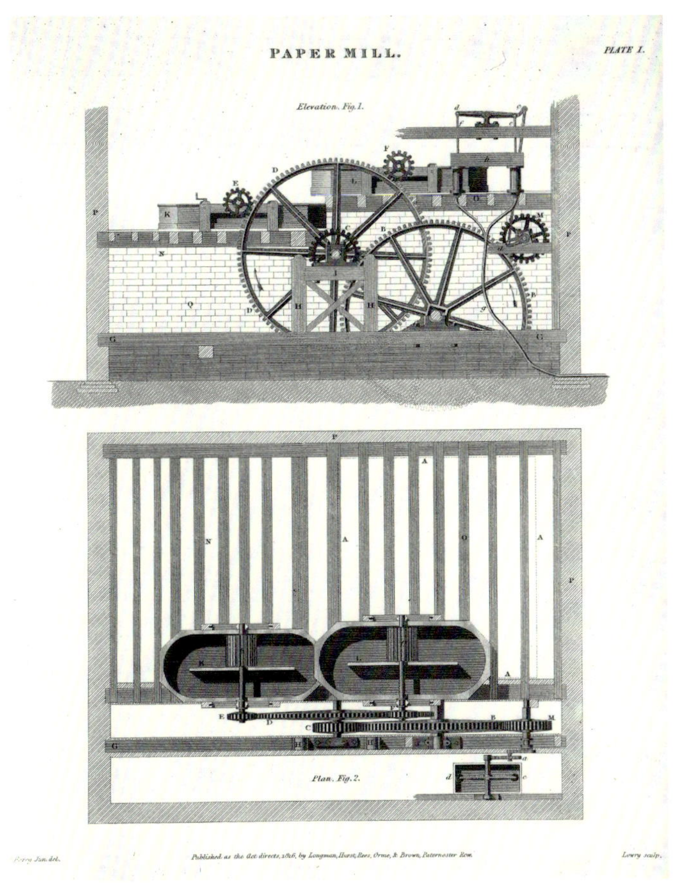

4

WILSON LOWRY AFTER JOHN FAREY

4 **Elevation and plan of a Breaker and Beater** 1816

Steel engraving
263 x 202 (10 x 8¼)
Trimmed within the plate mark
Dated 1816 in the inscription

White Wove
Unwatermarked, but other plates are watermarked 1811

Peter Bower

WILSON LOWRY AFTER JOHN FAREY

5 **Elevation and plan of Hollander Beater and details of Screw Press** 1814

Steel engraving
263 x 202 (10 x 8¼)
Trimmed within the plate mark
Dated 1814 in the inscription

White Wove
Unwatermarked, but other plates are watermarked 1811

Peter Bower

Both plates are from the entry for 'Paper' in Abraham Rees' *Cyclopaedia or Universal Dictionary of Arts, Sciences and Literature* published by Longman, Hurst, Rees, Orme and Brown, 1819. The account in Rees' encyclopaedia is perhaps the best description of papermaking by hand dating from the first half of Turner's career, and, to some extent, was based on the observation of

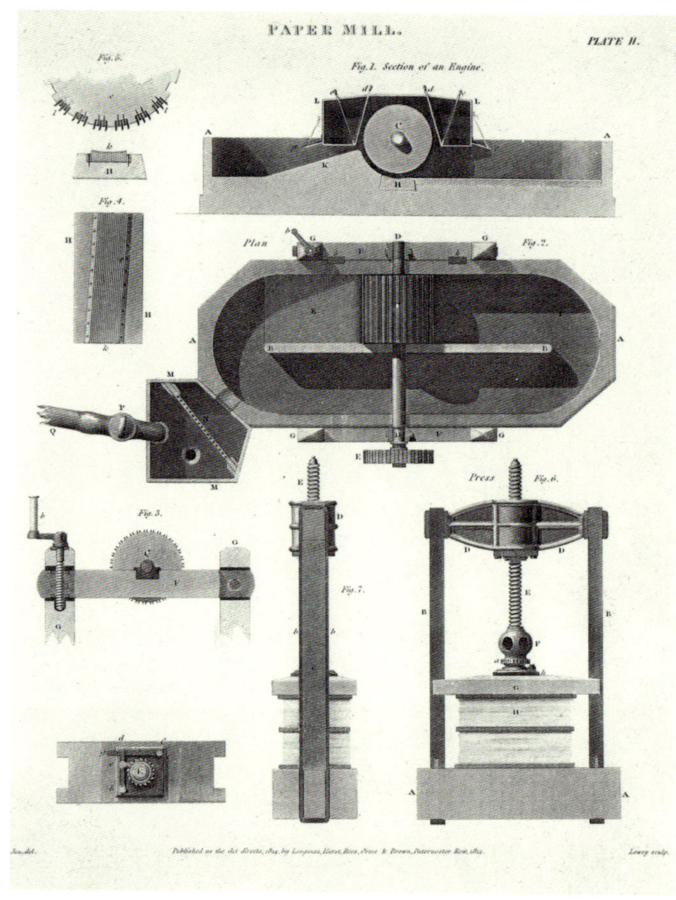

working practices at Balston's Springfield Mill, which Rees described as 'A very large and capital paper mill, at Maidstone in Kent, which is the principal seat of the paper trade in England'.

By the early years of the nineteenth century papermakers, users of paper, and commentators on paper and its making, had become much more sophisticated. The author of this text, in Abraham Rees' encyclopaedia has a much greater understanding, and far fewer errors, than the author of the piece for the *Universal Magazine* (see cat.no.3). Whilst the texts of many eighteenth and nineteenth century encyclopaedia and journal entries on paper and its making should be treated with some scepticism, the illustrations often repay careful study. The artists employed seem to have understood what they were looking at much more than the writers, who sadly are often only repeating earlier innaccuracies.[1]

It is one of the oldest truisms in papermaking that 'paper is made in the beater'. It does not matter how good the rags, how good the formation of the sheet, how well sized or finished the paper is, if the rags are not beaten and blended in just the right ways and proportion, the sheet will not behave as it should.

This particular text emphasises the quality and nature of rags suitable for various papers:

> The sorting of the rags is of no small importance in the art of making paper; for unless the rags, which are ground at the same time in the engine, are all of the same quality, both as to substance and condition, then the finest and best parts will be ground away in the mill.

Different qualities of rags were often beaten separately and then blended together to achieve particular qualities and characteristics in the finished paper: 'care in sorting the rags produces a great beauty of the paper'. The late eighteenth century saw an increasing understanding of the capabilities of different rags, and of ways to develop the potential of the fibres, in English papermaking, of, for example

> mixing a pulp, which will form the strength of the paper, with another which will give it softness and lustre; and thus two qualities may be united which otherwise existed seperately.

Some rag dealers and some paper mills, 'who have the perfections of their work at heart', observed every precaution in the sorting of all the different qualities of rags, but

> As to small country mills it is scarcely possible for them to make so great a choice. They are often obliged to lay up for fine many rags which are properly middling, and their middling may with better reason be reserved for making the coarser sort of papers.

This exhibition contains several examples (see cat.nos.9, 11, 17 etc) of such a 'coarser sort' of paper, which whilst not of the best, had some quality of tone, texture, feel or handle, which attracted Turner's interest. The off-white papers, for example, that make up the bulk of TB CLXXXIX, the *Rome C. Studies* sketchbook (see cat.no.52 and 53), made by Alexander Cowan, at Valleyfield, near Edinburgh, would probably have been made as the best quality white paper, but an admixture of lower quality rags has led to some deterioration over time, visible despite the grey wash used to prepare the sheets before use.

1 Artists of all sorts of skill and reputation were used on such illustrative work. Cornelius Varley for instance did all the drawings for the Bleaching entry in Rees' encyclopaedia.

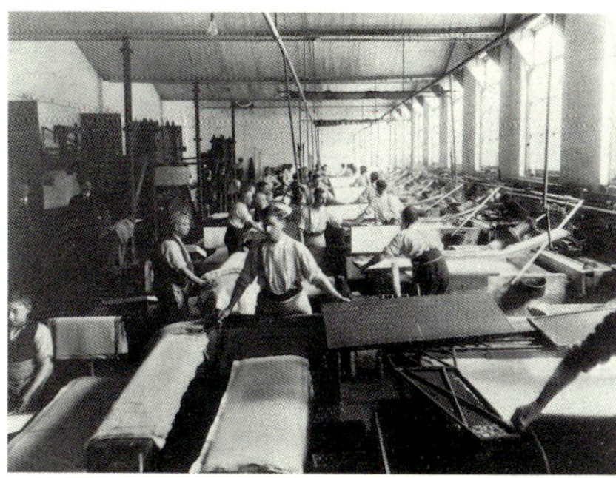

6

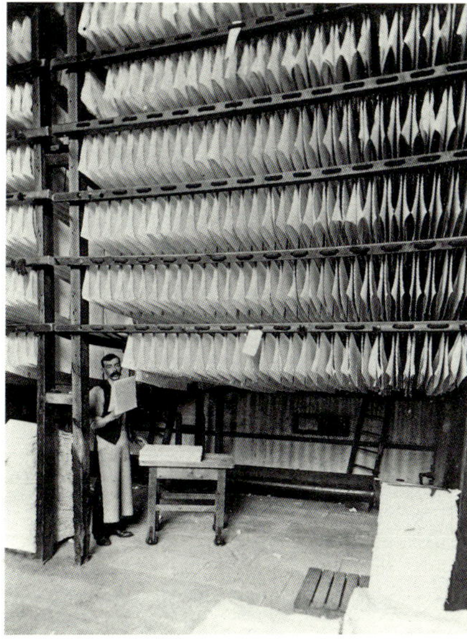

7

ANONYMOUS

6 The Vat Room, Springfield Mill, Maidstone, Kent 1906

Photograph

178 × 238 (7 × 9⅜)

Peter Bower

ANONYMOUS

7 Drying Handmade Paper, Springfield Mill, Maidstone, Kent 1906

Photograph

237 × 178 (9 5/16 × 7)

Peter Bower

The period covered by this exhibition, 1787–1820, is unfortunately not well served by contemporary illustrations of papermakers at work. Whilst there are some engravings of paper equipment (see cat.nos.4 and 5) and one or two water-colours and drawings of particular papermills, (see cat.nos.15 and 40)[1] it has proved impossible, so far, to trace any illustrations of people making paper from this period.

These two photographs come from a sequence of pictures taken at Springfield Mill, Kent, which produced the bulk of the Whatman papers used by Turner from 1807 onwards, to celebrate the centenary of that Mill. They date from perhaps the heyday of English hand-made papermaking. The equipment shown is technically more sophisticated than it would have been when William Balston built his new mill, but the actual process of making paper by hand had changed little in the intervening century. Each vat had a crew of at least three: the vat man to form the sheets, dipping the mould into the pulp and taking it out, allowing the water to drain through, leaving the pulp as a thin flat sheet on the surface of the mould. The coucher, who transferred the wet sheet from the mould to the felt, and the layer, who separated the sheets and felts after pressing.

The vat room shown here, with its nine vats, was one of two large vat rooms at Springfield by this date. When Balston designed the Mill he intended to start with ten vats, but often only six or so were actually working.

The second photograph shows one of the drying lofts, with the newly pressed sheets hanging over ropes, which were covered with horse or cow hair, to prevent the wet paper being stained by the hemp of the ropes. Many papers in the Bequest show the marks of the 'back', the distortions caused by the paper drying, either unevenly or too fast, over the drying ropes. (see cat. nos.26,27) Though difficult to remove, the normal fold caused by the paper hanging over the rope, could be made to disappear, by opening the sheets out and piling them on top of each other, and letting them stand under a light pressure.

The small tags of paper that can be seen at certain points on the drying rack contain the details of that particular 'post' of paper: who chose the raw material, who beat it, who formed the sheet, who couched it, who pressed it, who hung it up to dry etc. As the paper travelled through all the different stages of production, its particular history would be recorded so that in the case of any complaint the cause of the fault could easily be found.

When James Whatman had retired in 1794, his original mill, Turkey Mill, together with two other papermills he had owned, Poll and Loose, had been worked by a partnership between William Balston and the Hollingworth Brothers. In 1805 Balston decided to build himself his own mill on the other side of Maidstone. Springfield Mill did not open for business until 1807, so in the intervening period, Balston took a short lease on Loose Mill, which he and the Hollingworths had previously been working together.

From this period until 1859 there were two mills, owned by two different companies, producing paper with the Whatman Watermark. When the partnership split up Balston had wanted to keep the Whatman name for himself, feeling that he was Whatman's true heir,[2] but the Hollingworths also had the rights to the name:

> . . . before you began your mill Counsell had pronounced that no law could prevent their continuing the name and that they would have a verdict in their favour in a Court of Justice . . . the opinion is very plain – no more room for any more doubt.[3]

In order to distinguish between the products of the two mills, those papers produced by Balston, at Springfield, carried only the J WHATMAN name and a date.

Those papers made by the Hollingworths at Turkey Mill, were watermarked J WHATMAN TURKEY MILL (or occasionally, MILLS) and a date.[4] The position was finally resolved in 1859, when the Hollingworths turned Turkey Mill and all their production over to the finest machine made papers, and the Whatman name and watermark reverted finally to the Balstons at Springfield mill.

There was a considerable rivalry between the two companies at various times in their histories, but when times were difficult they kept an eye on each other, and to some extent helped out. After all, most of the public could not tell which mill made which particular Whatman papers: it was all the same to them. If one mill faltered, the other could equally suffer. When, early in 1813, the Hollingworth's dropped their prices, Balston was worried:

> I find the measures of the Hollingworths have injured them most materially – and I doubt much if they will ever again meet the same days as those which are past.[5]

Later that year the Hollingworths were in real difficulties and we find Catharine Balston writing to her husband

> Fausett says the Hollingworths will send you two or three tons of rags in their own wagon this week. Their people told him that their horses had not so much employment as usual, as they are only working two vats at Turkey.[6]

The earliest Hollingworth-made 'Whatman' paper that I can find in the Bequest comes from as late as 1817.[7] Until that date Turner seems to have consistently used Balston made 'Whatman'. After 1817, he used both, but with a bias towards the Balston papers.

1 Hand made paper mills, which were usually situated on the banks of clear and swift flowing streams, often in rather beautiful valleys, have regularly been drawn and painted. Besides the Illustrations of Egglestone Abbey Mill in this exhibition (cat.nos.15, 40 and 41) a watercolour of the first Whatman Mill, 'Vintners and Mr Whatman's Turkey Mill', was exhibited by Paul Sandby at the Royal Academy in 1794. This picture was illustrated in Balston, 1957.

2 Balston's early life is somewhat unusual. His father had had him admitted to Christ's Hospital because he was 'not able to maintain them [his wife and children] without assistance, being in poor circumstances.' When James Whatman was looking for an apprentice, someone he could train up to take over the business, he asked his brother-in-law, Samuel Bosanquet, to find him a boy. William Balston was that boy. That Whatman had something more than the usual apprenticeship in mind for him, can be seen by the facts that he took Balston into his own home, brought him up as one of the family, paid him well, and gave him an excellent grounding in the mill. On Whatman's retirement, it was Whatman who provided the funds for Balston's share of the new partnership, see Balston, 1954.

3 Letter from Susanna Whatman to William Balston, May 1810. James Whatman's widow Susanna was a tremendous support to Balston in all his endeavours, helping him with finance and involving members of her family in various aspects of the running of the mill. Whatman and Balston Archives, Kent County Archives U2161/Z1/2.

4 See cat.no.48, footnote 1, for a discussion on the particular difficulties of Whatman watermarks in Antiquarian papers during this period.

5 Letter from William Balston to Catharine Balston, 7th January 1813. Whatman and Balston Archives, U2161/Z1/2, Kent County Archives.

6 Letter from Catharine Balston to William Balston, 27th July 1813. Whatman and Balston Archives, U2161/Z1/2, Kent County Archives.

7 The only Whatman papers in the Bequest made by Hollingworths at Turkey Mill after 1805 and before 1820, are as follows:

TB CLXIX The *Aesacus and Hesperie* sketchbook.
Watermarked: J WHATMAN / TURKEY MILLS / 1817
Demy 16mo.

Several loose sheets in 'The Perspective Diagrams.':

TB CXCV – 52, 53, 149
3 sheets, Imperial
Watermarked: J WHATMAN / TURKEY MILL / 1817

TB CXCV – 4, 8, 19, 20, 26a, 36–46, 49, 51, 132, 133, 136, 175, 23 sheets, Super Royal
Watermarked: J WHATMAN / TURKEY MILLS / 1817

TB CXCV – 5, 6, 12
3 sheets, Elephant
Watermarked: 1818 / J WHATMAN / TURKEY MILLS

TB CXCV 134
1 sheet, Super Royal
Watermarked: J WHATMAN / TURKEY MILLS / 1819

The Early Years (cat.nos.8–18)

When Turner first began drawing and painting, the concept of a 'drawing' paper was beginning to undergo a great change. Although the phrase 'drawing paper' had been in common usage amongst English artists from at least the middle of the eighteenth century, it did not originally refer to papers made specifically for drawing, but rather to any paper that artists found suitable for the purpose. When talking of 'drawing', they included work in watercolour as well as pencil and chalks. By the end of the eighteenth century many mills were beginning to make papers specifically for particular uses, including both 'plate' papers, for copperplate engraving and, a little later in the century, for drawing.

At the outset of the eighteenth century the British paper industry had consisted mostly of very small mills, producing mostly brown, brown-white and blue papers. The white paper industry was only just beginning again after a hiatus during the 17th century, when most, if not all, fine white paper had been imported. But by the end of the century the industry had undergone a transformation, with well established, and often much larger, mills producing an increasing range of very fine papers for a variety of very distinct uses.[1]

This change had come about as part of an increasing awareness in papermakers, and a growing sophistication amongst their customers, as to the possibilities of paper.[2] The makers realised that by changing some of the details of the various stages of the production process, different potentials in the fibres used (mostly linen and hemp at this date) could be developed to produce specific properties and behavioural characteristics in the finished paper. The traditional definitions of 'writing', 'wrapping' and 'printing' papers could be expanded to cope with an increasing range of end uses that were gradually being perceived as needing increasingly specific papers to meet their demands.

Many different processes and events had contributed to such changes. Perhaps the greatest single impetus, early in the century, was the enormous benefit provided to the English paper industry by the influx of Huguenot papermakers and their families, fleeing persecution in France.[3] Not just the wealthier refugees who set up mills of their own, such as Henry Portal, but the mainly anonymous, rag women, vatmen, couchers, pulpmen, pressmen; papermakers who brought with them years of highly practical experience and the tricks of the trade that were never really written down. Papermaking has always passed its secrets on empirically, the youngster working with the more experienced, learning his trade by example in the day to day production of the mill. The example the Huguenot workers set, would play a dramatic part in lifting the general quality of English papermaking.

It is very important, when considering Turner's choice of papers, to understand their properties and characteristics in the way he and his contemporaries would have done. When Turner began buying paper it was described quite simply. It was made for Writing, Printing or Wrapping. Colours were white, brown, blue or drab, which covered a small range of browns, buffs, greys, blue-greys and olive-green papers. A purple paper was also made as a wrapping paper. Quality might be described as superfine, fine, retree, or bastard.[4] Even by the end of his career, the industry was still somewhat haphazard in its description of many of its products.

Despite Turner's innovative methods and his continuous self-education, it would appear that many of the qualities and characteristics shown by these early papers, continued to condition his choice of paper throughout his career. There are great similarities in the weights, textures and tones of many of the papers used in the first thirty years of his career. Even the development of a greater range of much higher quality coloured painting and drawing papers in the early years of the nineteenth century made little change in the nature of the tones and colours which he chose to work on. But the actual surface and internal strengths of these new papers were in fact very different and better suited to such developing techniques as the bodycolour and watercolour that Turner used on the range of blue papers he employed for his Petworth drawings in the late 1820s and the views for the 'Rivers of Europe' in the 1830s. These blue papers had their origins in blue sugar loaf wrapping papers, such as those used in cat.nos. 11 and 16. Even many of the surfaces which he prepared with his own colour washes were to repeat the 'drab' colours of the early wrapping papers.

Even with the very deliberate choices in papers that Turner made, it is important not to lose sight of the part chance played in some of them. In his earliest years he was living amongst many of the best stationers and paper suppliers in London, whose premises were clustered around the Strand. Being accustomed to seeing good quality paper from a very young age must have played some part in training his naturally 'good' eye. The earliest papers he chose to work on were all, in their own ways, quality products.

A range of other experiences also gave Turner further insights into the properties and possibilities of different papers, before his more formal training began at the Plaister Academy of the Royal Academy Schools in 1789. While staying with his aunt and uncle at Brentford in 1784 and 1785, he attended John White's school and also began to colour engravings. The experience of washing colour onto a soft-sized, but hard pressed surface, would have given him a good grounding in the complexities of the relationship between degrees of sizing and the finish, the actual open or closed texture of the paper surface, underneath that sizing. He had also begun to sketch from nature in pen and ink and watercolour.[5] In 1788 he went to work with the architectural draughtsman Thomas Malton, and the architect Thomas Hardwick. The combination of his own sketching practices on writing papers, suited to the pen, and the kind of draughtsmanship needed in such practices as theirs, would have reinforced his liking for smoother surfaces and for a hard crisp size rather than the softer and slightly rougher surfaces he would have experienced when colouring engravings (see cat.no.8).

At the Royal Academy schools we find him, in common with most of his contemporaries, exploring, in chalks and pencil and stump, the textures and subtle tones of various blue, brown and buff wrappings (see cat.nos.9 and 11). Over the next few years, whilst still a student at the Royal Academy Schools, he was to sketch from nature, in a variety of media on a range of different papers, on tours of England and Wales (see cat.nos.10–18); he continued to colour prints for engravers and print sellers; begin his copying with Girtin for Dr Monro and in 1794 began a small amount of teaching as a drawing master. Each of these quite distinct ways of working gave him something different. His own demands on his skill were growing and the surfaces he was trying them out on were becoming increasingly varied. But in some ways, it could be said that he had already found the basis of his vocabulary of papers.

Choosing a particular paper to work on involves a complex set of considerations, some of them technical, some aesthetic, and some the product of one's understanding of the capabilities of any particular paper, which is only gained through experience. The experience of both working on a large range of papers, and also learning how to judge them before working on them. When handling a sheet of paper, there are several simple tests that will give a fair idea of that particular paper's capabilities and potential for whatever process or medium is under consideration. Such handling becomes almost second nature as one's experience increases. One does not need sophisticated analytical tools, which can only tell one the facts of the sheet and nothing about the actual and vital process of using the paper.

Several swift shakes of the sheet will indicate the internal strength of the sheet. The higher the relative tone of the resulting 'rattle' of the sheet, the better bonded and stronger the sheet will be, though it must be borne in mind that a large thick sheet will obviously give a deeper 'rattle' than a smaller, lighter weight sheet. Moving the paper around in the light will show the details of the texture and the light reflecting capabilities, the 'brilliance' of the sheet, essential when using transparent or translucent colours on the paper.

Turner's sometimes startling predilection for working on coloured grounds, whether on coloured papers or grounds that he had prepared himself, presupposes an intimate understanding of all these qualities in a sheet, especially when that sheet has been altered with a coloured wash. For any such change to be effective one must also know the depth and degree of sizing in, or on, the paper. This can easily be ascertained, either directly in the initial application of a coloured wash to the sheet, or by testing a small corner of the sheet by applying a small drop of water, or saliva, to a corner of the sheet and watching its rate of absorbtion into the paper.

Tearing the papers will also tell you much about the relative strengths of particular papers. Turner appears to have torn down his papers more and more as his career developed, though it is a little difficult to be certain about this, as many sheets which were perhaps originally torn have since been trimmed.[6]

Bending or folding the paper gives an indication of both the surface strength and the hardness of any surface sizing present. Both sides of the sheet should be examined, as there will be subtle differences between the 'wire' and the 'felt' side of the paper.[7] When working in watercolour, on single sheets of paper, Turner seems to have gone through phases of working only on the wire side, and then only on the felt side of the paper, before returning to another period of working on the wire side. More research is needed to understand quite what this means in terms of both his working methods and the papers he was using. This does not apply to watercolours in sketchbooks, where the folding and binding of the sheets throws up wire and felt sides in complex arrangements throughout the book, often as the opposing halves of one opening.

The texture or finish of the paper affects both the colour and appearance of any mark made on that surface, even with white papers. The rougher texture will weaken the effect of washes, the colour being altered by the shadows cast into the hollows in the surface by the raised areas of the texture. But working with a drier brush over the same rough texture has the opposite effect, brightening the same colour, because the paint will sit only on the high points, leaving the natural white in the hollows of the sheet to show through. Turner, especially for his finished watercolours, seems to have mostly worked on relatively smooth papers. As the finishing of paper became more sophisticated and more specialised during his career, he appears to have quite consistently gone for the smoother surfaced papers, often choosing relatively hard sized writing papers. When he did use drawing papers, designed for watercolour work, again it was usually the smoother surfaces that he preferred. Writing papers, despite their heavy gelatine size, would have had a 'nap' or 'tooth' to them, sometimes erroneously called 'grain',[8] designed to give a small amount of friction to the quill, or the newly popular steel nib, as it glided across the surface of the paper, facilitating the adhesion of the ink, or in Turner's case, paint, to the surface of the sheet.

1 At the beginning of the eighteenth century there were probably some hundred paper mills in England, mostly one or two vat mills, producing chiefly the lower grades of paper, with perhaps a quarter of the mills attempting to produce white paper, and most of that not of the highest quality. By 1800 some 400 mills were in operation, many of them equipped with three, four or more vats, with an increasing number of mills making white papers of various qualities, often alongside the production the coarser sorts, the browns, brown-whites (usually a pale buff colour) and blues.

2 Paper and its making were becoming 'something' in the eyes of many who were not directly involved. William Hickey, in his *Memoirs*, describes 'escaping' by boat from London, for a few days with friends, and much to his father's disapproval, to spend five days

> very agreeably at Maidstone, our headquarters being Mr Watman's, a great paper manufacturer, who entertained us in a princely style. His mills and extensive works were a source of amusement to us several hours in each day, every one of our party making (awkwardly enough) a sheet of paper. . . . Early in the morning of the 30th we once more went on board, leaving the good humoured and unostentatious hospitality of Maidstone with much regret.

3 An indirect benefit to the paper industry, as it was in others, was the Huguenot tradition of women's involvement in the actual running of such businesses: papermaking, silk weaving, glass-blowing, etc. Catharine Balston, Suzanna Whatman, Anne Dickinson, the wives of the best and most innovative papermakers of this period, were all of Huguenot descent, and all contributed much to the running of the mills.

4 Bastard was not always a description of the quality of the paper. It was occasionally used to describe an odd size or quality of paper, a nondescript paper difficult for the Excise men to categorise in terms of the duty payable.

5 See W 1–4.

6 Turner was, almost always, working on handmade paper, where the internal strengths of the paper should be similar across both directions of the sheet, if it has been well formed. But both cylinder-mould and machine-made papers have a 'grain', the fibres being aligned inside the sheet in the direction in which the paper travelled through the machine during its manufacture. They will tear more easily with the 'grain' than across it.

7 The 'wire' side of the paper is the side of the sheet that was next to the wire on the mould, or on the machine, during its making. The 'felt' side is the other side, and takes its name from the first surface the wet paper comes in contact with, after formation.

8 'Grain' is strictly the machine direction of the paper. (see footnote 6, above).

8 Folly Bridge from Bacon's Tower, Oxford 1787

337 × 432 ($12\frac{1}{8}$ × 17)

White laid writing paper

Chain lines: 2.3–2.6 cm (approx 1 in) apart, variable

Laid line frequency: 8 per cm. (20 per in)

Watermarked: I TAYLOR

Heavy Shadows present: Single faced mould

Excellent formation, some process dirt present

Made by James Taylor at Poll Mill, Maidstone, Kent[1]

Worked in ink and watercolour with some pencil underdrawing on the felt side of the paper

Turner Bequest: I A
D00001

W5

8A Transmitted light detail of watermark and look-through, reversed.

8B Raking light detail of ink and surface texture. × 7 magnification.

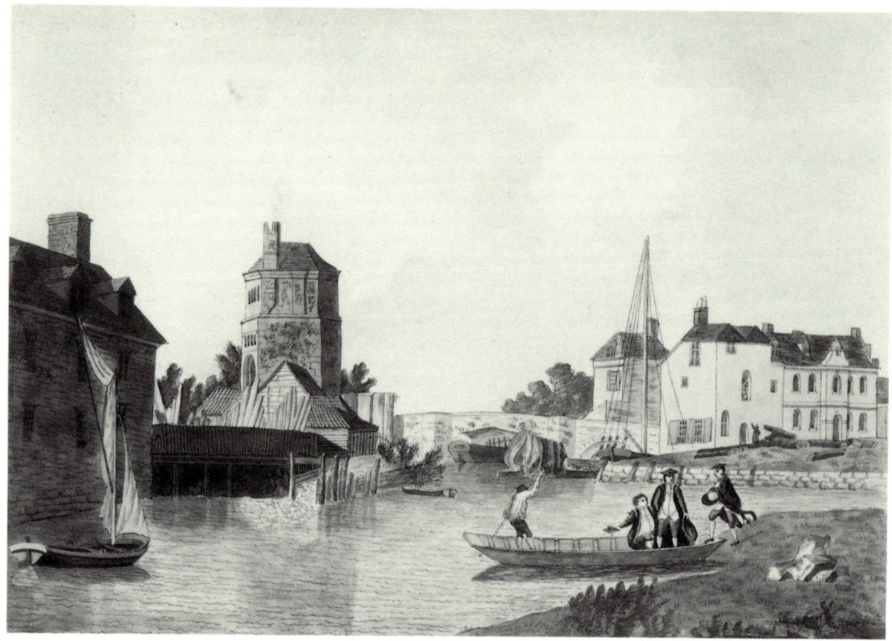

8

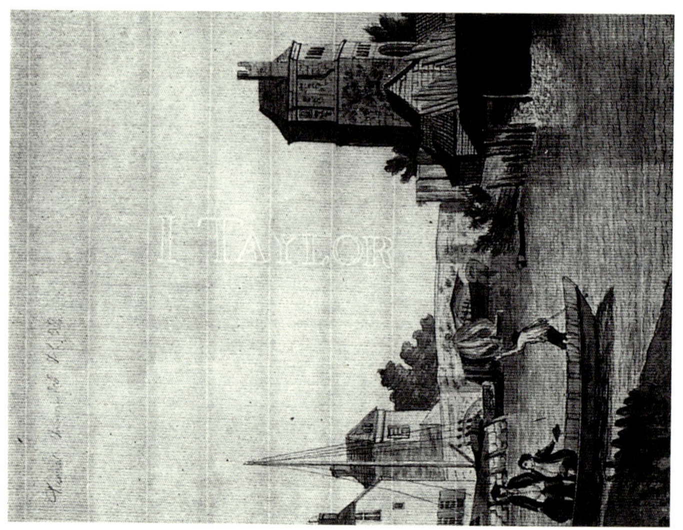

8A

This work, one of the earliest in the Bequest, a copy from an engraving of the 'North West View of Friar Bacon's Study' by Edward Rooker after Michael Angelo Rooker, is worked on paper originally made as a writing Foolscap, and is an interesting choice for a youngster to use. It is a quality sheet, which would not have been cheap. Its rich warm tone is not a product of ageing, but has come from the fermentation process used in preparing the linen rags for beating. Such writing papers are almost perfectly suited to the combination of ink and watercolour used in this work, the basic tone of the sheet lifting the rather restrained, even drab, traditional washes. Turner's pride in his own work is already apparent. He wants it to look good and knows, even at this young age, what will look good.

He chose the same maker's paper for other early works[2] and would probably have gone on using Taylor's paper if he had continued to make paper at Poll mill. It is highly likely that Turner continued to use paper made at this mill, by the same workers. On James Whatman's retirement in 1794 the mill passed to the Balston and Hollingworth partnership, which continued to make paper there, as well as at the main mill, Turkey, and at Loose Mill, until the dissolution of that partnership in 1805.

The Taylors at this date had a good name both in the trade and amongst their customers; it rested largely on the reputation of James Taylor's father, Clement. But in the years following their departure from Poll Mill they managed to alienate much of this goodwill, particularly by attempting to register a patent[3] for a bleaching process that was in fact in common use already all over the British Isles. Other makers objected

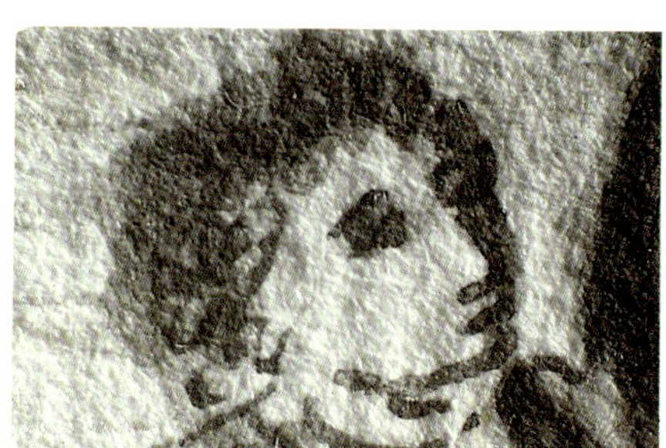

8B

to being asked to pay royalties on a process which in many instances they had developed themselves.

Turner, like all young artists (and when this work was done he was only twelve years old) would have had little idea as to what papers would have suited his particular needs; but living in the Strand he was in easy walking distance of many Artists' Colourmen and stationers. In addition, some of the mills were beginning to acquire warehouse premises in the streets to the east of the Strand and over the river in Southwark.[4]

[1] By the time Turner was actually using this paper, the Taylors had ceased production at Poll Mill and the mill had passed, after a long and complex lawsuit, into the possession of James Whatman, though various members of the family continued to work other Kent mills for some years to come (Balston, 1957, p.73 ff.). Relationships between papermakers, particularly those working in the same small area, were often complex. They were often bound by family ties and a web of partnerships and interests, and often by friendship and a mutual respect born of a common understanding of a highly specialised process, whose deceptive simplicity hid hundreds of years of sometimes very subtle development. Equally, great rivalry and sometimes personal enmity grew up between particular individuals. The Quarter Sessions Books in the Buckinghamshire Record Office record that in 1803 Joseph Mack, paper maker, of Hemel Hempstead, Hertfordshire, undertook to keep the peace and be of good behaviour towards Richard Elliott, paper maker of Chesham Bois, Buckinghamshire, whose mill he had threatened to burn down. For examples of Elliott's paper in the Bequest see cat.nos.54 and 55 (TB CCLXIII 14 and 170. *Watermills of Buckinghamshire*, unpublished researches from The Simmons Collection, Science Museum Library Archives, London.)

[2] TB I B, probably TB I C, and TB II, the *Oxford sketchbook*. All these papers exhibit slightly different characteristics, and include different watermarks, such as the Fleur de Lys / Strasbourg Bend / GR of TB II and the Fleur de Lys / GR mark of TB IC. In TB IV C there is also a C TAYLOR watermark, the mark of Clement Taylor of Upper Tovil Mill, Maidstone, Kent.

[3] Most of these developments in bleaching were in fact based on variations of Hector Campbell's Patent No.1922 of November 1792.

[4] At this date at least two Colourmen were in business in the Strand: Reeves and Blackman were at no.299 and Rudolf Ackermann at no.96. The stationer, William Dickie, from whom Turner was to purchase many of his sketchbooks in later years, was at number 120. Staples, 1984, p.27.

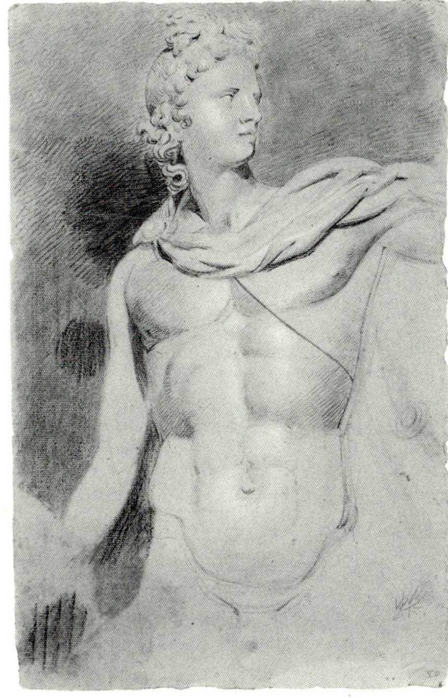

9

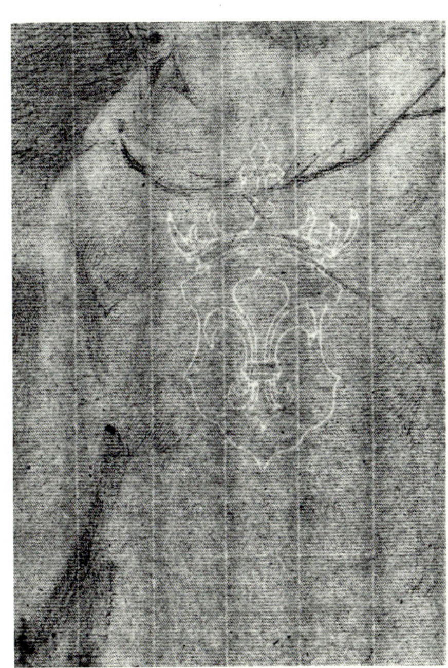

9A

9B

9 The Belvedere Apollo: Head and Torso *c.*1792

419 × 260 ($16\frac{1}{2}$ × $10\frac{1}{4}$)

Brown laid wrapping paper
Chain lines: 27 mm ($1\frac{1}{16}$ in) apart
Laid line frequency: 8 per cm (20 per in)
Watermarked: Ornamented Fleur-de-Lys

Shadows present: single faced mould
Unidentified maker

Black and white chalk and stump

Turner Bequest: V D
D00057

9A Transmitted light detail of watermark and look-through.

9B Raking light detail of chalk, fibre and rugged surface. × 25 magnification.

This drawing comes from Turner's early days as a student at the Royal Academy Schools. On the reverse of the work can be found, in his hand, a note on etching practice:

1 Get an Etching Ground, 26.
2 Heat the back of the P.
3 Rub it over with the Ball.
4 Dab it over with the Dabber of.
Well Hot 5 Smoke it over with Wax Tapur
6 Put some (?) at back of the Palte.
7 Re of Wax
Turpentine Varnish and Lamp Black.

Amongst the many works which have survived from Turner's time as a student at the Royal Academy, many are on various brown, blue or blue-grey (see cat.no.11), drab papers. One cannot be certain as to the actual colour some of these papers would have been when Turner worked on them. We do not know whether they are still undergoing colour changes, or whether they have reached a measure of stability. It is obvious that they have changed since Finberg catalogued them in 1909. Whilst Finberg had the advantage of being some 80 years closer than we are to the date of their making, some of his colour descriptions appear to be somewhat idiosyncratic. One wonders under what light he was examining some of the papers. This brown, for instance, looks quite different in daylight or under fluorescent lighting.

These variously coloured papers appear to have come from a variety of sources: both French and English watermarks can be found.[1] Most of them seem to have been made as wrapping papers, rather than for drawing. Some were possibly resized a little before use.[2]

Resizing a single sheet, or even a batch of papers, would have presented few problems, particularly in an age when artists did not necessarily expect to work directly on to paper, but expected rather to dampen sheets before printing, and were used to toning papers to change their colour, and often prepared their writing papers with sandarac to reduce the greasiness of heavily gelatine sized surfaces. If only one sheet was to be resized, the hot gelatine solution would be applied with a brush, but if several sheets were to be prepared at once then the sheets could be soaked in a gelatine solution and then given a light press to help the size 'bite'.

1 Amongst the coloured papers in this group are:

TB V A Grey laid, watermarked: HR
TB V C Grey Laid, watermarked: HR
TB V G Brown Laid, watermarked: HR
TB V I Brown Laid, watermarked: Fleur-de-Lys
TB V L Brown-grey laid, watermarked: C.A&C
TB VS Buff Wove, watermarked: COUPIALIN

The last paper is of some interest, being a very early French wove coloured paper. Coloured woves at this date are comparatively rare. The first French wove paper had been produced at Annonay, in the Ardêche, by the Johannots and the Mongolfiers, in 1777. It is also difficult to ascertain which mill actually produced the paper. I have found no record, as yet, of either a maker or a mill called Coupialin. There is however a famous French mill called Courtalin, part of the Marais group of Mills run by the Delagarde family at this date. (see cat.nos.29, 30, 31 and 36).

2 This judgement has been arrived at by comparison with many similar French and English wrapping papers in several collections of papers from this period. Many of the wrappings produced at this date would have been quite heavily sized, but others would barely have had any gelatine applied.

10 A Waterfall among Rocks 1792

205 × 162 ($8\frac{1}{8} \times 6\frac{3}{8}$)

'Blue' laid writing paper
Chain lines: 2.7–2.8 cms ($1\frac{1}{8}$ in) apart, variable
Laid line frequency: 9 per cm 24 per in
Watermarked: (partmark) Crown
Shadows present: single faced mould

From comparisons made with papers in my own collection, this watermark appears to be part of a Britannia watermark, found in combination with a J WHATMAN, undated, countermark. The Britannia mark denotes a foolscap sheet, ($17–16\frac{1}{2} \times 13\frac{1}{2}–13\frac{1}{4}$ in.), which takes its name from the continental use of the Fool's Cap or Jester's head with its cap and bells.

Worked in pencil and watercolour on the wire side of the sheet

Turner Bequest: XII K
D00140

10A Transmitted light detail of watermark and look-through.

10B Raking light detail of pencil and watercolour. × 7 magnification.

This sheet was probably made as a lightweight writing, possibly a letter paper, which would have been sold folded, giving the foolscap folio size, 13 × 8 in. when trimmed, that came to be popularly known as foolscap.

This work, from Turner's first sketching tour of Wales in the summer of 1792, appears fairly typical of one of his early ways of working, where the pencil sketch is later coloured at his leisure, Wilton believes that this work was 'possibly the first time that Turner had tackled the representation of a waterfall direct from nature.'[1] He also relates this work to another, slighter, sketch inscribed 'First fall, Monack' (TB XII H).

It is possible that TB XII M, a pencil sketch of a mountain, is another part of the same sheet sited below this sheet, giving a watermark Crown / GR. The pencil sketch is worked on the felt side. This differentiation between pencil on the felt side and colour on the wire side would suggest that the pencil sketch was never intended to be coloured. This difference occurs sufficiently often, with the loose sheets in the Bequest, for it to be more than a merely chance occurance. Obviously such distinctions are not applicable to the work in sketchbooks, where both sides of the paper would often be used, particularly when running the drawing over both leaves of an open book.

This paper is a particularly good example of what is sometimes called a 'corrected white' paper, and variously known as blue and even yellow. The name derives from attempts by papermakers to counteract the yellow cast that often resulted from an over-fermentation of the rags prior to beating, by adding blue dyes to the pulp in the beater or the vat. It was possibly made as a ledger paper, but its relatively light weight would suggest a letter paper. It takes both the pencil and the pigment well, but would not have been capable of standing up to the vigorous handling Turner was to use on a later visit to Wales (see cat.nos.25, 26, 27).

Whatman had first begun to 'blue' his paper in 1765, though makers on the continent had been using the technique since early in the sixteenth century, utilising a variety of different blue substances, from smalts (finely ground cobalt blue glass) to indigo or even small amounts of pulped blue rag added to the furnish. Amongst the evidence given by Whatman in a forgery trial[2] was a discussion on the blueing of white papers and the permanence of the process, at least in the 1760s, when the process was still new to him. He was asked if he was

> able from a sight of any paper, to know whether that paper was manufactured at your mill, and at what time manufactured?
>
> Whatman: Yes. . . . here is an improvement in our manufactory in this sheet, with regard to blueing it; formerly our papers were of a very yellow cast; we have improved the manufactory, by throwing blue into it, as people to in washing linen, in order to take off the yellow cast; the first of my doing was in april 1765; this is very blue; so that I do not believe it has been made more than a twelvemonth; if you please to compare it with paper made seven or ten years ago, there is an amazing difference.

During cross-examination the jury asked him if the blueness would wear off in time and Whatman replied 'Yes; and this is so blue, it convinces me it has

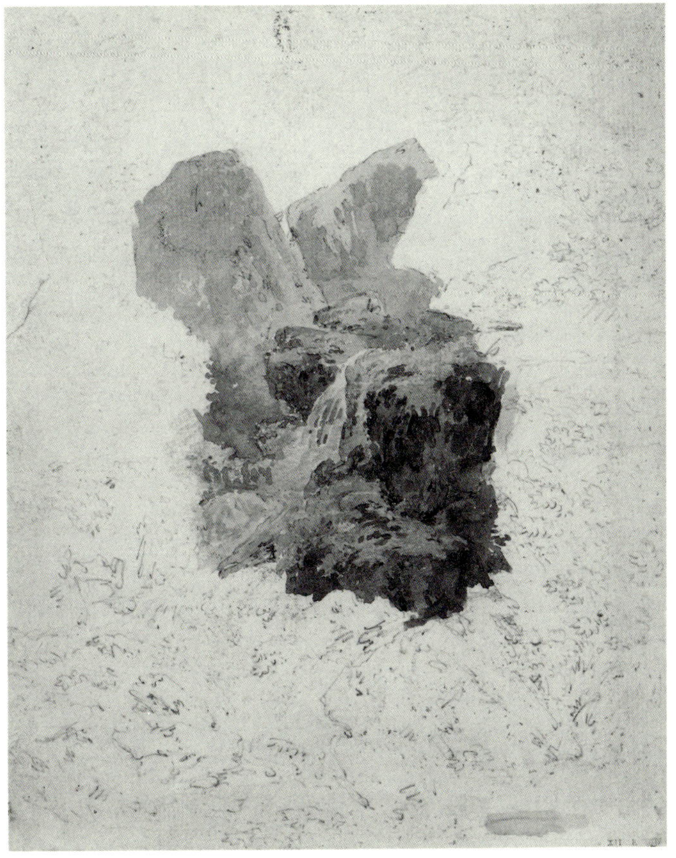

10

been made but a short time.' Such contemporary information is of great importance; it counteracts a tendency to make assumptions as to the original colour and tone of papers that could well be very inaccurate. Some of the 'blued' papers, and indeed the coloured papers generally, appear to have survived or reached a position of relative colour stability, but it can be very difficult to realise quite what the original tone of the sheet would have been. Sadly, the written or published evidence which has come down to us cannot always be trusted. Much of what was written, in various encyclopaedias or journals, was written by people who had no actual experience of papermaking. It is rare to have documented evidence from papermakers themselves in the eighteenth century. It is likely that this sheet was originally rather bluer than it is now, which would change our view of the actual colours used in the painting.

1 Wilton, 1984, p.36.

2 The *Proceedings at the Old Bailey, 1770–1*, No. VII, case 610, on the Trial of Edward Burch and Mathew Martin, accused of forging the will of Sir Andrew Chadwick who had died in 1768. The will purported to have been written in 1764 but Whatman gave evidence that the paper had been made at his mill in 1768. Both men were found guilty and sentenced to death.

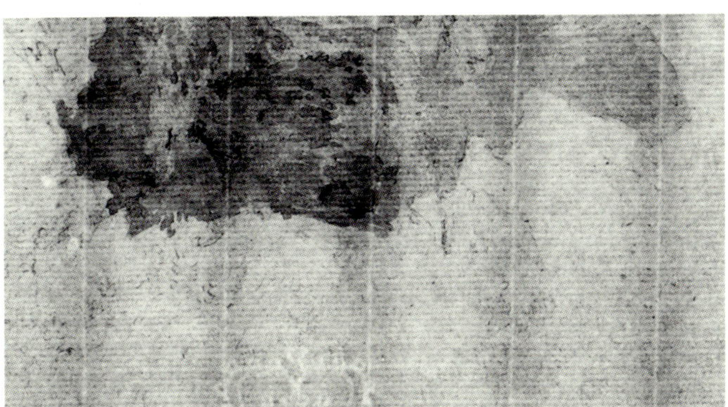

10A

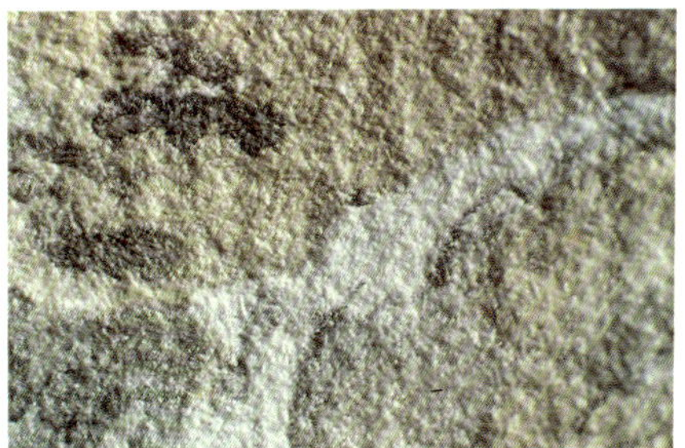

10B

11 Back view of Striding figure with right arm upraised *c.*1797

514 × 365 ($20\frac{1}{4}$ × 14)

Blue laid wrapping paper
Chain lines: 27 mm ($1\frac{1}{16}$ in) apart
Laid line frequency: 8 per cm (20 per in)
Watermarked: '6' or '9'
Shadows present: single faced mould
Unidentified maker

Black and white chalk with touches of body colour

Turner Bequest: XVIII G
D00202

11A Transmitted light detail of watermark and look-through.

11B Raking light detail of chalk, bodycolour, fibre and surface. × 15 magnification.

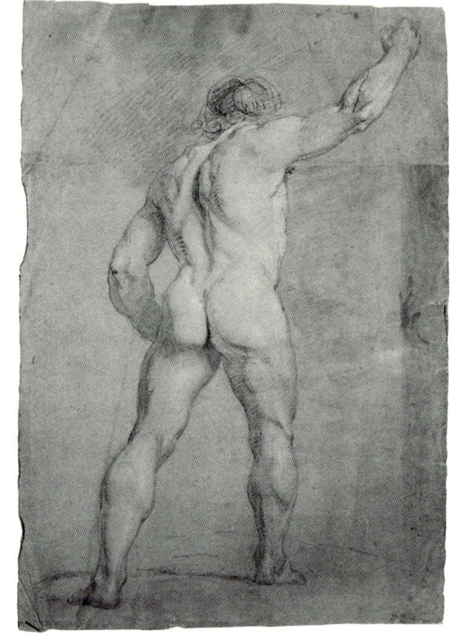

11

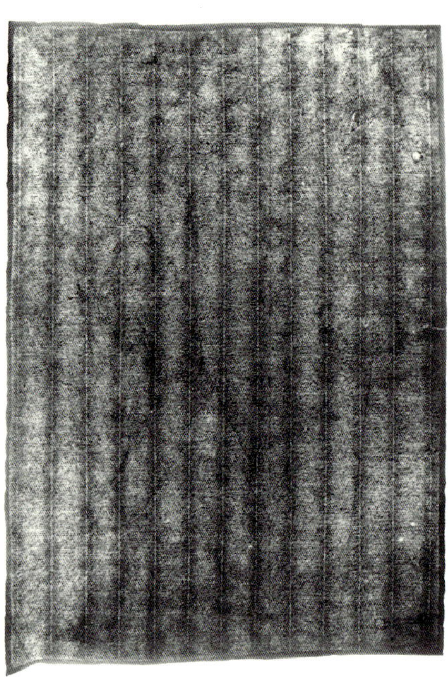

11A

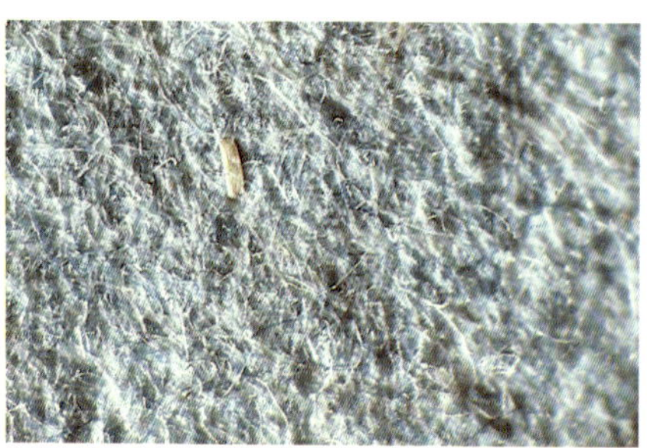

11B

After some years drawing from plaster casts in the Royal Academy Schools, Turner entered the Life Class in June 1792. Many of the papers he was to use in these sessions are very similar to those used in the earlier plaster cast drawings.[1] This sheet has changed colour considerably over time, probably starting off a much richer deeper blue. Many of these blue wrappings were made of blended fibres: old linen clothes, the coarser grades of white rags (that had gone beyond hope of cleaning up) and old hemp sailcloth and ropes, and sometimes even with a small proportion of wool. The newly developed bleaching processes, which were coming into vogue in many of the mills that made white papers, would not have been considered either necessary or desirable in a mill making only such coloured papers. The quality production of coloured papers was only just beginning.[2]

1 See cat.no.2, especially footnote 1. eg: TB XVIII J, a brown-grey laid is watermarked with a Fleur-de-Lys and countermarked: C.A&C.

2 The patent that had ushered in the age of chemical bleaching, which was later to cause so much trouble both to the paper industry and to users of paper, was that taken out by Hector Campbell: Patent no.1922, 28th November 1792. 'Destroying and taking away the carbonic, oleaginous, and colouring elements in rags and other materials used for making paper.'

The first patent taken out attempting to increase the quality of coloured papers and to introduce new colours to the range available was: Thomas Cobb, Patent no.2147, 19th November 1796, 'Making coloured paper for writing, printing, drawing and for various other purposes.'

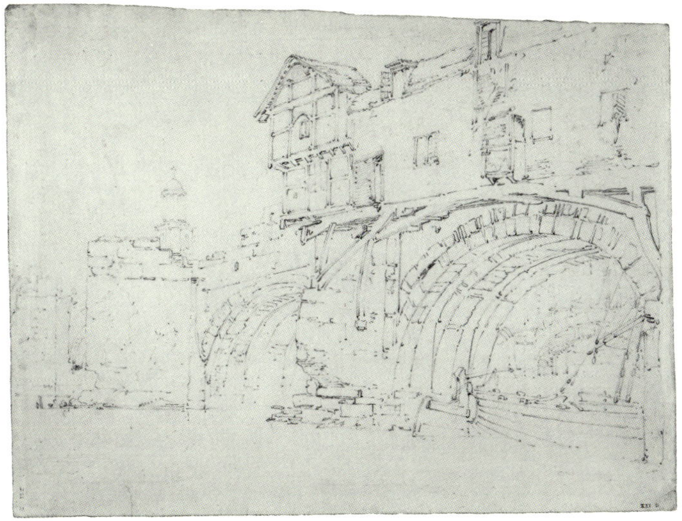

12

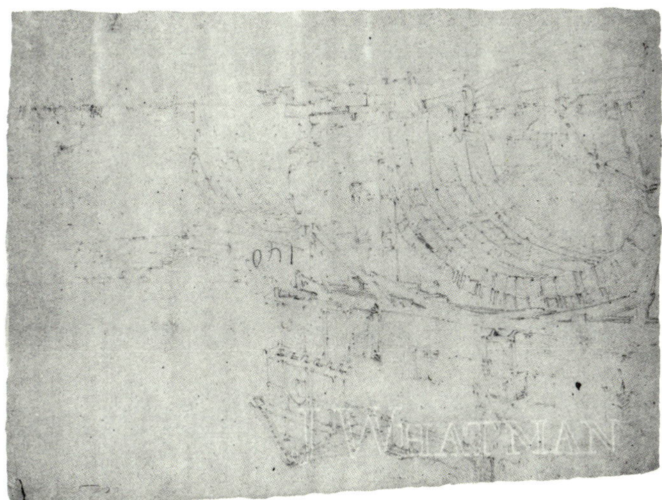

12A

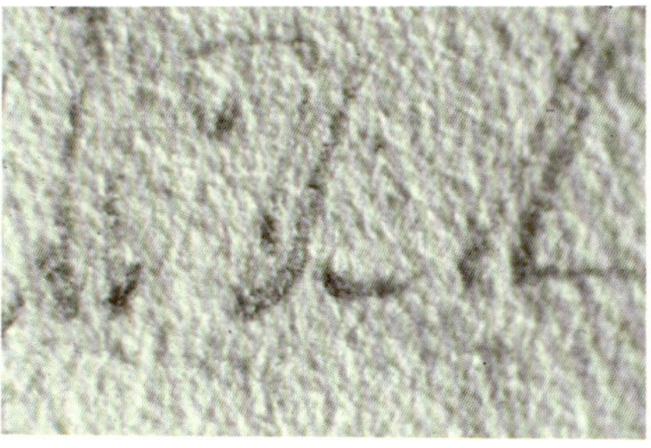

12B

12 The Old Welsh Bridge, Shrewsbury 1794

215 × 276 ($8\frac{1}{2} \times 10\frac{7}{8}$)

White wove writing paper
Watermarked: J WHATMAN
Made by James Whatman the younger, at Turkey Mill, Maidstone, Kent

Worked in pencil on the wire side of the sheet

Turner Bequest: XXI D
D00330

12A Transmitted light detail of watermark and look-through, reversed and inverted.

12B Raking light detail of texture, graphite and particles of smalts in the surface of the sheet. × 7 magnification.

The Bequest contains many cut down sheets similar to this work, which could well have come from sketchbooks. Many of those from this period are of a similar format: Large Post Quarto (approximately 210 × 270 mm or 8 × 10 in). It is possible that some of them have come from sketchbooks no longer extant, but a lot of further research would have to be done in order to establish particular connections between them.

The watercolour, which was worked up from this sketch, was done on a very similar paper, but of slightly different dimensions.[1] Turner has expanded the height by about $1\frac{1}{2}$ inches to increase the expanse of the river, giving more prominence to the reflections in the water, an area completely ignored in the pencil drawing.

The particular qualities of this type of Whatman writing paper appear to have suited Turner. Its hard, gelatine sized but slightly 'toothed' surface, developed for writing in ink with a quill or steel pen,[2] was versatile enough to adapt equally well to both pencil and watercolour. It can be found most often in the Bequest in both sketchbooks and torn or cut down sheets derived from the Large Post size; also, more rarely, in the Double Foolscap and Post sizes.[3]

James Whatman the younger was an extraordinarily innovative papermaker, constantly experimenting and developing his ideas and techniques. The specific drying and sizing processes he developed for his different papers allowed him, in the case of these writing papers, to combine in one sheet considerable internal and surface strengths, a light weight and surface finishes that gave the sheet great versatility. Perhaps more importantly, he developed a tradition of quality control in the mill, enabling consistent batches of papers to reach the markets.[4]

Besides the careful choice, preparation and beating of the rags, and the skilled formation of the sheets, the two elements that contributed so much to Whatman's eminence as a papermaker were the methods of sizing and drying the sheets. To a great extent papermakers kept their ideas and techniques to themselves, but the American papermaker Joshua Gilpin, visiting England at the end of the eighteenth century, recorded various details about Whatman's methods which seem to accord with the actual papers he was producing.

Whatman paid particular attention to the sizing of his paper, both in the materials and the techniques involved. He used some 13 tons of 'scrowls' (or 'scrolls') a year. These were trimmings or scrapings from leather, particularly vellum and parchment parings. Added to this was some 8 tons a year of 'pieces', from rabbit, calves, bullocks and oxen.[5] These were boiled to produce the gelatine, which was then diluted in a 1:10 ratio with water. A small proportion of potash alum would be added to this solution to help the size 'bite' the surface of the paper. Gilpin records that:

> The informed think Whatman's sizeing machine is a large box which holds a whole press full of paper at once. This box has a bottom, but the sides are only standards. In this the paper is laid horizontally and loose. The size is in a very large vatt or tub so deep as to cover the whole quantity in the box. The box with the paper is then raised and brought over the size vatt by a lever on the end of which is a pulley, and lets down into the size, where it remains for an hour or until fully saturated, when it is taken out of the tub and put under the press.[6]

The sizing of a large batch of sheets at one time was one way of ensuring consistency, providing all the utensils were kept as clean as possible. It was also much less time-consuming than the earlier method of laboriously dipping a few sheets at a time into the size tub. Whatman was prepared to save time if he could thereby enhance, and not interefere with, the quality of the finished paper. But in the drying of paper, speed is a definite disadvantage, and Whatman took great pains to carry out his drying very slowly:

> Salmon informs me that Whatman for his best paper has double shutters and curtains inside the drying loft, and will admit no air while it is drying, letting it dry very slowly. Hardens the paper by hanging it in the saule or close store room.[7]

It was the hardness of the size and the internal stability of the sheets, that made it capable of taking the often vigorous handling that Turner gave it. The slow drying allowed all the different tensions, between the fibres inside the sheet, to resolve right out to the edges of the sheet, as it shrank during drying. Quick dried sheets leave these tensions unresolved, making them much less stable, so that when a wet wash of colour is applied to the surface, the tensions are reactivated by the water and the sheet buckles and cockles.

1 Hartley, 1984, p.14 cat.no.5.
2 The first recorded maker of steel pens in England appears to have been Samuel Harrison of Birmingham, *circa* 1780. The new pens rapidly became popular and were in general use by the early years of the nineteenth century.
3 For other Whatman Large Post writing papers in this exhibition, see cat.nos.12, 15, 24, 40, 41, 45 and 50.
4 The traditions of excellence, reliability and innovation begun by the Whatmans at Turkey Mill, were inherited and then further developed by Balston and the Hollingworth Brothers, at first in partnership, and then separately after the dissolution of their partnership.
5 Balston, 1957, p.59.
6 *Journal of Joshua Gilpin*, Vol.XXIII, Sept 17th 1796. Pennsylvania State Archives. From an unpublished transcription by A.P. Woolrich.
7 *Journal of Joshua Gilpin*, Vol.V, November 10th 1795. Pennsylvania State Archives. From an unpublished transcription by A.P. Woolrich.
The 'saule' referred to, is more usually called the 'salle' and is the room in a paper mill where dry paper is finally finished, counted, sorted and graded before going for sale.

13 A Transparency of a Cottage
1794/5
325 × 234 ($12\frac{7}{8} \times 9\frac{3}{8}$)
White Wove drawing paper
Watermarked: none visible
Unidentified maker

Worked in watercolour on the felt side. Areas of the verso have been coloured with indigo and black

Turner Bequest: XXVIII H
D00693

13A Transmitted light showing the effect of the transparency.

13B The verso, showing the back painting that achieved this effect.

Finberg considers that this work and a second transparency, the wash drawing in black and brown inks, 'Moonlight through Trees', date from 1796 and to be connected with the South Wales tour of 1795.[1] Wilton connects this work with an earlier tour of the Midlands in 1794.[2] If this earlier date is correct then Turner had anticipated and discarded the process before the vogue for transparencies which began in London in 1796 and was to last into the early years of the nineteenth century. A contemporary account of this fashion, merely part of a fascination with 'Fancy' paper work that had a brief flowering at the turn of the century, and was to become almost a mania later in the nineteenth century, speaks of

> Transparencies being now so generally admired by the fashionable world, as to be a necessary apendage to every entertainment that can boast of elegance and taste, . . . For painted lamps and lanterns, to hang in a hall, or placed on a supper table, they surpass, for taste and elegance, everything that has yet been invented . . . The most interesting subjects are moonlights, forges, conflagrations, banditti in caves with torches, internal views of Gothic buildings with painted glass . . . .[3]

The second transparency, the almost monochrome, 'Moonlight between Trees' would seem to accord with such fashionable taste, but this work has a different feel to it. A cottager stands outside his home, having a last pipe before retiring. The somewhat drab 'daylight' image is subtlely transformed

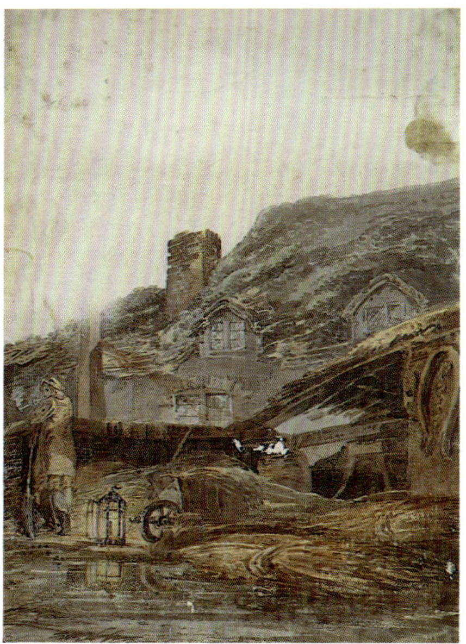

13

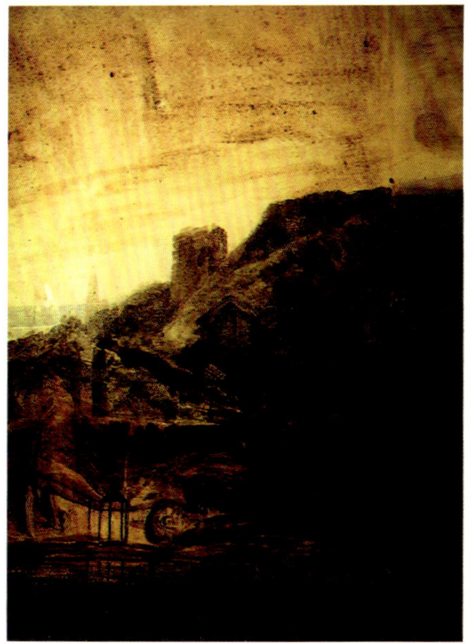

13A

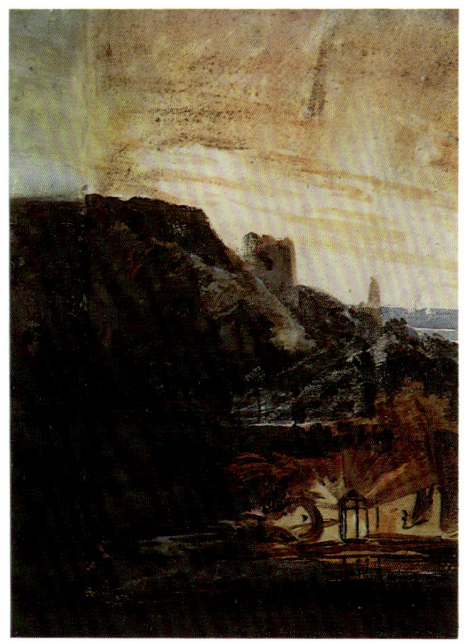

13B

when a light source is placed behind it: the cottage windows and the lantern on the ground cast a warm and welcoming light that lifts the mood.

One method of making a paper transparency was to treat selected areas of a watercolour or print with a resin such as Canada Balsam or a mastic varnish, increasing the translucence of the paper so that when the work was placed in front of a light source the image was changed from a daytime to a nighttime scene.[4] It is interesting that Turner does not appear to have used this technique, preferring to rely more on the natural translucence of the sheet of paper: though there are slight indications that the paper has perhaps been oiled lightly, which would have had a similar effect, but would also have yellowed the paper somewhat.

No other transparencies appear in the Bequest and one wonders what Turner himself thought of the process. It seems to have had sufficient interest for him to make these two attempts at it, each being executed in a slightly different technique. He does not seem to have had any desire to take transparencies as such any further; perhaps considering such tricks only the 'distraction' they would come to be for so many amateur artists. There is, however, a small group of views of Norham Castle,[5] dating from 1798, in which Turner explored the natural translucence of paper in a quite different way: in these works the backs of the sheets have been washed with colour to create a glow or resonance behind the image. They depend for their success on the effect of the light falling on the surface of the work passing through the paper and being reflected back at the viewer. A blank sheet of white paper would have been placed behind drawings executed in this manner.[6]

The transparency or more correctly, translucence, of paper depends on the fibrillation of the fibre during beating, the colour and purity of the water used in the making of the sheet, a good even formation and sound pressing practices: all these contribute to packing the fibres closely together, allowing light to pass through the sheet more or less unbroken or unreflected. Such translucence is often an indication of quality. The dirtier the water, the more loadings used, the less well beaten the fibre, the more opaque the sheet will be.

The two large colour studies of Norham Castle in the Bequest are preparatory workings of 'Norham Castle on the Tweed, Summer's Morn', a large watercolour exhibited at the Royal Academy in 1798. These two studies are on different papers, each washed on the verso with different tones: in TB L B the verso wash is a dusty ochre, whereas the wash used in TB L C is a richer yellow, blended lightly towards the top of the sheet with some red. Turner was developing the most effective way of creating the rich and evocative sunrise to illuminate the castle ruins and suffuse the whole picture with light, despite the depth of the dark tones used in much of the work.

1. Finberg, 1909, Vol.1, p.57.
2. Wilton, Revised Catalogue of the Drawings in the Turner Bequest. In preparation.
3. 'Transparencies' from the *Ladies Monthly Museum*, London, Vol.9, July 1802, pp.59–60. Krill, 1987, p.116.
4. Krill, 1987, p.116.
5. W 225 at the Cecil Higgins Art Gallery, Bedford and TB L B and C, in the Bequest. A second finished watercolour, W 226, has possibly been worked in a similar manner. The papers used for the two studies in the Bequest are:

   TB L B: 663 × 840 ($26\frac{1}{8} \times 33\frac{1}{16}$) on a white wove watermarked 1794 / J WHATMAN and made by the Balston and Hollingworth partnership at Turkey Mill, Maidstone, Kent.
   TB L C: 539 × 742 ($21\frac{1}{4} \times 29\frac{1}{4}$) on a white wove, watermarked J WHATMAN and made by James Whatman the younger at Turkey Mill.

   All four works are of different sizes and have been trimmed after being stretched over boards before working. It is a little difficult to determine the original surface of the two colour studies, owing to the considerable scrubbing they received during working, and later conservation.
6. A similar technique based on the natural translucence of well beaten fibre can be found in the portrait drawings of John Downman, particularly those works executed between 1780 and 1800 when he was living in London.

14 Small boats beside a Man of War 1796

354 × 593 (13 15/16 × 23 3/8)

Off-white laid printing paper
Watermarked: mostly indecipherable, but apparently the Dupuy T with some lettering
Made by Depuy at La Grandrive, Marsac, Auvergne, France

Pencil, watercolour and bodycolour

Turner Bequest: XXXIII e
D00902

14A Raking light detail of prepared surface and paint layer. × 7 magnification.

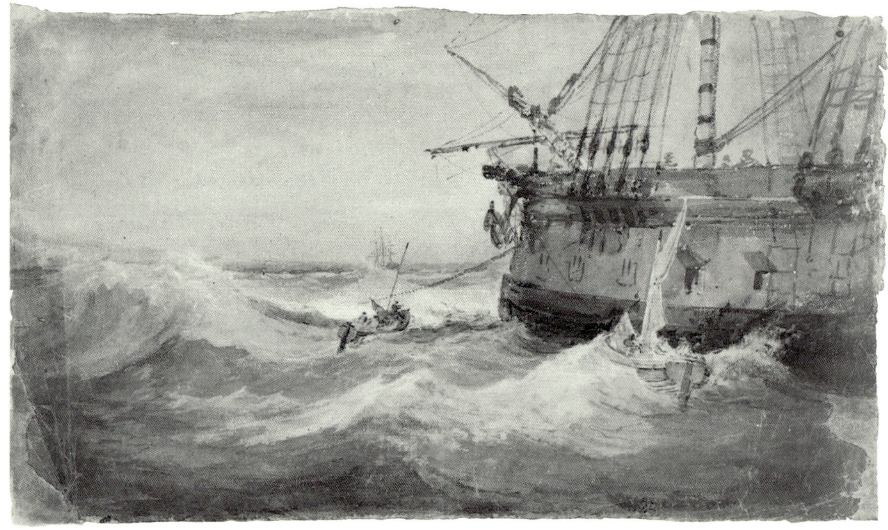

14

Finberg catalogued this paper as being 'sugar loaf paper'.[1] Anne Lyles describes it as buff,[2] it would appear in fact to be a prepared white sheet, which has been washed with a very pale grey-brown wash and then painted. Whilst many of the 1796 sea pieces are produced on buff-grey papers that were made as wrapping papers, this sheet is in fact a printing paper, similar to the papers that Turner was later to use for the printing of the early editions of the *Liber Studiorum*. It is possible also that this sheet has been sized prior to painting, in an attempt to increase its surface strength.

Given the fact that the sheet has been backed and is heavily worked, its colour and apparent coarseness make it very like some of the wrappings that Turner was using for similar works at this period. The nature and character of such papers were well known to him from his work in the Royal Academy Schools (see cat.nos.9 and 11)[3] but perhaps he wanted something more from the paper, some element of strength or durability whilst it was being worked, that he could not get from the wrapping itself. One wonders if he actually attempted to reproduce some of the characteristics of these wrappings in a stronger and better quality paper.

This sheet is certainly one of the earliest prepared papers in Turner's career. The *Studies near Brighton* sketchbook,[4] a blue wove laid paper prepared with a red wash, also dates from this year, the first in which he appears to have prepared the paper with colour before working on it.

Many of the works in the Bequest are backed and it is to be hoped that the gradual process of lifting them will reveal much more about their history and character, as well as revealing other drawings and annotations which have long been hidden.

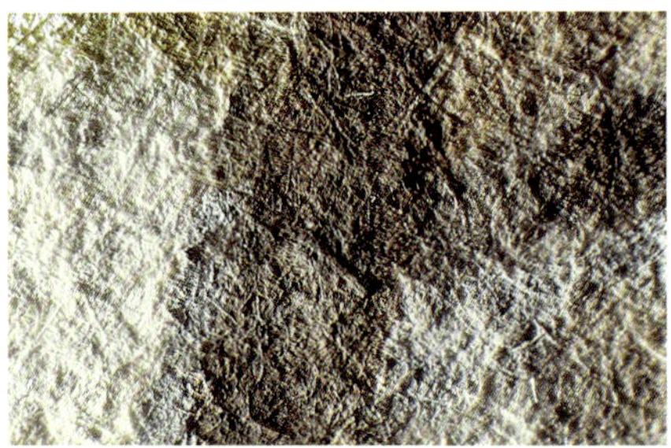

14A

1 Finberg, 1909, p.68.
2 Lyles, 1989, p.29.
3 Such toned papers were in the early years of the nineteenth century to become known as Academy papers. But by the time colourmen were selling 'olives, drabs, buffs and greys' under this name, they were in fact no longer just ordinary wrappings, rather very high quality coloured papers made specifically for artists to work on. The Winsor and Newton Archives at Harrow contain various trade catalogues from the late 1830s onwards.
4 TB XXX. This sketchbook contains two separate papers besides the endpapers: Page size: 114 × 126 (4 1/4 × 5)

(a) White wove
Watermarked: 1794 / J WHATMAN
Made by Balston and the Hollingworths at Turkey Mill, Maidstone, Kent.

(b) Blue laid strong wrapping paper.
Chain lines: 2.3–7 cms (9/10–1 1/10 in) apart, variable.
Laid line frequency: 9 per cm (23 per in)
Shadows present: single faced mould.
Watermarked: none visible.
Unidentified maker.

Owing to the similarities between them, it is possible that this paper was made by the same maker as that used in the *Wilson* sketchbook (cat.no.16), and was probably washed with colour at the same time, prior to binding.

The Whatman paper is possibly a Royal folded 16mo, and the blue laid a Crown folded 12mo. The blue laid paper has been folded so that the chain lines run horizontally across the page rather than vertically.

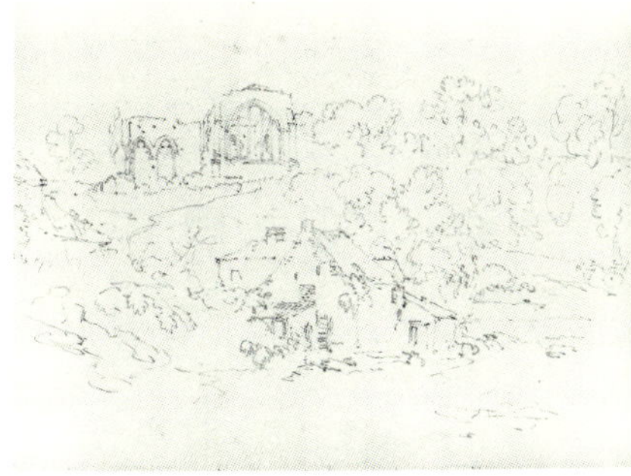

15

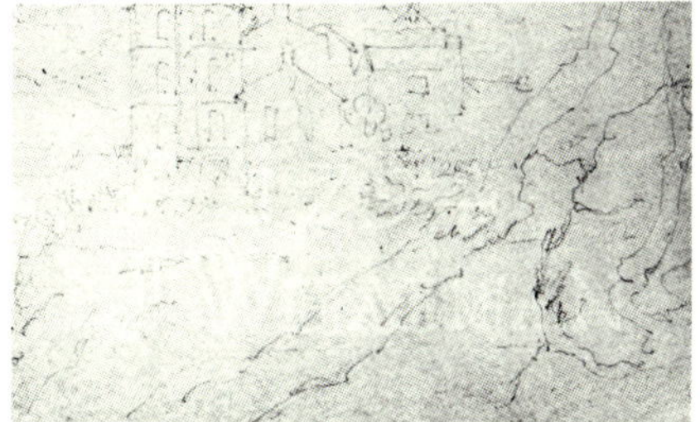

15A

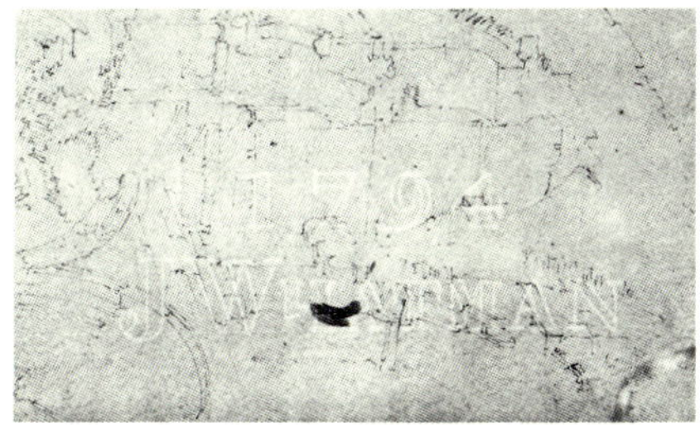

15B

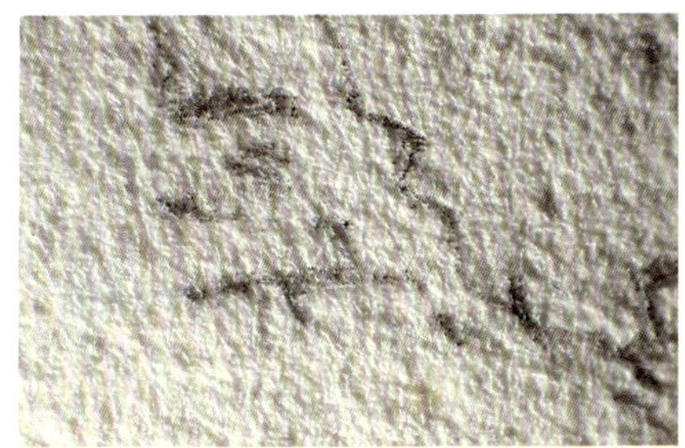

15C

15 Egglestone Abbey and Henry Cooke's Paper Mill 1797

From the *North of England* Sketchbook.
Calf bound sketchbook, with four brass clasps
222 × 276 × 23 ($8\frac{3}{4} \times 10\frac{13}{16} \times \frac{9}{10}$)
Page Size: 209 × 270 ($8\frac{1}{4} \times 10\frac{5}{8}$)

Large Post Quarto. White Wove
Watermarked: 1794 / J WHATMAN
Made by the Balston and Hollingworth Brothers Partnership at Turkey Mill, Maidstone, Kent

Worked in pencil and some colour on both surfaces of the sheets

This sketchbook probably bound by William Dickie, of 120 The Strand, London[1]

Turner Bequest: XXXIV 27
D00933

15A Watermark and look-through of TB XXXIV 18, taken with transmitted light, showing the small M in the watermark.

15B Watermark and look-through of TB XXXIV 52, taken with transmitted light, showing the broken H in the watermark.

15C Raking light detail of pencil and paper surface. × 7 Magnification.

This drawing is the original drawing for the watercolour of 'Egglestone Abbey, near Barnard Castle' (cat.no.41) and relates to another drawing (cat.no.40). The paper used in this sketchbook was produced on a pair of moulds, one bearing a broken 'H' in the watermark and the other with the 'M' smaller than is usually found in the Whatman mark. These watermarks show the paper to be part of a batch of white wove Large Post Writing paper that Turner was to use over a considerable period of years. Unlike many of the other sketchbooks containing this paper, this one has not been prepared with a coloured wash prior to binding.[2] It is possible that the sheets were not washed with colour because they were faulty: there appears to be some evidence of size 'bloom' on sheets 74, 75 and 83. Such 'blooming', caused by applying the size too cold during production, or allowing the newly sized paper to chill in a draught just after the size has been applied, would mean that any colour wash applied to the surface would not take as well in the damaged areas, causing a mottled appearance. The application of gelatine size to the new sheet of paper is a difficult art, needing considerable skill to judge the precise degree of sizing wanted for a particular purpose. A highly sized writing such as this would probably have had more than one application of gelatine.

Another indication that these papers are perhaps not the best quality lies in another sheet, no.40, in which the watermark is very blurred. Some of the pages in this part of the sketchbook would appear to come from sheets that are very badly formed. Some such as 42, 44, 50, 59, and 64 are both yellower and more opaque than others.[3] They may form part of one of the outside quires of a particular ream. The outside quires were usually formed of lesser quality papers, those that were still usable, and sometimes called 'retree' by the mill, to give some protection to the bulk of the good sheets in the ream during its transportation and storage.

Careful examination of the 24 sheets of paper that originally made up this sketchbook shows faults in the manufacture of a good proportion of them. A very bad air bubble in 89 was caused during the couching of the sheet.[4] Other couch faults, where the mould has slipped slightly, or the edge of the sheet has been folded whilst still wet, can be found in 32 and 42. There are also formation faults in 36, 37 and 40. These were caused by a careless knocking of the mould against the side of the vat.[5] The Whatman papers already had a considerable reputation for quality by this date, but any hand-made paper mill always produces its share of bad sheets. Whilst the worst of the sheets, called 'broke', would never have left the mill, being repulped to make new sheets, papers which were not 'broke' would be used as the 'outsides' of reams.

1 See further examples of Dickie's work in this exhibition, particularly cat.no.31.
2 For a complete list of the papers Turner used from this batch of paper, see footnote 2 to cat.no.24.
3 These are the parts of individual sheets that bear the watermarks. This sketchbook is a Large Post Quarto, giving four leaves out of each sheet.
4 Such large air bubbles are common in the first sheet or two of a new post of paper. For

some reason, still not fully understood by papermakers after hundreds of years, when starting to couch a new post of paper air may get trapped under the first sheet as it is transferred from the mould by the coucher. As the post grows this becomes less likely to happen. Papermakers have tried many different ways of avoiding the problem, couching onto a curved surface or onto a wad of wet couch felts, but it still occurs often enough to be a great nuisance. Couch faults are often found in bound books, whether sketchbooks, ledgers or printed books. Bound into a book they become much less noticeable than they would be in a loose sheet.

5 The particular nature of these faults would lead me to suppose that the vatman who formed these particular papers had been drinking, and rather more than would have been usual at this time. Most English handmade paper mills, until well on this century, particularly after the vats had started to be steam heated, would have provided the vat crew with a barrel of ale, in the vat room, which they would have drunk consistently whilst working, as an aid to stopping dehydration caused by the hot atmosphere. Drunkenness while working was rare, but did occasionally occur. Papermaking must be one of the few crafts where such drinking occured, and not only in England: a barrel of wine was very common in many French vat rooms.

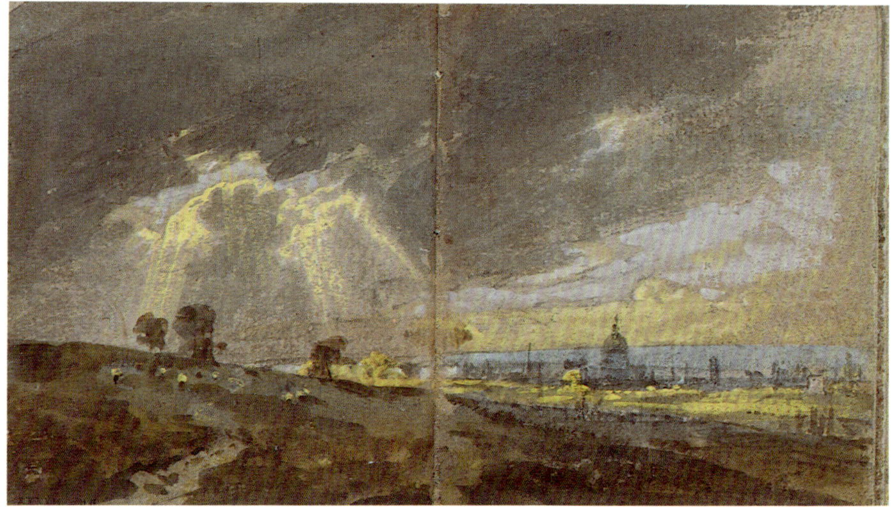

16

16A

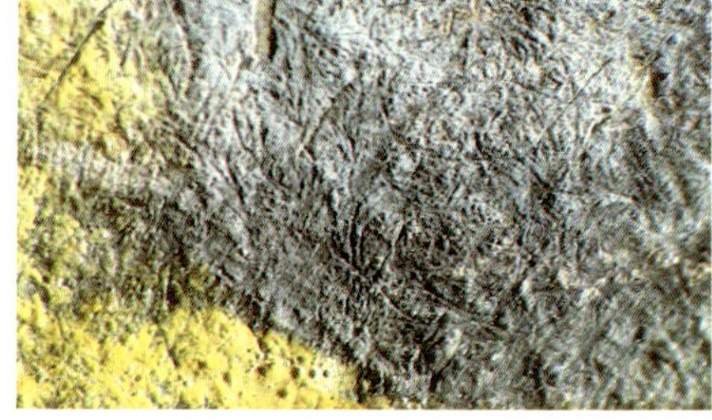

16B

16 Distant View of London from Nunhead? with the sun breaking through stormy clouds 1796–7

From the *Wilson* sketchbook
Small green, leatherbound pocket book, with one brass clasp
115 × 97 × 15 ($4\frac{9}{16} \times 3\frac{3}{4} \times \frac{9}{16}$)

Page Size: 114 × 92 ($4\frac{1}{2} \times 3\frac{5}{8}$)

Crown 16mo
Blue laid wrapping paper
Chain lines: 26–8 mm (1–$1\frac{1}{8}$ in) apart, variable
Laid line frequency: 8 per cm (22 per in) variable
Shadows present: single faced mould
Watermarked: '6' or '9'
Unidentified maker

Pencil, watercolour and bodycolour

Turner Bequest: XXXVII 56, 57
D01173, D01174

16A Transmitted light detail of indistinct watermark and look-through of XXXVII 43.

16B Raking light detail of watercolour, body colour and the rich prepared ground. × 15 magnification.

Every sheet that makes up this book has been washed with a red colour that would, originally, have given a deep red-brown ground.

The *Wilson* sketchbook is so called because it contains several copies after the eighteenth-century Welsh landscape painter Richard Wilson, who was to be an important influence on Turner's early work. Besides these copies, the sketchbook contains many studies of skies, sunsets, seascapes and figures, in which Turner has used the deep ground to explore the complex relationship between the translucence of watercolour and the opacity of bodycolour.

The nature of the particular paper used in this book is such that one doubts whether it would have taken the working it has without the addition of the deep ground. The washing of a layer, or more, on some of the sheets, would have given a considerable increase in surface strength to an otherwise soft-surfaced sheet, especially if the colour had been mixed with a hot gelatine solution before application, and then left to dry out thoroughly before use.

The paper contains a fair measure of wool, which gives a good friction to a brush, nib or even pencil or chalk.[1] Such additions were typical of the low grade wrappings produced by some mills at this period. The paper is possibly of the same origin as that used in other red-washed blue laid sketchbooks used by Turner in the late 1790s.[2]

Watermarks of single numbers, or letters, can often be found in late eighteenth- and early nineteenth-century wrapping papers (see cat.no.18). Many contain only parts of watermarks, sometimes only the broken fragments of marks that are no longer decipherable. Most of the small 'brown', 'brown-white' and 'blue' paper mills of this period would not have had their own mould-maker, and would have bought in old moulds from other mills, moulds which while no longer suitable for the production of the finest papers, either because they no longer retained enough rigidity, or were considerably worn, would still have been serviceable enough for the less exacting qualities of wrapping papers.

This sketchbook is also unusual in that the paper has been folded and bound so that the chain lines are aligned horizontally across the page, rather than in the more usual vertical arrangement.

[1] The inclusion of a percentage of wool in the later nineteenth-century coloured laid papers that were to become known as 'Ingres paper', was to give those sheets their characteristic flecked appearance, and to contribute much to the actual physical qualities of the sheet as it was worked.

[2] TB XXX, *Studies near Brighton* sketchbook of 1796 and TB XLIII, the *Academical* sketchbook of 1798.

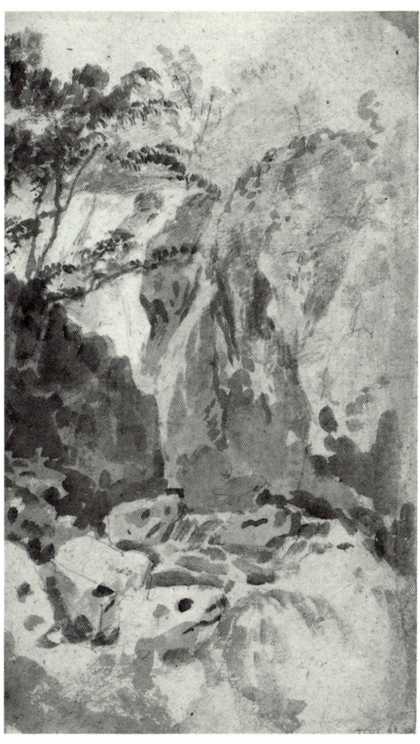

17

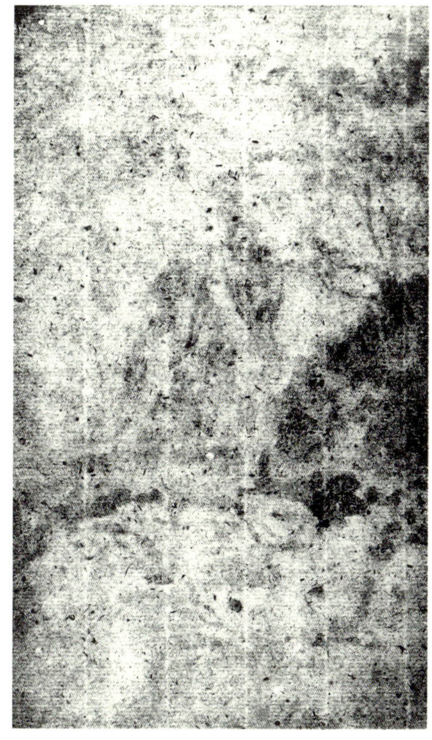

17A

17B

17 A Rocky Stream with a Waterfall 1798

From the *North Wales* sketchbook
Calf bound sketchbook with two brass clasps, now broken
180 × 274 × 27 ($7\frac{1}{8} \times 10\frac{3}{4} \times 1\frac{1}{8}$)
Page size: 167 × 265 ($6\frac{5}{8} \times 10\frac{1}{2}$)

Deep buff, heavily flecked, laid wrapping paper which has probably yellowed considerably over time (pages 44–60,89,92,93)
Watermark: none visible
Chain lines: 2.8–3 cms. $1\frac{1}{8}$–$1\frac{1}{4}$ in. variable
Laid line frequency: 9 per cm, 22 per inch, variable
Shadows present: single faced mould
Unidentified maker

Turner Bequest: XXXIX 93
D01457

17A Transmitted light detail of look-through XXXIX 93, from the verso.

17B Transmitted light detail of watermark and look-through of J Whatman: XXXIX 5.

17C Composite transmitted light detail of watermark and look-through of XXXIX 65 and 68, countermark and look-through of XXXIX 61 and 62.

17D Raking light detail of marks, media, colour of paper and surface of XXXIX 93. × 7 magnification.

17E Raking light detail of marks, media, colour of paper and surface of XXXIX 66v. × 7 magnification.

17F Raking light detail of marks, media, colour of paper and surface of XXXIX 25. × 7 magnification.

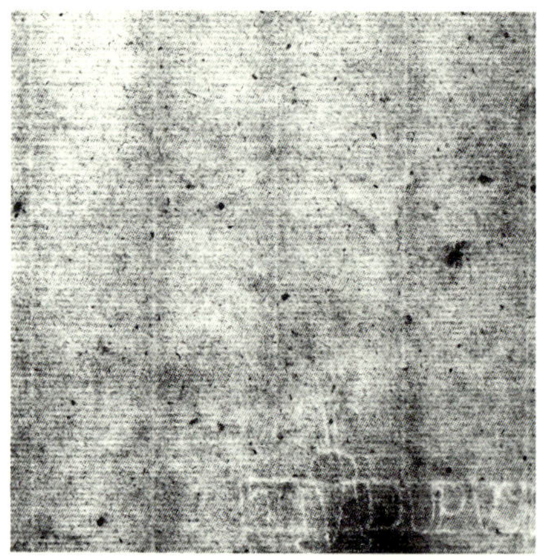

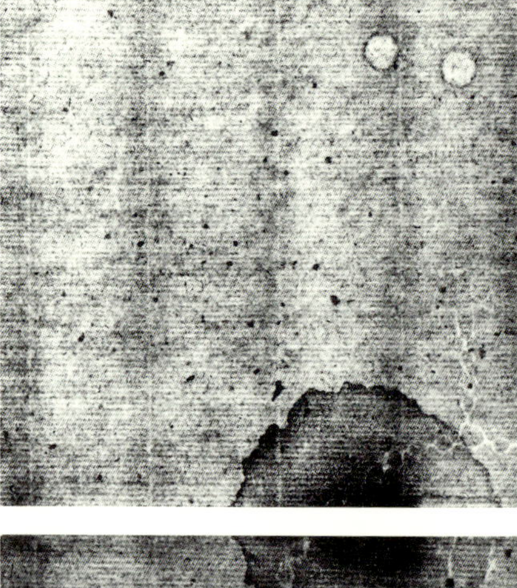

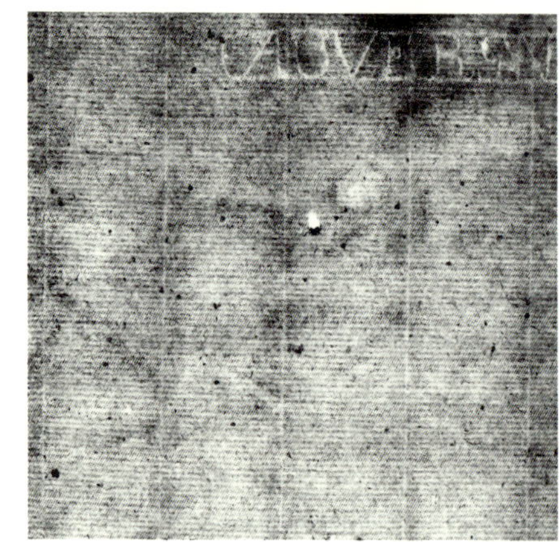

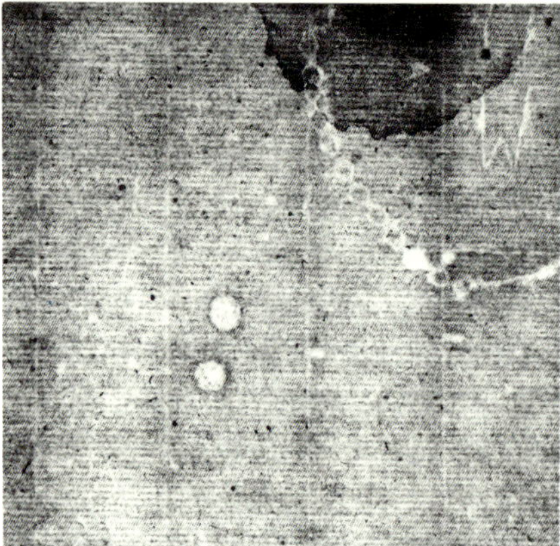

17C

The length and general state of the fibre in this sheet would seem to show a stamper beaten, rather than Hollander beaten pulp, which, at this date would indicate a French origin for this paper. It is not impossible that it was produced at a small English mill, producing brown and brown-white wrappings, which had not yet been modernised by the installation of a Hollander beater.

Besides the paper described above, this sketchbook contains two other papers, from very different sources. Whilst three such different papers may well have been bound up together by a stationer for stock, given the very distinct natures of all three of them, I feel it more likely that these papers were chosen by Turner precisely for their different qualities and characteristics and then bound up for him.

The two other papers are:

(a) White wove writing paper, (pages 1–43,87,88,89,95,96.)
Watermarked: 1794 / J WHATMAN
Made at Turkey Mill, Maidstone, Kent.
These sheets have been drastically trimmed during binding to correspond in size with the second paper in the sketchbook.

(b) Heavy white laid printing paper, which has been very unevenly tinted with a pink wash, (pages 61–68)
Watermarked: T DUPUY / AUVERGNE in lozenges, with traces in two sheets of the ubiquitous 1742 date,[1] as countermarks to a typical Auvergne CIRCLET & CROSS watermark.
Made by Dupuy at La Grandrive, Marsac, Auvergne, France.

The strongly sized white wove Whatman is probably from the same 'Broken H' batch of paper that we have found in several other sketchbooks and amongst the loose sheets. This paper is a heavily trimmed Large Post Writing, which at this date would have been described as 'thick' with a surface now known as 'hot pressed', a term that only came into general use later in the nineteenth century. The surface may well have lost some of its smoothness over time. Turner has mostly worked only on the wireside of this paper.

The smooth polished dark buff, probably wrapping, paper, contains various blue, red, brown and black fibres, the latter two probably coming from old tarred hemp rope. Traces of the deckle are visible on several pages. Both the other papers have been trimmed to accommodate this.

The pink washed French paper has a relatively smooth surface, but the original felt impression remains clearly visible on both sides of the sheet. It is softer sized than the Whatman, and was possibly made as a printing paper. Dupuy papers were well known in England as Plate papers, for copperplate engravings, and had been imported since the middle of the eighteenth century. Turner himself was to use papers made by Dupuy for the early impressions of parts of the *Liber Studiorum*,[2] and there are other examples of Dupuy papers in the Bequest (see cat.no.14). Despite the continuing war with France, considerable stocks of imported French papers, especially for engraving and etching, would still have been available in London. It is possible that some unofficial trade was still continuing in very specialised papers; but more research is necessary to determine this.

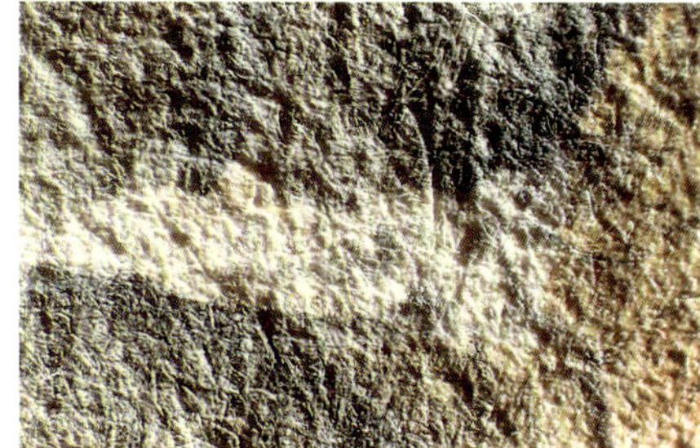

17D

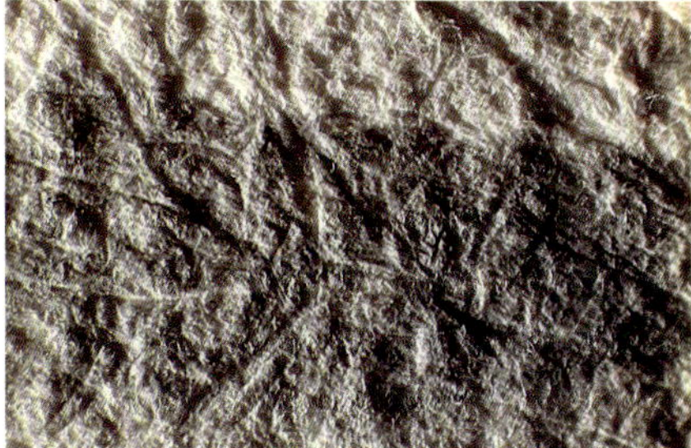

17E

17F

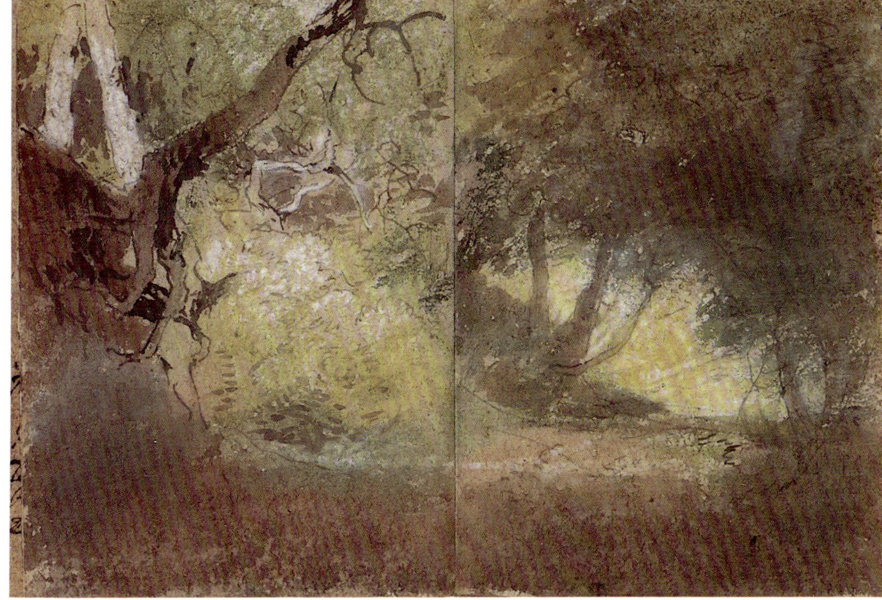

18

18A

18 A Woodland Scene 1798–9

From the *Swans* sketchbook
Calf bound sketchbook with one brass clasp
133 × 180 × 25 ($5\frac{5}{16} \times 7\frac{1}{8} \times 1$)
Page size: 174 × 125 ($6\frac{7}{8} \times 4\frac{7}{8}$)

Imperial 16mo
Self-coloured coarse brown laid
Chain lines: 28–30 mm ($1\frac{1}{8}$–$1\frac{1}{4}$) apart, variable
Laid line frequency: 6–7 per cm (15–20 per in.) variable
Watermarked: 5 (in XLII–80) plus indistinct traces in 10, 24 & 70

Worked in brush and ink, watercolour and bodycolour

Turner Bequest: XLII 136, 137
D01812, D01813

18A Transmitted light detail of watermark and look-through of XLII 80.

18B Raking light detail of bodycolour, entangled fibre and surface. × 30 magnification.

The majority of this sketchbook is worked in pencil, chalk and colour on both sides of the paper. It was generally a low quality paper, but such papers provided artists with a different tonal ground, almost impossible to achieve by tinting the paper with a wash, or even

[1] This date is probably not the date of manufacture. It relates rather to an official ordinance of Colbert's, from 1741, which regulated the manufacture of particular papers. Makers continued to use the moulds with the date 1742 for many years without changing the dates. Many of the 1790s English papers, dated in the watermark, used by Turner suffer from the same kind of inaccuracies. It was not until the early years of the nineteenth century that English makers regularly changed the dates on their moulds.

[2] These *Liber Studiorum* papers were a white laid Colombier, approximately $23\frac{1}{2} \times 34\frac{1}{2}$ in., watermarked with the Dovecote which gives its name to this size of paper, and countermarked (T DUPUY / AUVERGNE / 1742). This particular paper size was originally developed by the Auvergne papermaker, Colombier, who used the Dovecote as a play on his name. Finberg in *The History of Turner's Liber Studiorum*, 1924, makes some errors in his descriptions of the papers used in the Liber, not realising that the watermark he read as 'La Grande', and presumed to be a reference to the paper's size or quality, actually reads 'La Grandrive' and is the name of the mill.

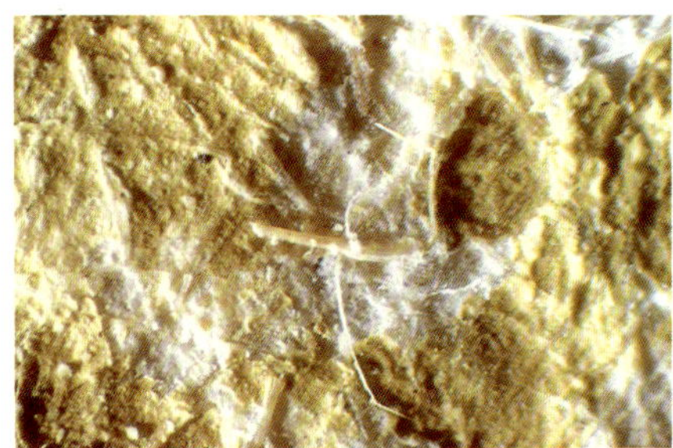

18B

by dying, whether during making or after. The colour comes purely from the 'furnish', the pulp used in its manufacture.

It is possible that this is a French paper, though the war had put paid to most of such trade. The lone number '5' could possibly refer to the Revolutionary Year 5 (September 1796–Sept 1797). The actual style of the watermark '5' is similar to other French numbering from this period and later. Another single number watermark in the Bequest is the '6' or '9' found in the red washed blue laid paper of the *Wilson* sketchbook, (TB XXXVII) cat.no.16.[1]

Where certain pages have been exhibited they have gone very brown indeed; this coupled with the crackle of the paper would suggest the presence of the short crisp fibres of straw in the furnish.

Straw can be found in many Western European papers, generally those of the lesser qualities, almost throughout the seventeenth century and onwards, and was usually used as a cheap, locally available filler to bulk up the rags. By the end of the eighteenth century, with the increasing demand for raw materials from a greater number of mills, straw was being seriously looked at as an alternative to rags. Matthias Koops registered his patent, No. 2481, in London in 1802 for the manufacture of straw papers at both Neckinger Mills in Bermondsey and his new mill at Millbank.[2]

Not all straw paper was as coarse as the paper in this sketchbook. The second edition of Koops' book *An Historical Account of the substances which have been used to describe Events, and convey Ideas, from the Earliest Date to the Invention of Paper*, published in 1801, was printed on paper of a very high quality, 'manufactured solely from straw'. Joseph Farington refers to Koops' paper in his diary:

> Murray the Bookbinder in Princes St shewed me today a quire of straw paper. He said that manufacture had not answered and the partners had each lost several hundred pounds. The quality of the paper was good, but they could not manufacture it so cheap as the paper made of rags.[3]

1 For a discussion of single numbers in watermarks at this date see entry for cat.no.16.

2 Papermakers seem to have had recourse to straw in various times of shortage, in the French Revolution or the Second World War for example. Such troubled times have generally led to inferior papers being made, some of them from straw, when simply getting the paper made was of more importance than the strength or durability of the sheet. But it is easily possible to make excellent papers from straw. Indeed the use of straw is rapidly increasing today, with a new 'greenfield' pulp mill in prospect for this country and the increase in the blending of this annually renewable resource with other fibres to produce very high quality printing papers.

3 The Diary of Joseph Farington, Yale 1979, Vol.6, 9th June 1804.

The paper used for TB CCX A, 'Two Studies for *The Fall of Jericho*', was made on a mould that originally came from Koops' Neckinger Mill. It is a half sheet watermarked N. . . . . ./M. . ./18. . . The missing lettering was probably removed when the moulds and all the equipment were put up for sale on 27th October 1804, after the mill failed. It has proved impossible to identify which mill actually made this paper.

Experiments with Drawing Papers (cat.nos.19–27)

Turner experimented with paper surfaces, and the working methods appropriate to them, throughout his life. Indeed, the evolution of both his painting and his understanding of grounds and materials was inextricably bound up together. One of the most concentrated and productive periods of such experimentation began in 1798, the date when he appears to have started working on papers that can definitely be described as having been designed for drawing.[1]

The next few years were a time of intense activity for him, with tours to Kent, the Welsh Marches, North Wales (twice), Lancashire, the Lake District and Scotland, culminating in his first continental tour in 1802. Despite his travelling, he appears to have been obtaining most, if not all, of his papers in London. The identifiable papermakers are all, with one exception, Kent-based: they naturally sent their wares to London stationers and merchants at this date.[2]

A noticeable feature of Turner's work on paper during this period is his constant exploration of surface strengths and textures. In many cases the papers are not as obviously different from each other as some of the papers he had been working on earlier, but as his techniques developed he came to focus more on very specific details of the papers that might suit his needs. The London colourmen and stationers were handling a greater variety of sizes, weights and textures of paper, of increasing quality, and sometimes made specifically for drawing.

He must have seen or been shown many of these new papers. There are isolated sketchbooks, individual sheets, various small groups of sheets that were probably obtained for trials throughout the Bequest. But what seems to have preoccupied him with regard to paper during this period, despite all the different media he was using, were surfaces upon which he could work out various technical problems, particularly those associated with applying colour in ways that would create the kind of atmosphere that would reflect his own vision. The two Stourhead subjects (cat.nos.19 and 20) are just such attempts to enlarge his pictorial vocabulary. He comes close to success but the surface of the papers used are not resilient enough for his needs.

The large works done from nature in North Wales, and those

executed in the studio, on his return, (see cat.nos.25,26 and 27) show him beginning to succeed in his complex washing and scrubbing and lifting out of colour. When we examine the three different papers used we find a cut down Whatman Antiquarian drawing paper, which has been stretched on a board before working, and two somewhat inferior quality drawing papers, probably bought as seconds. These two sheets were taken with him, still folded, as they would have come from the mill, on his travels. They were worked on flat and then folded up again for transportation. They both show signs of a 'back' and repeated folding.[3] What seems to have concerned him with these three papers, was the behaviour of his relatively coarsely ground pigments on subtlely different surface textures, which were also sized to different degrees.

These early ventures into a range of complex painting techniques are all executed on quite a large scale. A fascinating part of Turner's exploration lies in his ability to work equally well on so many different scales, matching the texture of his surface to the detail and intensity of the marks he makes with equal facility, regardless of the size of the sheet. A large heavyweight Not surfaced drawing paper is usually rougher than a smaller, thinner sheet. This is a result of the papermaking process, where the felt mark bites deeper into the greater bulk of the thicker sheet than into the thinner, and is consequently harder to remove in the finishing of the sheet. Faced with two weights of paper of the same size and nominal surface, Turner seems to have gravitated towards the lighter weight sheets, which for the above reason would have had smoother surfaces. Another factor that must be borne in mind with the thin linen-based sheets of his time, is that the relative strength of the surface increases with the thinness of the sheet: the surface of a thinner sheet being more compressed and consolidated in the first wet press during making, an action that is reinforced by any further pressings that the sheet is subjected to. A fascinating and perhaps unique example of Turner using two very different papers together in the same work is 'Edinburgh from Calton Hill' (cat.no.23). In this work a very lightweight smooth paper has been cut and pasted down onto a much heavier textured paper. The thin paper used for the bottom half of the sheet shows the kind of paper Turner liked to use, when he had begun to understand the relationship between paper weights and surface strengths.

As Turner painted, some of his actions changed the very nature of the working surface. This happened too often, and with too much fine discrimination, for it to be anything less than deliberate. He was beginning to know precisely what his surfaces were capable of, discovering their potential as he worked: 'Turner has no settled process but drives the colours about till he has expressed the idea in his mind.'[4] In some ways Joseph Farington's description of Turner's working methods in 1799 describes very adequately what was happening in 'Dolbadarn Castle' (cat.no.25), but a few years later, about the time of 'Edinburgh from Calton Hill' Farington was to describe a much more particular and controlled Turner:

> The lights are made out by drawing a pencil (the old name for a brush) with water in it over the parts intended to be light (a general ground of dark colour having been laid where required) and raising the colour so dampened by the pencil by means of blotting paper; after which with crumbs of bread the parts are cleaned . . . A rich draggy appearance may be obtained by passing a camel hair pencil nearly dry over them, which only flirts the damp on the parts so touched and by blotting paper the lights are shown partially.[5]

He was beginning to find the surfaces that would give him precisely the responses that he needed, and not just for watercolour. His explorations into monochrome pencil and chalk in the 'Scottish Pencils' (see cat.no.21), a technique that was to be repeated to more effect in the 'Grenoble' sketchbook of 1802 (see cat.nos.30 and 31), were done on another drawing paper, a medium weight Super Royal. The way the chalk and different hardnesses of pencil could be worked into the very textures of the paper would have given him yet more insight into the potential of such sheets.[6]

Not all the white wove papers he was using during this period were drawing papers. He continued to use the Large Post writings he was to favour throughout his career, and was still working on coloured grounds, either coloured paper or surfaces that he had prepared himself (see cat.nos.17, 18 and 21). Though the identifiable papers used during this period are predominantly watermarked Whatman, several other makers are represented, and the Whatman marks hide a great range of paper types, sizes and surfaces.[7]

[1] Though cat.no.13, 'A transparency of a cottage' may well have been done on a drawing paper.

[2] The exception being TB XLIX, the *Salisbury* sketchbook which was in use between 1799 and 1800. The makers of the paper, John and Edward Gater, had an excellent reputation for fine papers. They did send paper to London, but given the nature of much of the subject matter, it is likely that it was purchased in Salisbury, rather than London. Its specifications are:

Calf bound sketchbook
155 × 131 × 23 ($6\frac{1}{8} \times 5\frac{1}{8} \times \frac{7}{8}$)
Page size: 149 × 125 ($5\frac{7}{8} \times 4\frac{7}{8}$)

Foolscap Quarto, radically trimmed.
White laid writing paper
Watermarked: Crowned Brittania with an initial G
Countermarked: GATER / 1799
Made by John and Edward Gater, Up Mill, South Stoneham, Hampshire.
Worked in pencil.

This sketchbook was bound with the chain lines running horizontally rather than vertically, as would be more usual.

[3] Though earlier in the eighteenth century, a visible 'back' in a sheet had been a fashionable conceit amongst some artists, many would despair of getting large flat sheets to work on. Much soaking and stretching could remove it, to some extent, in a fairly newly-made sheet, but not always successfully. An alternative drying method was developed, early in the nineteenth century, which by the 1860s was being heavily marketed by artists' colourmen. This drying method involved laying the wet sheets flat, in spurs of several sheets at a time, dependant on their size and weight, on canvas 'sails'.

Winsor and Newton, in their Trade Catalogue for 1861, were describing

> Whatman's Seamless drawing papers in Not, Hot-Pressed, Rough . . . perfectly flat, and without any seam mark across the centre of the sheet. . . . great advantage will be found to result from the Antiquarian having been dried on the new flat principle, whereby the line mark across the centre is avoided, and a uniform surface presented.

It would appear that this method of drying was not new in 1861, but had been developed in various forms earlier in the century, specifically for drying newly sized sheets.

[4] Farington, 1979, 16th November 1799.

[5] Farington, 1979, 28th March 1804.

[6] 'Black Lead' pencils, of solid plumbago (or graphite), encased in cedarwood, had been available for some time, but as the demand for pencils outstripped the amounts of fine quality plumbago available, several ingenious solutions were devised to make use of the poorer grades of this material. Powdered black lead was bound with gum, resins, sulphur, antimony and isinglass. The most successful process however was that developed, in 1790, by Nicholas Jacques Conté and Joseph Hardtmüth, working, independently of each other in Paris and Vienna. They produced very satisfactory leads by mixing finely powdered graphite with china clay and firing it in a kiln. This had the additional advantage of producing leads of varying degrees of hardness, according to the proportions of the materials used.

Some pencil makers were rather unscrupulous:

> Genuine cedar pencils must cost at least sixpence each. Pencils of a spurious kind are however sold as low as $4\frac{1}{2}$d per dozen. . . . the most successful attempt at deception is where the pencil has all the outward form and semblance of being well made, but where a process of anatomisation shows the purchaser that the amount of black lead is marvellously small, the central part of the groove being filled with a different substance.

from *A Series of Articles on Writing Materials originally Published in the Saturday Magazine, 1838–9*, and reprinted in 1984.

[7] The makers represented during this period include:
- William Elgar (see cat.no.27)
- John and Edward Gater (see footnote 2, above)
- Dupuy (see cat.no.17)
- John Larking: Upper Paper Mill, East Malling, Kent. TB LXII, LXV
- Robert Edmeads and John Pine Ivy Mill, Maidstone, Kent. TB LXIII, LXX L
- John Hayes and John Wise: Padsole Mill, Maidstone, Kent. TB LVII, LXX G, LXXX H (and cat.nos.28 and 34)
- Charles Willmott; Sundridge Mill, Kent. TB LVI

19 View over the Lake at Stourhead
*c.*1798

16 × 544 ($16\frac{3}{8} \times 21\frac{1}{2}$)

White wove writing paper
Watermarked: J W
Made by James Whatman the younger at Turkey Mill, Maidstone, Kent

Pencil and watercolour with some scrubbing of the sheet

Turner Bequest: XLIV f
D01908

19A Transmitted light detail of watermark and look-through, reversed and inverted.

19B Raking light detail of fibre and paint layers. × 7 magnification.

20 View over the Lake at Stourhead
*c.*1798

442 × 595 ($17\frac{3}{8} \times 23\frac{1}{2}$)

White wove writing paper
Watermarked: 1794 / J WHATMAN
Made by William Balston and the Hollingworth Brothers at Turkey Mill, Maidstone Kent.

Pencil and watercolour with scrubbing, scraping and stopping-out.

Turner Bequest: XLIV g
D01909

20A Transmitted light detail of watermark and look-through, reversed and inverted.

20B Raking light detail of fibre and paint layers. × 7 magnification.

Some thirty years elapsed between the making of these two papers. They both come from the same mill but are the products of different companies, and very different papermaking. The paper used in cat.no.19 dates from the 1760s, soon after James Whatman the younger had assumed control of the mill and the business, and is a very early example of a wove paper.[1] That in cat.no.20 dates from the period immediately after the transfer of ownership to the Balston Hollingworth partnership. By this time Turkey mill was operating five vats, Poll mill two vats and Loose mill a single vat. The scale of the operation had grown enormously from its start in 1740, as had its concerns: new markets were opening

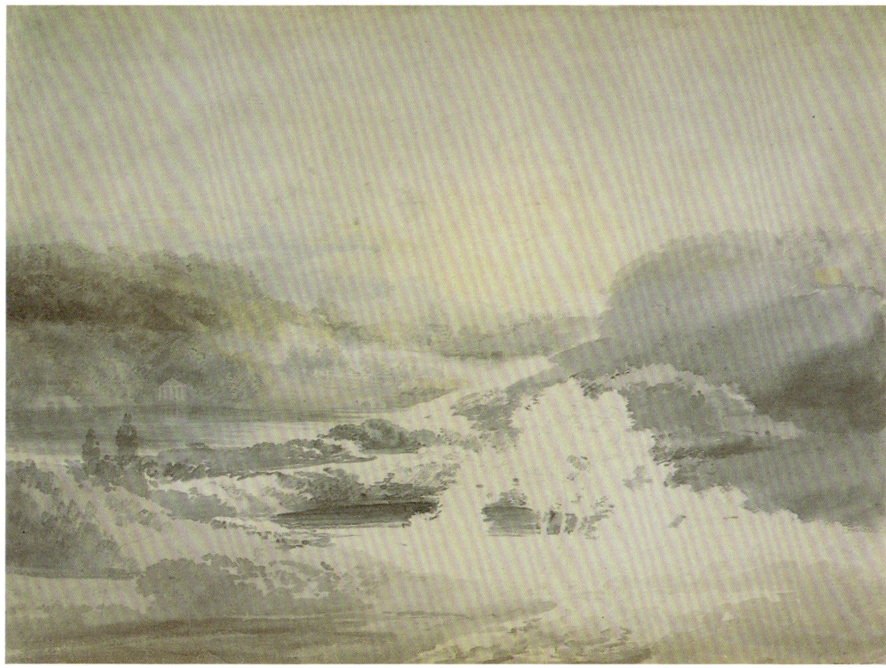

19

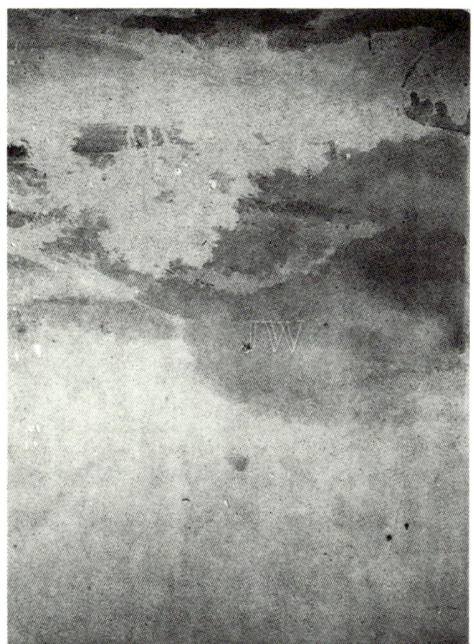

19A

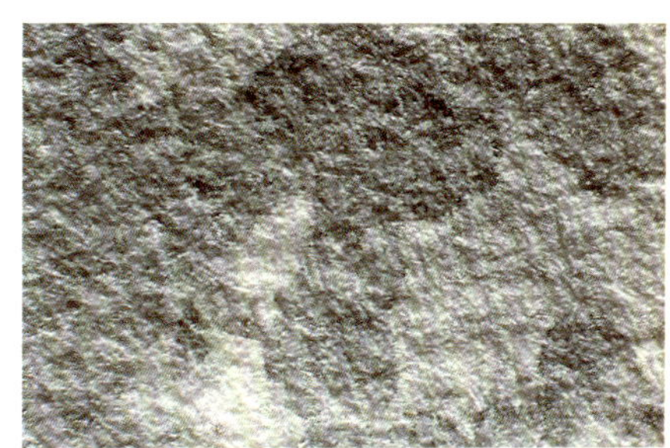

19B

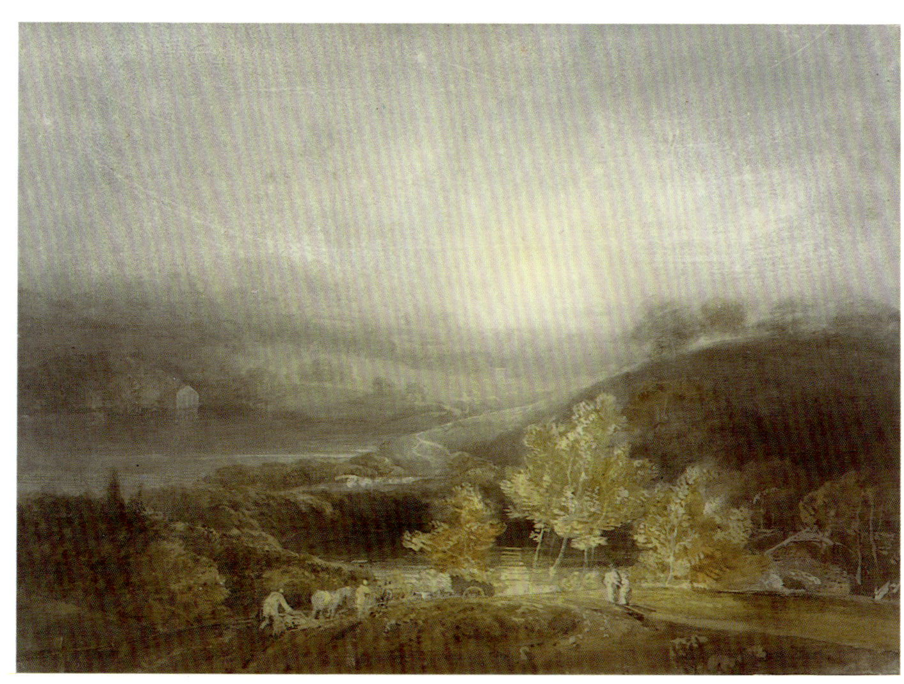

20

20A

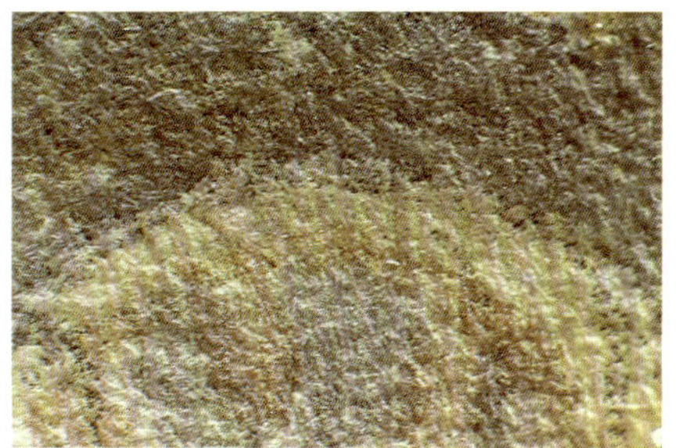

20B

up, and amongst all the various printing and writing papers the Whatman mills were producing, they were gradually developing the drawing papers that were to make their name.

These similar views of sunrise over the lake at Stourhead, the seat of one of Turner's most influential patrons Sir Richard Colt Hoare, are both unfinished attempts to capture the particular light and emotive power of sunrise in an idyllic setting. The cut-down sheets suggest that both these papers were stretched on boards prior to working: the only way that one could adequately control the washing and scrubbing necessary to achieve the effects Turner desired.

It would be difficult to say which was begun first; perhaps they were worked on together. Anne Lyles relates both to another unfinished work, a *View of the Bristol Cross, above the Lake at Stourhead*.[2] In cat.no.19, it is likely that part if not all of the sheet was washed with colour prior to working, and that in the sunrise area of the sky the sheet was then vigorously scrubbed back to the original colour of the sheet. Scrubbing the surface of the sheet changes the nature of the surface, breaks through the coating of gelatine size, making the fibre body of the paper very susceptible to water. If the scrubbing is done too vigorously it allows the colour partly into the paper itself, which means that to get back to the white one has to scrub harder, and eventually the surface of the sheet will start to break up, making it unworkable. This paper has been literally flooded with colour before scrubbing. Examination of the surface under a raking light reveals traces of pigment deep in the surface as well as on it. Working very wet on a rough paper will fill every depth of that texture. If one works drier, merely 'kissing' the high points of the surface, then the original colour of the sheet will still be there to reflect light back at the viewer, suffusing the image with light.

Turner, in common with other artists of this period, was developing the practical watercolour techniques necessary to give expression to the emotional power of landscape as they experienced it. The vigorous methods he was developing needed papers that could stand up physically to his demands. These works illustrate what was to become a constant preoccupation with the effects of light, not just in the actual landscape, or in the images that he made, but in the actual physical process of 'lighting' a picture: how Turner can work the surface to return the light falling on it to the viewer, enhanced and made vivid by his colours.

For whatever reasons, neither of these works satisfied him, and neither was completed. Besides the inability of the paper on this occasion to stand up to perhaps an overenthusiastic experiment, there would appear to be other reasons why they were abandoned. In cat no 20 particularly, the light falling on the trees and figures in the central foreground are lit from a point just in front of the viewer, rather than by the sun just rising on the far horizon.

1 The earliest wove papers appear to have had as their watermark a very small W on the edges of the sheet. The JW, centred in one half of the sheet, as this one is, only appears in 1764, in a rare issue of W Caslon & Son's 'Specimens of Printing Types' printed by Dryden Leach. After this period, Whatman woves were usually watermarked J WHATMAN, (Balston, 1957, p.159.).

2 Lyles, 1989, p.39, TB XLIV e. A white wove paper, in which can be found traces of an undated J WHATMAN watermark along the extreme edge of the sheet. Neither of the Whatmans appear to have dated their papers in the watermark. The Whatman marks with the 1794 date were all made after April 1794, when the Act of Parliament which led to the dating of English papers in the mark, came into force. Though the actual transfer of ownership from Whatman to Balston and the Hollingworths was not completed until October 1794, they had in fact been operating the mill for some months.

21 Kilchurn Castle on Loch Awe
1801

362 × 457 (14¼ × 18¾)

White wove

Watermarked: 1794 / J WHATMAN

Made by the Balston and Hollingworth partnership at Turkey Mill, Maidstone, Kent

Black and white chalk, pencil and chinese white, on a prepared ground

Turner Bequest: LVIII 16

D03395

21A Transmitted light detail of look-through, watermark and uneven nature of the prepared ground.

21B Raking light detail of surface colour, chalk and texture. × 7 magnification.

The *Scottish Pencils*, the group of sixty drawings from which this work comes, date from a nineteen-day tour of Scotland taken in the summer of 1801. With the exception of some sketchbooks[1] and the loose sheet exhibited as cat.no.14, this is the first large body of work produced by Turner on prepared surfaces. Apart from LVIII 43, all these papers are Whatman white woves, dated in the watermark 1794 and in one case 1797.[2] The sheets vary in size from 285 × 432 (11¼ × 18) to 368 × 495 (14¼ × 19½). They are mostly worked in a combination of black and white chalk, soft lead pencil and some white bodycolour. Farington gives details of the preparation used to colour this paper before use:

> Turner I drank tea with. He shewed me his sketches made in Scotland – Those made with black lead pencil on white paper tinted with Indian Ink and Tobacco water and touched with liquid white of his own preparing, are much approved.[3]

Turner was to return over and over again throughout his career to working on such coloured grounds, preferring to prepare them himself, rather than purchase them already prepared. He had already worked on coloured papers (see cat.nos.9 and 11) and was to continue to do so throughout his career, some of the papers used in the late 1820s and 1830s being particularly fine examples of hand made coloureds specifically produced for artists.[4] The actual colour of the tints used on the *Scottish Pencils* sheets varies quite considerably, as does the weight, texture and size of the sheets. They are generally papers with three deckles remaining, the fourth side either cut or torn. The variations in the surface textures might well be the product of the washing and staining given to the sheets, rather than any result of the production of the papers.

All this group of papers were, at one time, mounted in a large leather-bound album with the words 'Italiaanse Tekeningen' on the front cover. It is unlikely that these papers originally formed part of a sketchbook, because although they all bear the same watermark they do not appear to have been made in uniform

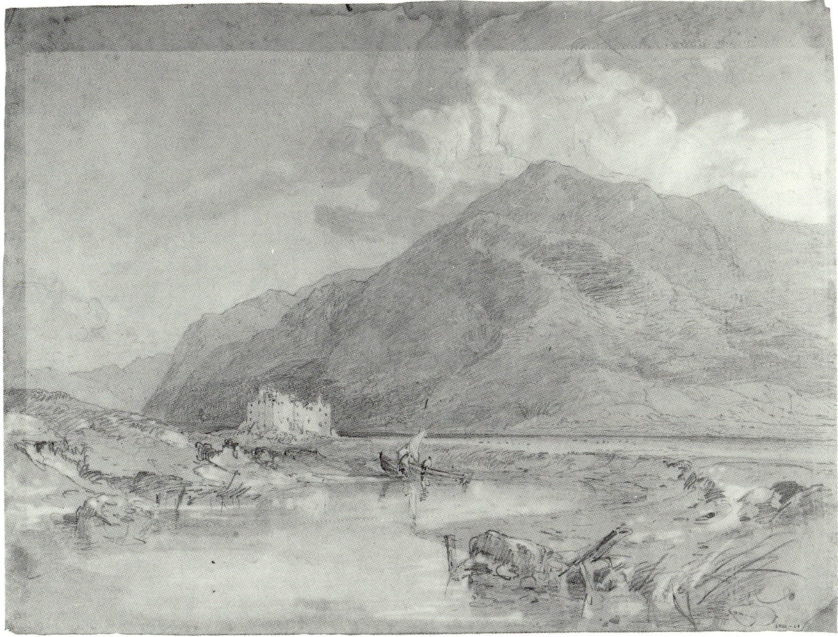

21

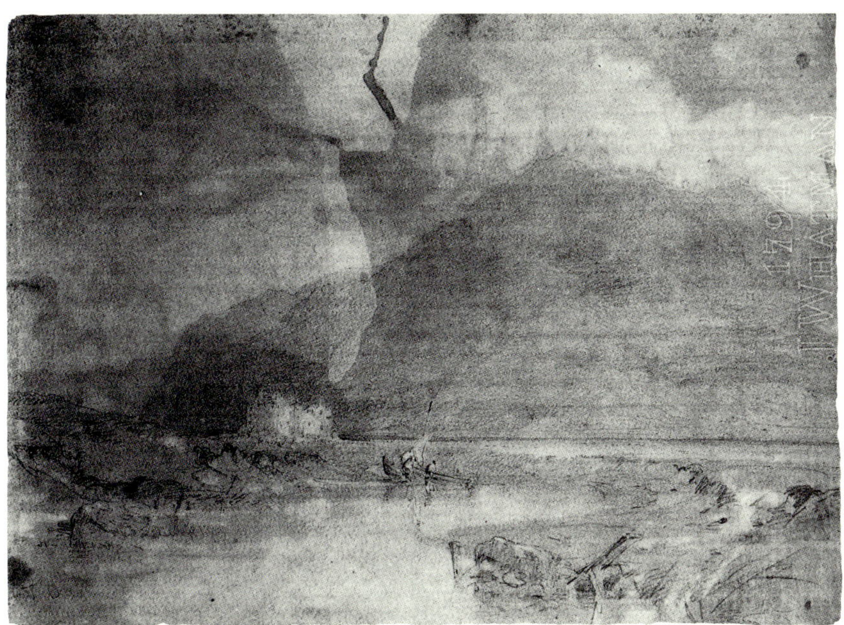

21A

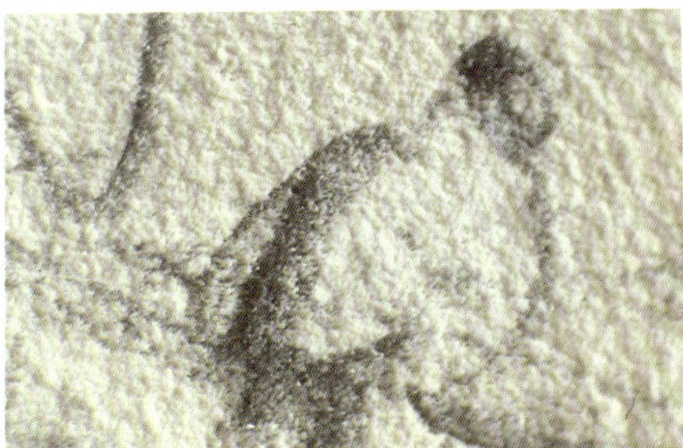

21B

size sheets. The majority appear to be cut or torn down Super Royal ($27\frac{1}{2} \times 19\frac{1}{2}$ in approximately). This particular size of Super Royal would indicate that these sheets were actually made as drawing papers, rather than as writings or printings, which were generally made $\frac{1}{2}$ in smaller in each dimension.[5] Some of the sheets, however, do not quite fit this category. It would seem likely that these papers were originally a quire (24 sheets, which would give 48 half sheets) with some other pieces of different paper added.

Even so, Turner seems to have treated them in some ways as if they were the leaves of a sketchbook, perhaps carrying them and working on them still folded as a quire. Turner seems to have had very particular habits at this stage in his career, governing which side of the sheet he worked on. In the case of these *Scottish Pencils* he appears to have worked almost indiscriminately on both the wire and felt sides of the sheets, something that would happen if the papers were worked on still folded in half. If he worked on the wire side of the first fold of a sheet, as he worked down the folded papers he would arrive at the other half of the sheet, but this time he would be working on the felt side. Most paper at this date was sold folded in quires, which would have helped Turner considerably in terms of carrying the sheets as he travelled. Such folds in the paper can be seen quite clearly in cat nos 26 and 27.

1 TB Nos XXX, XXXVII, XLIII, XLVI, LIV and LVII. This latter sketchbook, the *Tummel Bridge* sketchbook, also comes from this tour of Scotland. In this case the paper, again a white wove Whatman, watermarked 1794, has been prepared with various washes of stone grey, with a purplish grey applied, in some cases, over the first wash.

2 TB LVIII 43. Cat.no.22.

3 *The Diary of Joseph Farington*, Yale 1979, Vol.5, 6th February 1802.

4 See, in particular TB Nos CCCXLI, CCCXLII, CCCXLIII and CCCXLIV, a large body of works in black and white, catalogued by Finberg in groups of Grey, Brown, Blue and White papers. Many of these were made by Bally, Ellen and Steart, at the De Montalt Mill, near Bath, Somerset, who besides producing the better qualities of Bath Wove Post, used for letter writing all over Britain at that date, also specialised in the manufacture of coloured

and toned papers, usually made Imperial 559 × 762 (22 × 30 in approximately) for artists; concentrating particularly on watercolour and drawing papers.

5 See Labarre, 1952, for a very thorough listing of paper sizes, linked to their designed uses.

22 A View Towards Snowdon from above Traeth Bach 1798

381 × 552 (15 × 21¾)

White wove

Watermarked: none visible

Unidentified maker, but probably Whatman

Worked in black chalk and stump with a little grey wash and white bodycolour

Turner Bequest: LVIII 43

D03422

22A Transmitted light detail of look-through.

22B Raking light detail of marks, media, colour of paper and surface. × 10 magnification.

This sheet, originally catalogued by Finberg as being of 'Taymouth' and part of the *Scottish Pencils*, would appear in fact to belong to an earlier tour of Wales, rather than the 1801 tour of Scotland. Wilton relates it to one of the group of works discussed in cat.no.25 and dates it to 1798.[1] Unlike the rest of the *Scottish Pencils* the sheet has not been prepared, and seems to be a half sheet of Imperial (21¾ × 30 in) rather than the Super Royal used for most of that group of works. The general tone and texture of the sheet suggest that it is a Whatman or perhaps Edmeads and Pine, another Kent Maker.

1 TB XXXVI V, A View towards Snowdon. Wilton, Revised Catalogue of the Drawings in the Turner Bequest. In preparation.

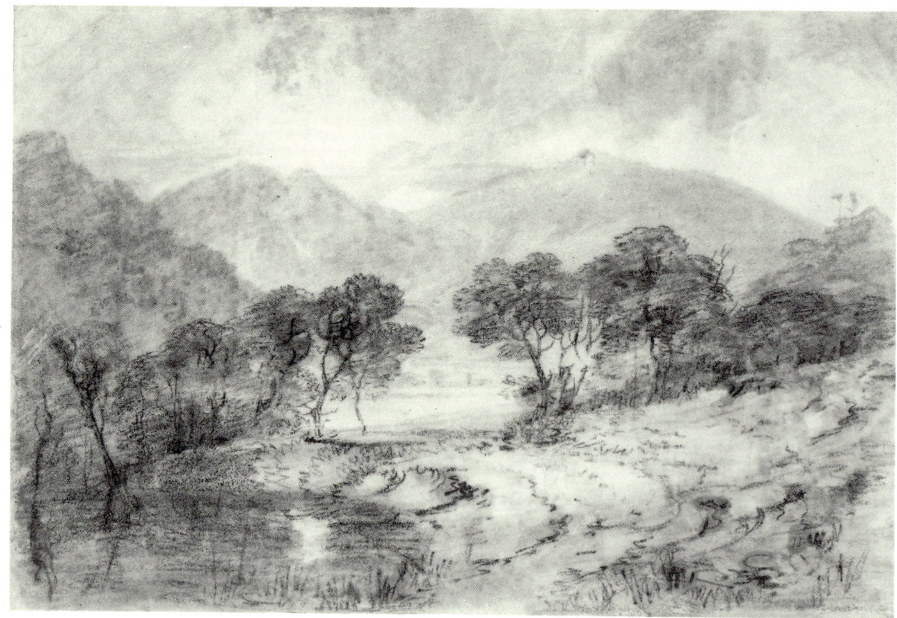

22

22A

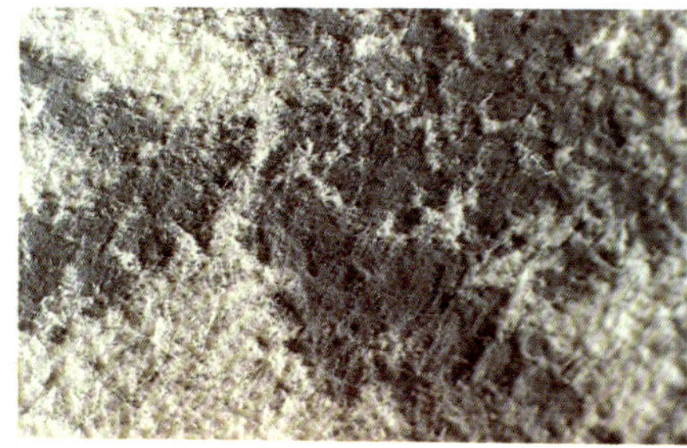

22B

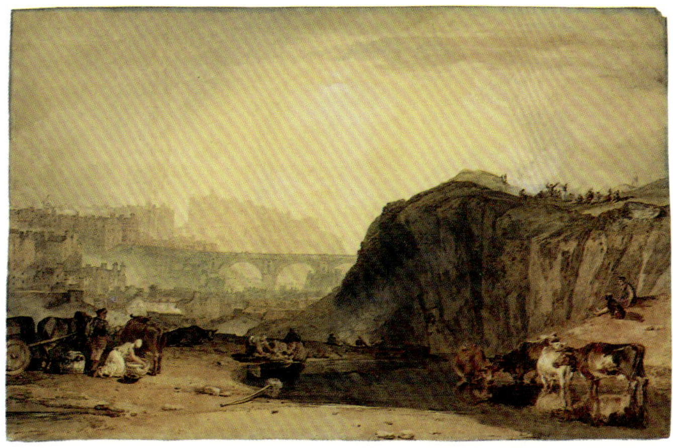

23

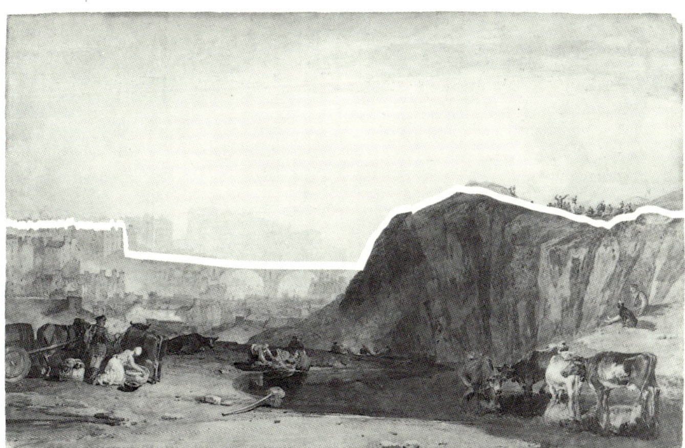

23A

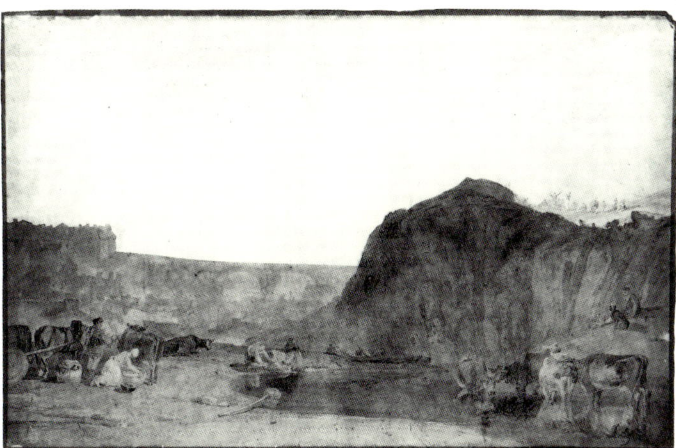

23B

23 Edinburgh from Calton Hill 1804

660 × 1000 (26 × 39⅜)

This work has been executed on two different papers with one laid down on top of the other as indicated in the illustration below. Both papers were probably made as Double Elephant (40 × 27 in)

(i) The paper used for the bottom half of the picture:
Lightweight white wove writing paper
Watermarked: none visible
Probably made by the Hollingworth & Balston partnership at Turkey Mill, Maidstone, Kent

(ii) The paper used for the top half of the picture:
Heavy weight rough surfaced white wove drawing paper
Watermarked: non visible
Unknown maker

Pencil, watercolour and bodycolour

Turner Bequest: LX H
D03639
W 348

23A The watercolour divided along the line between the two different papers

23B Transmitted light detail of look-through.

23C Raking light detail of join between the two sheets.

23D Raking light detail of paint layers. × 7 magnification.

Although it is not uncommon for artists to lay down pieces of paper on top of an area of drawing in order to rework that area, particularly in the case of works intended for reproduction, this work is perhaps unique in the Bequest in that it has been executed on two distinctly different papers. It would seem probable that originally the whole work was executed on the smooth surfaced, lightweight writing paper seen in the bottom half of this watercolour. At some point Turner decided that the sky was unsatisfactory and carefully cut the picture in half and laid the large area of the bottom part of the picture onto a heavier weight rougher textured drawing paper to complete the work. It may be that such a large lightweight sheet could not handle the contrasting tensions created in the paper between two areas of very

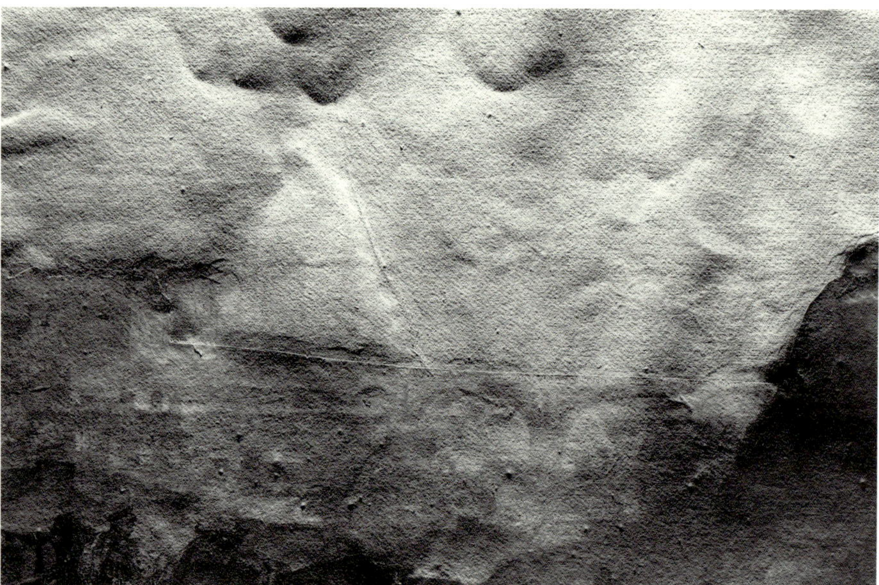

23C

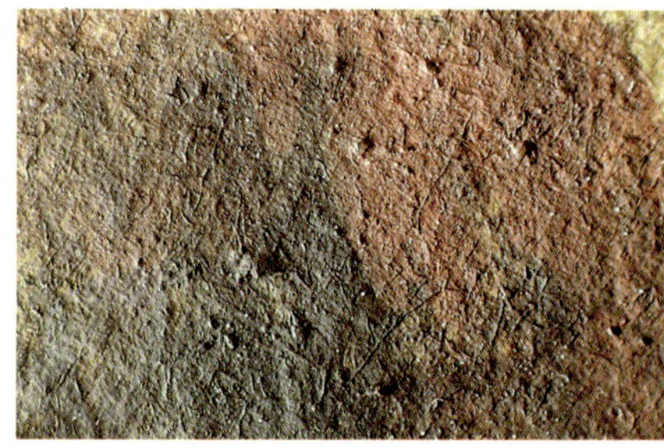

23D

different watercolour techniques: thick bodycolour paint layers and wet watercolour washes. Such different treatments could easily create cockling and creasing in the sheet particularly in the washed areas of the sky next to the heavier painted areas of the hill top, even though the paper had probably been stretched on a board prior to painting. Turner appears to have resolved the problem by removing the sky and replacing it with a heavier weight paper more able to take the strain.

This drawing, first exhibited at the Royal Academy in 1804, is based on studies from both the *Smaller Fonthill* (TB XLVIII) and *Scotch figures* (TB LXI) sketchbooks from Turner's 1801 tour of Scotland. It has been seriously damaged by light. The very edges of the sheet, previously hidden by earlier mounts, give us some idea of the original colours of the work.

A real curiosity amongst many of the 'fine' white papers used by Turner and other artists at this period, is how much yellowing has occurred in many of their papers, and not just amongst those works which were overexposed to strong light during the latter part of the nineteenth century and the earlier part of this. One expects the more fugitive pigments to fade and change over time, especially under the kind of prolonged exposure to light that this watercolour has been subjected to, especially with the presence of so much indigo in the blues and greens used. But in this work and others, it is not only the pigments in the paint which have yellowed and faded, but the paper itself has discoloured, particularly that used for the top half of the work.

Nowadays we are all used to the continuous and rapid discolouration, and increasing brittleness, of the various wood-based and sometimes highly acidic papers, such as newsprint, that we handle every day. We all see the effects of various atmospheric acids on the edges of older, and not so old books. But most of the papers used by Turner for large-scale watercolours like this, especially in the earlier part of his career, were made from the finest grades of linen rags, which should not yellow in this way. Linen has the property of getting whiter in direct light rather than yellower. Indeed, the sun-bleaching of paper in the open air was common in eighteenth-century English papermaking (see cat.no.41).

We have seen in 'A Waterfall' (cat.no.10) something of the nature of the 'blueing' of paper to correct the yellowness of much rag based paper. Whatman had begun blueing with smalts, but by the 1790s was adding indigo to the pulp to achieve the same effect, not liking the idea of bleaching the rags white.[1] It is probable that indigo has been used here as a whitening agent and has contributed greatly to the present very yellow cast of the work.

1 'Returned Maidstone & called on Hollingsworth at 4 went to dine with Mr Whatman at Vintners a fine seat elegant lawn, grounds etc. Mr W fine gent ab: 56 . . . his father formerly a papermaker – he bred up, a great study, in carrying it to perfection . . . blues with indigo which is much cheaper than smaltz . . . does not think highly of bleaching fine rags . . . thinks there a waste in the rags in this process and that it does not take the size well.' *The Journal of Joshua Gilpin*. Vol. VII, 17th March 1796. Pennsylvania State Archives. From an unpublished transcription by A.P. Woolrich. Gilpin was an American papermaker who travelled extensively in England and Europe at the end of the eighteenth century, visiting papermills and makers.

Both the Hollingworths and Balston continued Whatman's traditions of practical involvement with the actual processes of papermaking, unlike many of the entrepreneur mill owners, who would never have been able to make a sheet of paper. Balston, after his partnership with the Hollingworth brothers was dissolved, set up his own mill at Springfield in Maidstone, and in it established what was probably the earliest paper laboratory.

24 Boats on the Shore 1801

From the *Jason* sketchbook
Calf bound sketchbook with brass clasps
Page size: 207 × 132 ($8\frac{1}{8} \times 5\frac{1}{8}$)

Large Post Octavo
Flecked white wove, coarse printing paper. (pages 1–8 and 51–63.)
Watermarked: none visible
Unidentified maker

Pen and ink and pencil

Turner Bequest: LXI 61
D03717

24A Transmitted light detail of look-through.

24B Raking light detail of straw fibre, ink marks and colour differences in the paper surface. × 7 magnification.

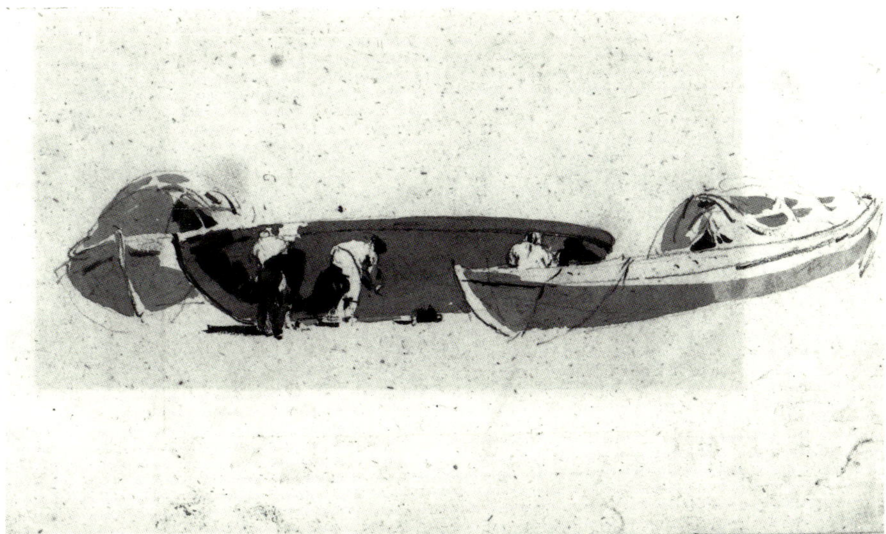

24

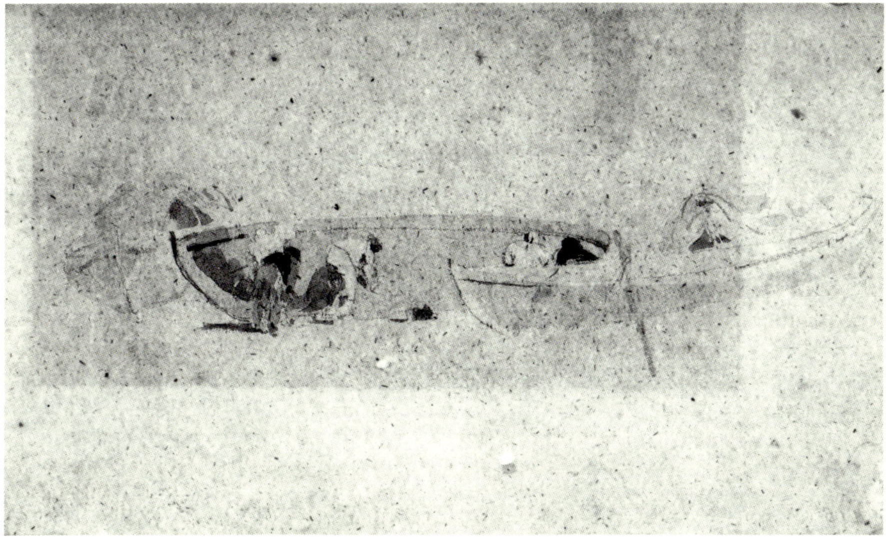

24A

This sketchbook contains two different papers, and originally had many more pages. It was rebound, probably in the 1930s, but not in the original order. From the details of the binding it would appear to have been produced by William Dickie.

The second paper is a white wove writing paper. (pages 9–50)
Watermarked: 1794 / J WHATMAN
Produced on two moulds, one bearing a broken H in the watermark and the other with the M smaller than is usual in the Whatman mark.[1] Made by the Balston and Hollingworth partnership at Turkey Mill, Maidstone, Kent.

Both these papers were made as Large Post, nominally 21 × $16\frac{1}{2}$ in, the Whatman paper being a lighter weight paper than the unidentified paper at the beginning and end of the book. All the Whatman sheets have been prepared, before binding, on one side of the sheet with various coloured washes. There were originally eight of these prepared sheets: three prepared with differing tones of grey, from a pale blue-grey (which might well have been a richer blue originally), to a deep grey-green; one pink; one sandy buff; one a deeper yellow; one salmon coloured and one pale blue.

This particular Whatman paper is part of a batch of Large Post paper that was purchased by Turner soon after its making, and which can be found in several other sketchbooks and amongst the loose sheets in the Bequest.[2] Given their appearance in sketchbooks that were in use from 1795 to 1806 and the very varied nature of the washes used on those sheets which were prepared before binding, it would seem likely that they were bound up at different times rather than all at once. It is the presence in the Bequest of the loose sheets of this particular batch of paper, which have never been part of any sketchbooks, that suggests that Turner purchased this paper as a lot and then had it bound up as and when he needed it.

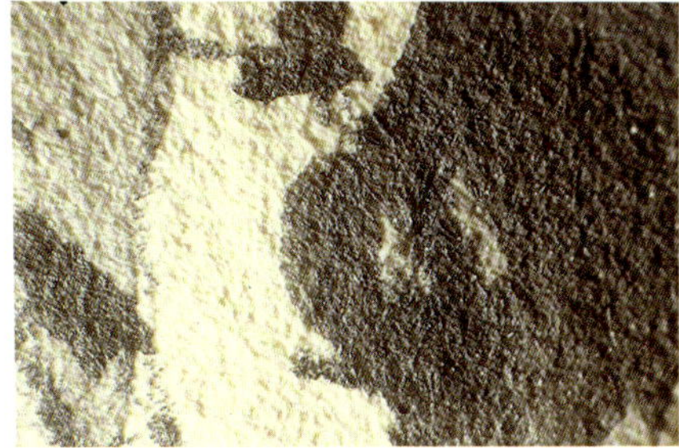

24B

While it would have been possible at this time to have bought such colour-washed sheets already bound from a stationer, given Turner's discrimination in terms of colour and light, and the very definite choices he made in terms of his papers and his various media, it seems out of character for him to have bought these books off the shelf. All the sketchbooks which contain this batch of paper were bound by the same binder. The same binder also bound many other sketchbooks, for Turner. These contain a range of other papers, many of which had been prepared, as loose sheets, with very distinctive washes, well suited to his considerations and preoccupations. This is particularly true of the red-washed blue laids, where he was to work in both watercolour and bodycolour on deep rich grounds (now aged into warm browns) more usually used in oil painting.[3]

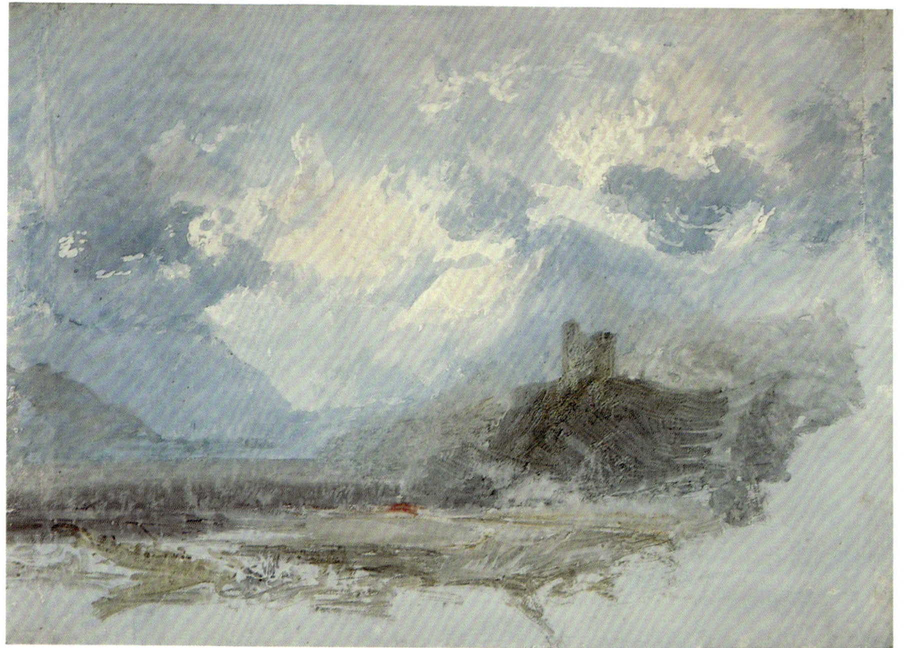

25

[1] Moulds are usually made and used as a pair, to speed up production, so in any given batch of handmade sheets one would expect two slightly different watermarks to be found. If the mould is designed to produce two sheets at a time, as were the two moulds on display in this exhibition, then one would expect to find four marks, with slight, but noticeable, differences between them.

[2] The particular sketchbooks and loose sheets concerned are as follows:

XXIV *Isle of Wight* sketchbook, in use in 1795.
XXV *Smaller South Wales* sketchbook, in use in 1795.
XXVI *South Wales* sketchbook, in use in 1795.
These three sketchbooks also contain papers watermarked E & P / 1794.
XXXIV *North of England* sketchbook, in use in 1797.
XXXV *Tweed and Lakes* sketchbook, in use in 1797.
This sketchbook also contains paper watermarked E & P / 1796.
XXXVI Subjects connected with the *North of England* tour, Loose drawings, Nos D,E,M,N,O,P,Q.
XL *Dinevor Castle* sketchbook, in use 1798.
XLVI *Dolbadarn* sketchbook, in use 1799.
L Miscellaneous: Oxford Salisbury etc. In use 1799–1801. Loose drawings, Nos H,J,N,O,Q,R,S,T,X,Y,Z.
LI Miscellaneous: Rural Scenes, 1799–1801. Loose drawings, Nos A,B,C,D.
XCI *Hurstmonceux and Pevensey* sketchbook, in use from 1804–6.

[3] XXX *Studies near Brighton* sketchbook, in use 1796.
XXXVII *Wilson* sketchbook, in use 1797.
XLIII *Academical* sketchbook, in use 1798.

25 Dolbadarn Castle 1798–9

677 × 972 ($26\frac{5}{8}$ × 38)

White wove drawing paper
Watermarked: none visible
Probably made by Balston and the Hollingworth Brothers, at Turkey Mill, Maidstone, Kent

Watercolour and stopping-out on a prepared pale blue ground

Turner Bequest: LXX O
D04166

25A Transmitted light detail of look-through.

25B Raking light detail of paper surface and paint layer. × 7 magnification.

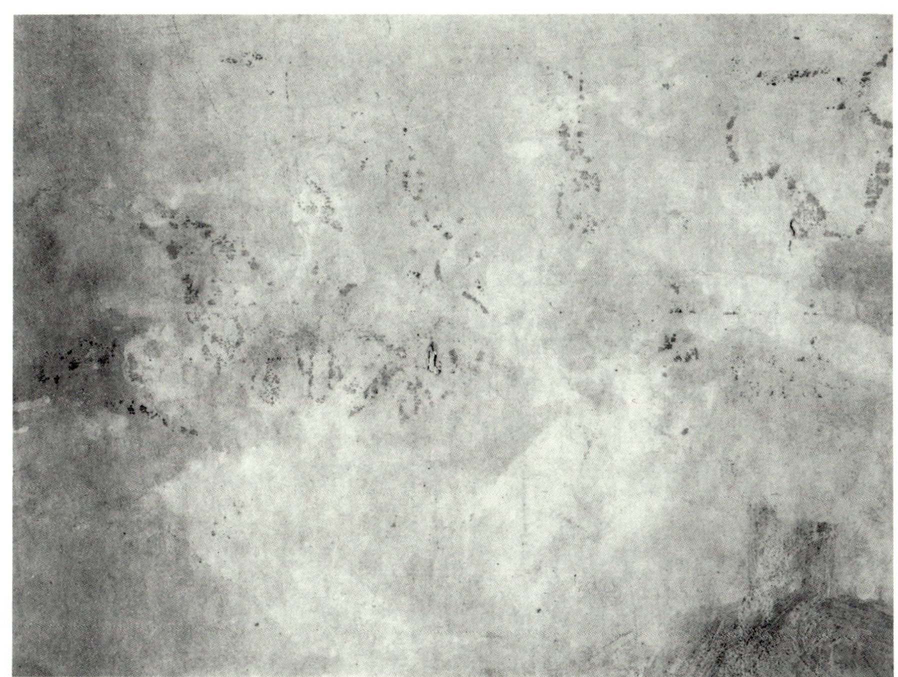

25A

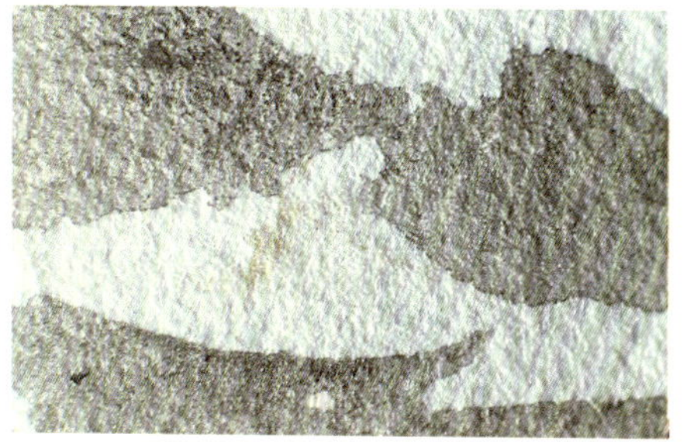

25B

This sheet, which had been cut down probably from a Double Elephant sized paper, has been stretched over a board. One of the most interesting, technically, of Turner's early works, it has been both washed with a ground colour, and then worked to different degrees, in different areas of the sheet. The washing and to some extent the rubbing of the surface has provided him with subtlely different areas of texture within the same sheet, actually making it easier for him to produce the variety of marks.

The method of stopping-out developed by Turner involved the removal of areas of dry wash by the use of a brush loaded with clean water. The newly wet area could then be blotted taking up some of the dry colour with the water.[1] A close examination of the surface of this work suggests that another technique has also been used: stopping-out using washes of gelatine, which would then be washed out themselves with warm water. One curious feature of the drawing is the viscous nature of the pigment used to paint the rock on which the castle stands. This deep rich brown pigment bears all the signs of being a natural earth, probably clay based; the only kind of earth that would produce such a viscous mark.

This work relates to two other large colour studies, also worked in the same subtle palette.[2] The drama inherent in these techniques was to reach its full expression later, when, in combination with others developed over the years, they would all gradually synthesise into a complex and vigorous exploration of all the capabilities of both the media and the surfaces used.

1 *The Diary of Joseph Farington*. Yale 1979. 28th March 1804.
As Farington's entry dates from some years after the work under discussion, it is possible that Turner had been working on a range of techniques of stopping-out. As none of this particular group of studies is finished, perhaps the technique proved too laborious, and washing the gelatine out adversely affected the remaining painted areas.

2 Wilton, 1984, p.59. TB LXX j and TB XXXVI U.

26 Llanberis Lake and Dolbadarn Castle, with Snowdon beyond

1799–1800

548 × 707 ($21\frac{1}{2} \times 27\frac{7}{8}$)

White wove drawing paper
Watermarked: 1794 / J WHATMAN
Made by Balston And the Hollingworth Brothers at Turkey Mill, Maidstone, Kent

Pencil and watercolour

Turner Bequest: LXX Y
D04176

26A Transmitted light detail of watermark and look-through.

26B Raking light detail of the 'back' of the sheet. × 20 magnification.

This work dates from the tour Turner made of North Wales in 1799, but it is possible that some of the group of large watercolours to which it belongs were worked up later in his studio. Like the rest of the group, the sheet bears the marks of its manufacture: the rope mark made when it was hanging up to dry shows clearly down the centre. But the paper also shows signs of having been folded both before use and after.

All the papers in this group of works are either whole, or slightly trimmed, Imperial sheets, mostly watermarked WHATMAN (but see cat.no.27), with the exception of this one which appears to be a nondescript size, somewhere between a Super Royal ($20\frac{1}{2} \times 27\frac{1}{2}$ in) and an Extra Royal ($21\frac{1}{2} \times 28\frac{1}{2}$ in).

It is difficult to ascertain exactly what state some of these papers were in when they left the mill. If this sheet was some form of Extra Royal originally, it would have had a rather smooth, almost Hot-Pressed surface: Extra Royal was made as a board rather than as a paper. A Super Royal sheet might have been made in any number of finishes, as the size was used for Writings, Wrappings, Drawings and Boards. The later history of these papers has sometimes obscured some of the information one might have hoped to gather from them: disasters such as the Thames flood having 'washed' many of them. It must also be said that sometimes the conservation measures necessary for the protection of the paper can also lead to a loss of information. Several of the sheets in this particular sequence seem to have been washed and cleaned, and been repressed lightly during the drying necessary after such cleaning, all of which has altered the original surface, making it difficult to determine the use they were originally designed for.

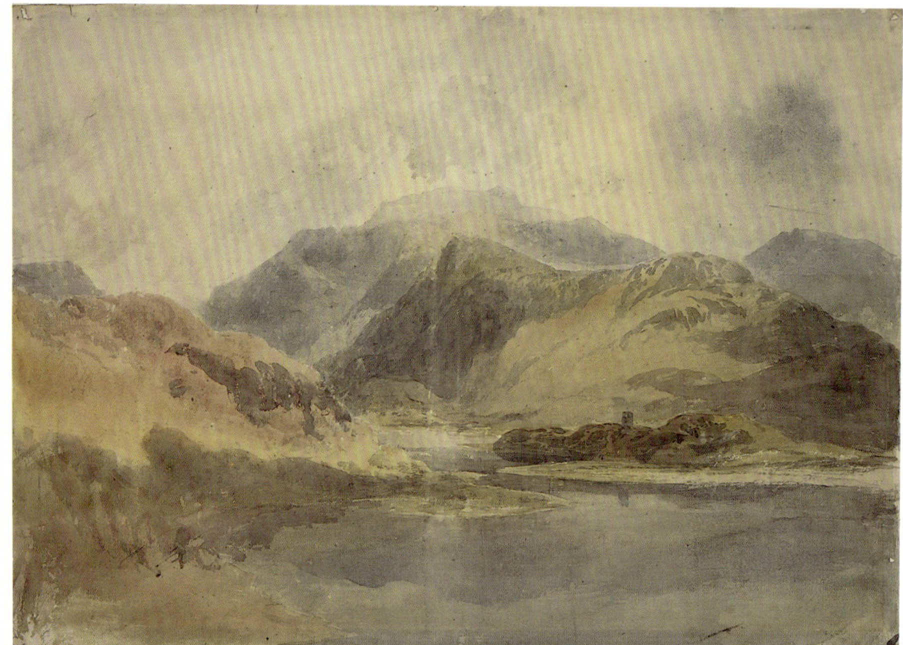
26

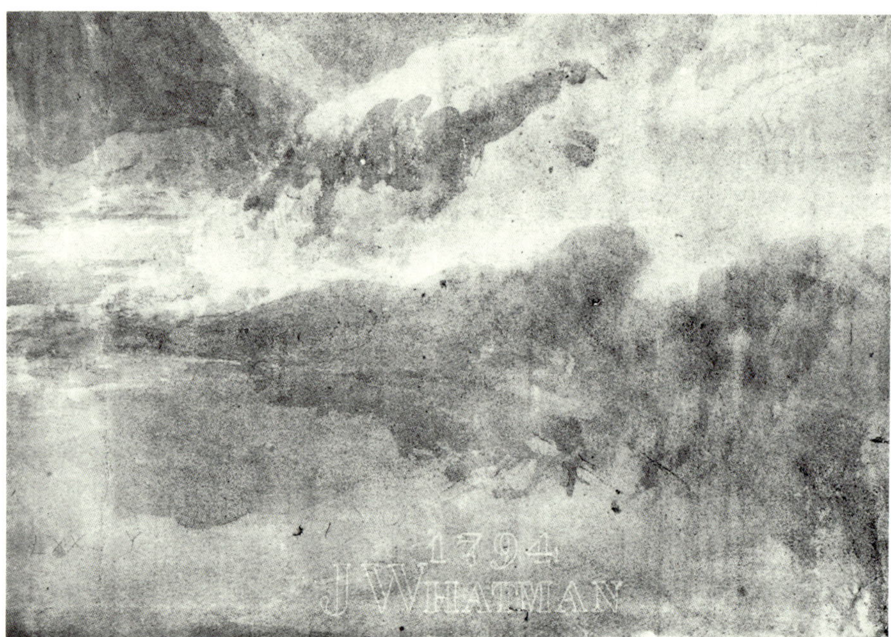

26A

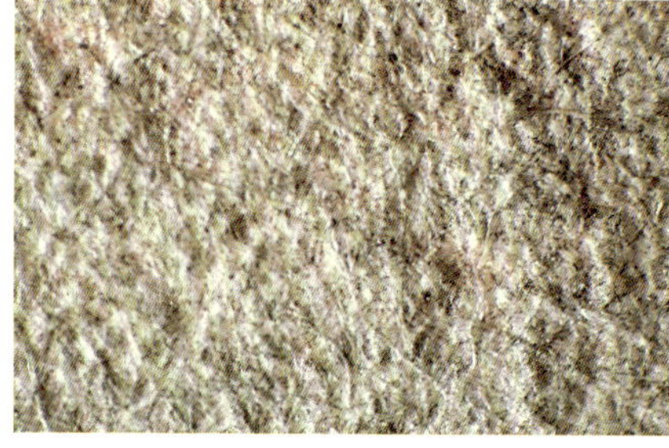
26B

27 Blair Atholl, looking towards Kiliecrankie *c.*1801

533 × 780 (21 × 30$\frac{11}{16}$)

White wove drawing paper
Watermarked: W ELGAR / 1796
Made by, or for, William Elgar[1]

Watercolour, with stopping out and some bodycolour

Turner Bequest: LXX B
D04179

27A Transmitted light detail of watermark and look-through

27B Raking light detail of surface and paint layers over the centre of the sheet. × 7 magnification

This watercolour had been previously identified as a 'Distant view of Snowden' and related to Turner's 1799 tour of North Wales but appears to be based on a pencil sketch in the *Scotch Lakes* sketchbook of 1801.[2] This work does have some things in common with the large Welsh subjects from the 1790s: large scale, similarities in technique and the fact that it had been worked on a sheet that was folded both before and after use. But all the paper used for the large Welsh subjects is watermarked J WHATMAN and this sheet is from a different source.

Besides the fold this paper does shows signs, down the centre of the sheet, of the stretch and distortion marks common in rope dried paper. As most paper was at this period sold folded, the 'back' had little direct significance in many uses. But here, where Turner has worked on a large scale the remains of the rope mark have remained clearly visible through the paint. There is no sign that this sheet was ever stretched, unlike cat no 25. Stretching the paper tight down on a board, and then washing and soaking it with colour, would have tended to reduce the 'back'.

This particular sheet has also become distorted somewhat over time, with some curvature of both the long edges of the sheet. Such distortions are often the result of the paper having dried too fast, say during a hot windy day in mid summer, when the part of the sheet immediately next to the rope dries slower than the rest of it, giving rise to considerable differences in the dimensions of the paper at different points across the sheet. These distortions are sometimes made worse during mounting

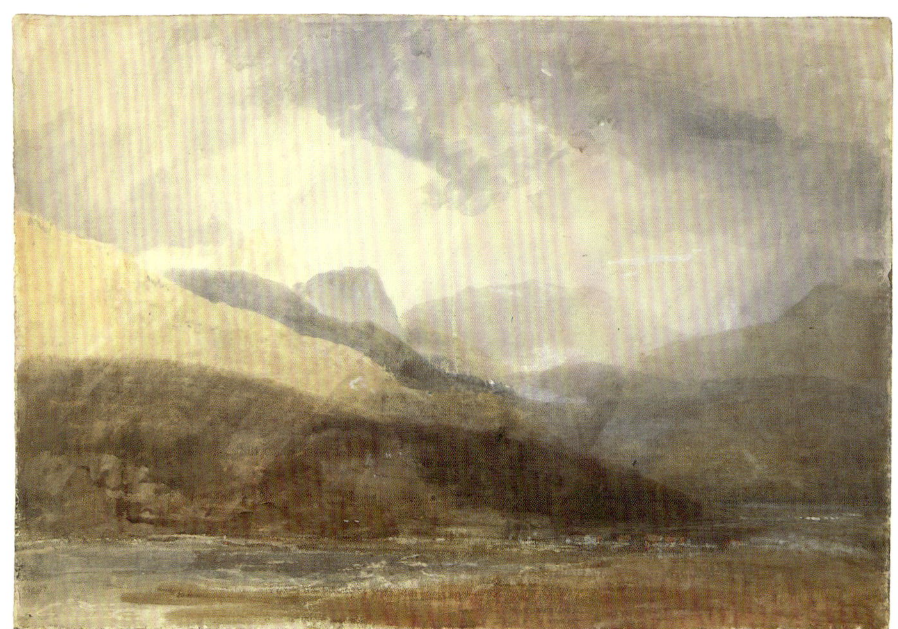

27

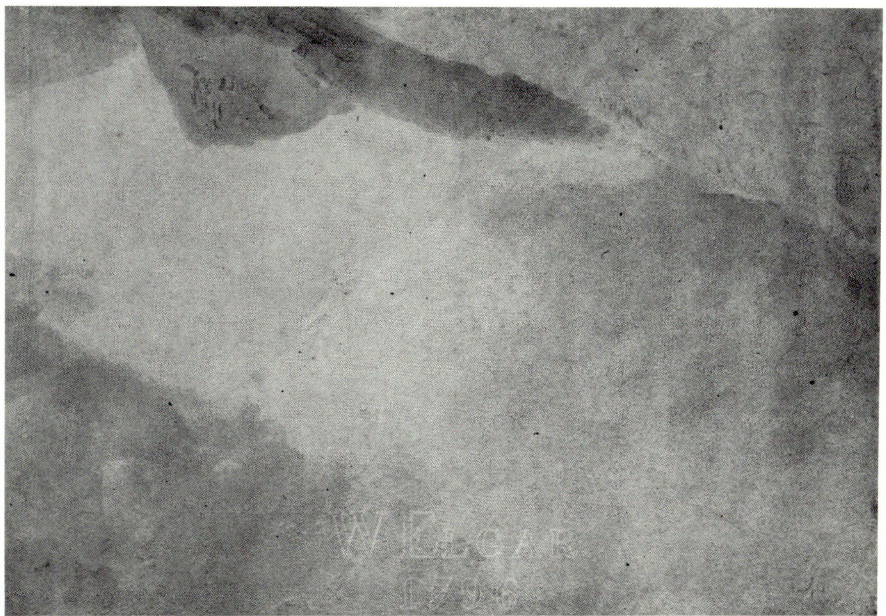

27A

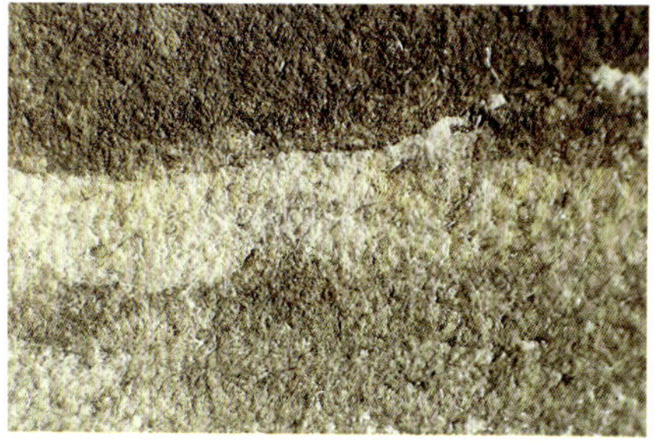

27B

and conservation, where wetting and pressing reactivate the different tensions inside the paper that led to the distortion in the first place.

[1] It has proved impossible, so far, to identify which mill was being worked by Elgar at this period, Shorter, 1957, p194, suggests that William Elgar was possibly working Little Ivy Mill or Upper Tovil Mill, Maidstone, Kent after the death of Thomas French, in 1795.
It is also possible that the watermark is not that of a papermaker at all, but of Elgar & Co, bankers in the Maidstone district who had had paper made for them.
The Elgar watermark occurs elsewhere in the Bequest:

TB XLIV Y, an unfinished watercolour of 'Caernarvon Castle' 1799.
White laid writing paper
Chain lines: 2.8–3 cms ($1\frac{1}{16}$–$1\frac{3}{16}$ in) apart.
Laid line frequency: 8 per cm (20 per inch)
Watermarked: (partmark) W ELGAR

TB LV, the *Edinburgh* sketchbook of 1801
Paper covered boards with leather spine.
Page size: 196 × 122 ($7\frac{3}{4}$ × 5)

Large Post Octavo
White wove writing paper
This sketchbook contains two different papers:
(i) Watermarked: 1794 / J WHATMAN
(ii) Watermarked: W ELGAR / 1794

[2] TB LVI, Wilton, Revised Catalogue of the Drawings in the Turner Bequest. In preparation. (58 ff 121v 122r)

The First Swiss Tour of 1802 (cat.nos.28–36)

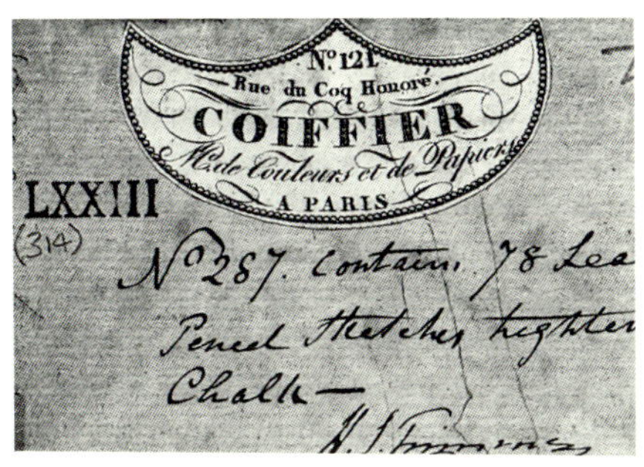

fig.16 TB LXXIII. Paper merchant's label.

Turner's first sketching tour on the continent provided an important impetus to his continued development. On June 15th 1802 he stepped ashore at Calais exhilarated by a fairly rough crossing of the Channel, and no doubt excited by the tour ahead of him. He was one amongst many hundreds of curious English men and women who, for various reasons, were taking advantage of the brief treaty of Amiens to visit continental Europe: foreign travel had been denied them since 1793 and would shortly be denied them again for another thirteen years of war with France.

In the three months that he was away, travelling down through France and into Switzerland, and then back to Paris for a time before returning to England, he produced some four hundred drawings, works which would provide him with images to explore for many years to come.

Only twenty or so of the four hundred drawings done on this tour were coloured, most of the work being done in pencil, with or without the addition of black and white chalk and with some use of white bodycolour for highlights and to enhance the detail in some of the drawings done on coloured grounds. The examination of this group of papers, assembled with such a specific purpose in mind, gives us insights into what governed Turner's choices. The two other continental tours before 1820 give us further opportunities from later periods in his career (see cat.nos.42 and 50–53), the Italian tour of 1819–20 being of particular interest.

Turner took some paper with him, in the form of sketchbooks and some larger folded sheets, and purchased others on his travels. With the exception of the *Fonthill* sketchbook[1] which he had already been using in England prior to his trip, all the English paper he took with him had been prepared before use with various brown and grey washes. The papers he bought abroad can be divided quite simply into two different categories: French-made coloured papers, either in sketchbooks or as loose sheets, with one exception (cat.no.35) all made by one mill, Marais, near Paris, and probably all purchased from the same stationer, Coiffier: and white, Swiss-made, paper, bound up into sketchbooks.

Given Turner's difficulties in learning other languages it is most likely that the Swiss servant, that Turner and his travelling companion engaged in Paris, actually made the purchases, but

Turner made the choices.[2] The tones, weights and surface characteristics, and the similarities and differences between the papers Turner had brought from England, and those he had been using prior to this tour would indicate a very careful choice. He knew exactly what he wanted.

Whether English, French or Swiss, these papers all have very distinct qualities, and provided Turner with a range of very versatile grounds for soft and hard pencils, for chalks and colour. For example both the *Small Calais Pier* and *Studies in the Louvre* sketchbooks exhibit some differences and some similarities. The Whatman paper used in the *Small Calais Pier*[3] book was probably made as writing paper, quite different from the heavier, stiffer sheet bound into the *Studies in the Louvre* book (cat.no.28). Judging by various details of the binding of both these books: the calf used, the edge-tooled designs, they both appear to have been produced by William Dickie, a stationer who produced many of Turner's other sketchbooks around this time (see cat.no.38). They are both prepared with a brown wash on one side of the paper and a grey wash on the other, though the tones and pigments used are very different. Careful examination of brush marks in the washes, and comparisons in tonal changes across the papers, all suggest that the papers were coloured prior to binding: that Turner prepared the sheets and then had his stationer make them up into books for him.

Working on such prepared papers was not a new departure for Turner. Though similar in some ways to the *Scottish Pencils*, the drawings in the *Grenoble* sketchbook (cat.nos. 30 and 31) are lighter and freer. They range from very rapid sketches to relatively worked up 'finished' drawings. The scale of the mountains, provided Turner with a new stimulus, something that grew in intensity the longer he stayed in the Alps. The later Schaffhausen (cat.nos. 34, 35 and 36) and St Gothard and Mont Blanc (cat.no.32) drawings have a power and intensity not really present in the *Grenoble* series: one feels that in those drawings Turner was in a sense 'working himself in', acclimatising to the sublime grandeur of the scenery he was exploring.

The French papers are softer than the harder sized English papers, taking chalks, pencil and paints differently. The many differences in whiteness, hardness or softness, and general behaviour between English and Continental papers at this time were much remarked on by many contemporaries. In a fascinating letter to James Whatman, dated 1796, the printmaker Poggi suggests that, besides differences in beating techniques, one cause of the relative hardness and softness of Northern and Southern European papers lay in the washing and preparation of the rags, not just prior to being turned into papers, but also when the fabrics were laundered during ordinary use, before being discarded as rags. In England soap was used to wash the cloth, but many mills and laundries on the Continent used a lye, made from boiling wood ash in water and letting it stand, before washing or soaking the rags in it. He seemed to feel that 'the corrosive nature of the lees enervates the fibres of the flax' giving a weaker fibre.[4]

Some makers and users were very particular about the sizing of their paper, because of its importance in determining many of the behavioural characteristics of the sheet. The printmaker Basire, for example, in his requirements for Antiquarian paper, demanded that kid leather be used for the gelatine. Whatman himself preferred 'scrolls', the parings left after vellum manufacture, when making for writing papers.

Turner's choice of papers for the tour seems to have been very deliberate. By this stage of his career he was confident as to what he wanted his papers to be capable of. There is a curious feeling of inevitability about so many of the marks he makes in his swift and sure sketches, fixing the image not merely on the paper but in his memory as well.

It is possible that he brought other Continental papers back with him from this tour, but few can be found in this part of the Bequest. Amongst the drawings catalogued together by Finberg as being connected with the Swiss Tour, there is a black and white chalk and stump drawing of Voreppe, near Grenoble, executed on a French made off-white laid paper with a partly decipherable watermark; C . . . E / FIN / DANGOUMOIS / 1742.[5] Paper from the mills near Angoulême are regularly found in eighteenth century English books, documents and works of art, indicating a continuity of imports from France despite opposition from the growing English paper industry. Whether or not this paper was acquired in France or Switzerland, or in England, it is impossible to say.

1 The *Fonthill* sketchbook, TB XLVII, white wove, watermarked: 1794 / J WHATMAN. This sketchbook was probably in use from as early as 1799 and perhaps until as late as 1804–5. Besides the Swiss drawings, it contains scenes of Fonthill, Cassiobury, Eton and Oxford

2 Cecilia Powell, 'Turner's Travelling Companion of 1802: A Mystery Resolved?' *Turner Society News* No.54, p.12–15.

3 TB LXXI *The Small Calais Pier* sketchbook
Rebound calf sketchbook
118 × 196 × 22 ($4\frac{11}{16} \times 7\frac{11}{16} \times \frac{7}{8}$)
Page size: 111 × 184 ($4\frac{3}{8} \times 7\frac{1}{4}$)
Post Octavo
White Wove, prepared with grey and brown wash, before binding.
Watermarked: 1794 / J WHATMAN
Made by the Balston and Hollingworth partnership, Turkey Mill, Maidstone, Kent.

4 A Poggi, letter to James Whatman. From a copy made in the *Journal of Joshua Gilpin*, Vol. LVII, Pennsylvania State Archives. From an unpublished transcription by A.P. Woolrich.

5 The date in this mark is probably not the actual date of manufacture (see cat.no.10, footnote 1). This work, like many in the Bequest, is at present backed, making the reading of watermarks and the examination of the internal structure of the sheet very difficult. It is unlikely, however, that this watermark will be any more decipherable after the work is removed from its backing. The wires making up the mark are considerably broken and distorted and would yield little further information.

28 Copy of Titian's 'Entombment'
1802

From the *Studies in The Louvre* sketchbook
Calfbound sketchbook with one brass clasp
134 × 117 × 25 ($5\frac{3}{10} \times 4\frac{3}{5} \times 1$)
Page size: 128 × 111 ($5\frac{1}{16} \times 4\frac{3}{8}$)

White wove writing paper
Watermarked: HAYES & WISE / 1799
Made by: John Hayes and John Wise, who were working Padsole Mill, Maidstone, Kent[1]

Watercolour and bodycolour

Turner Bequest: LXXII 32
D04315

28A Composite transmitted light detail of watermark and look-through of LXXII–9,2,7.

28B Transmitted light detail of watermark and look-through of LXXII 61.

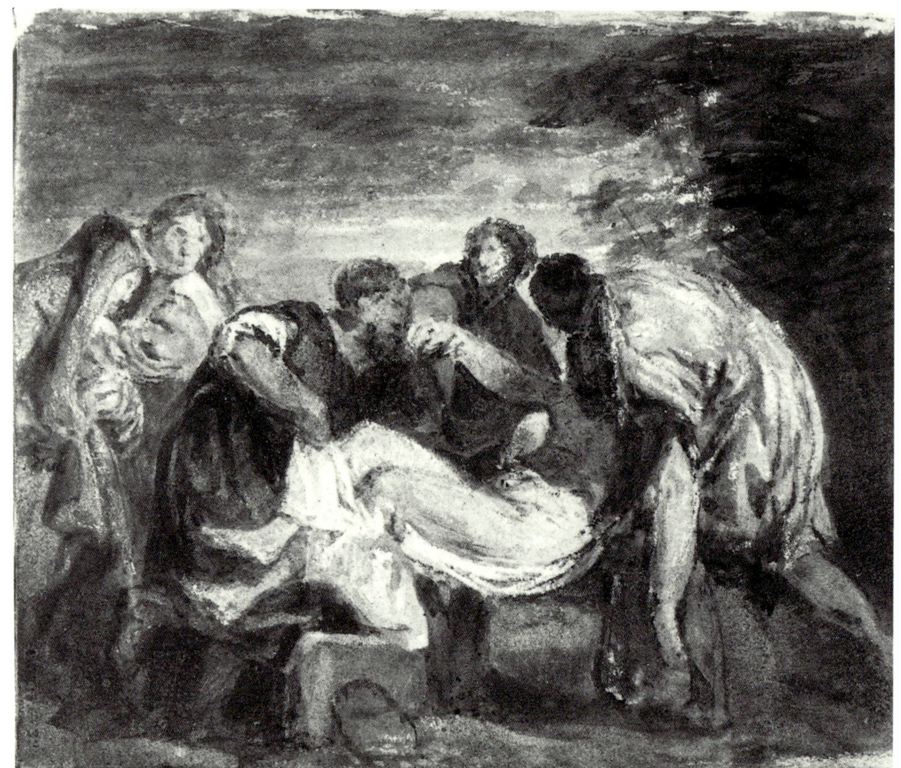

28

This sketchbook, bound by William Dickie, contains three different papers, the bulk of the sheets having been prepared with grey and brown washes prior to binding. The endpapers are a white wove writing paper, watermarked 1799, from an unidentified maker. One sheet of a different paper has been bound in with the Hayes and Wise paper: a white wove drawing paper, Watermarked: 1794 / J Whatman, made by the Hollingworths and Balston at Turkey Mill, Maidstone, Kent.

The colour washes used to prepare the

28A

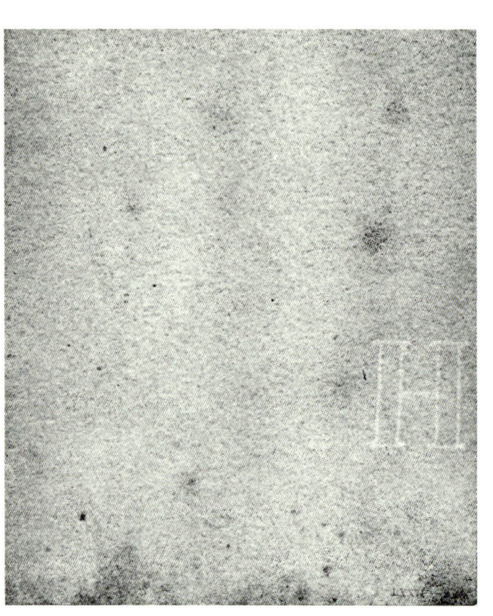

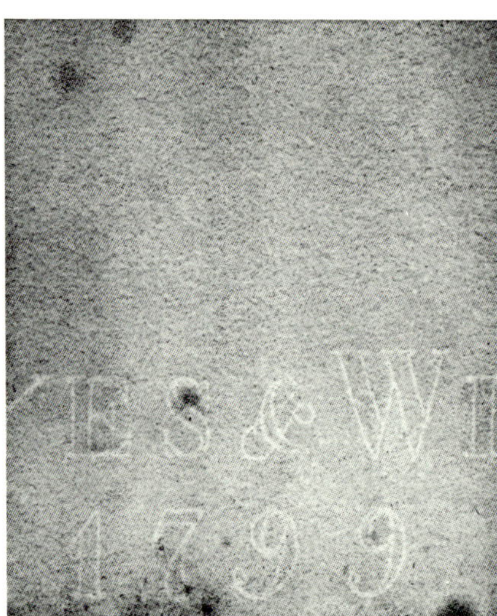

sheets show a great range, from very light grey (p.65, 66, 67 etc.) to very dark brown (p.61). Some sheets were folded in four prior to being washed, (see p.29,30,37 etc.). Some were probably rubbed with graphite or black chalk, perhaps after binding, as well as being washed (68v. and 69, 74v and 75, 82v and 83 etc.).

These deep-coloured grounds are admirably suited to the series of water-colour copies of paintings in the Louvre that Turner made in this sketchbook. Each of the copies is accompanied by detailed notes which reveal his intense preoccupation with both the emotional and structural use of colour in painting. Pages 29v–31v of the sketchbook discuss the actual colour structure of the 'Entombment', relating the colours and forms, in combination, to the emotional expression of the work, which Turner considered as ranking 'amongst the first of Titian's pictures as to colour and pathos of effect'.

[1] John Hayes and John Wise worked Padsole Mill from 1798 until Hayes' bankruptcy in 1804. (*London Gazette, May 1–5 1804*). The mill had originally been built on the site of an earlier mill by John Smythe and the Hollingworth brothers, who appear to have ceased working it when they went into partnership with William Balston at Turkey Mill in 1794. Various members of the Wise family continued working the mill until at least 1819. (*Watermills of Kent*, unpublished researches from the Simmons Collection, Science Museum Library Archives, London).

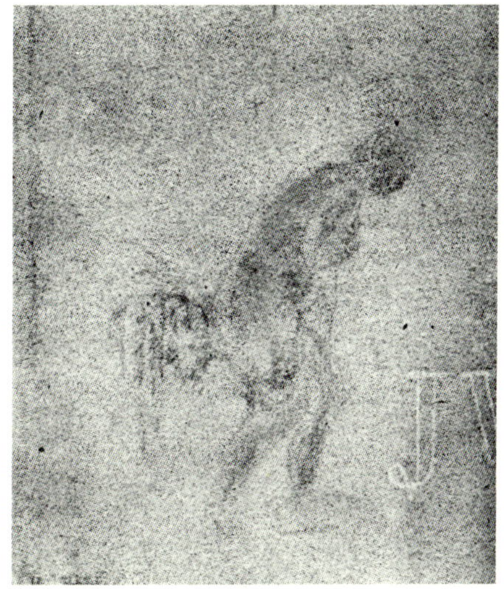

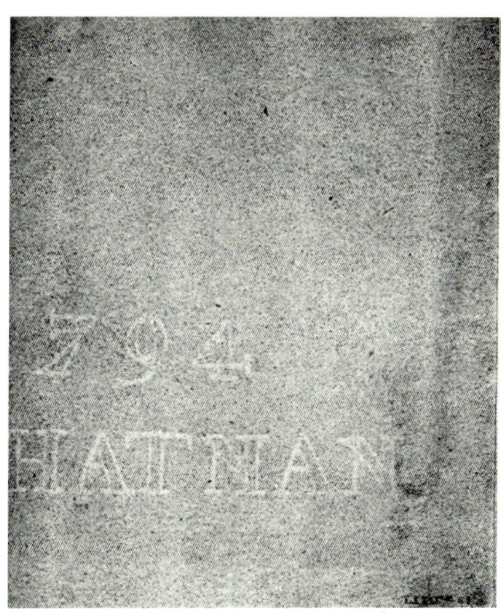

28B

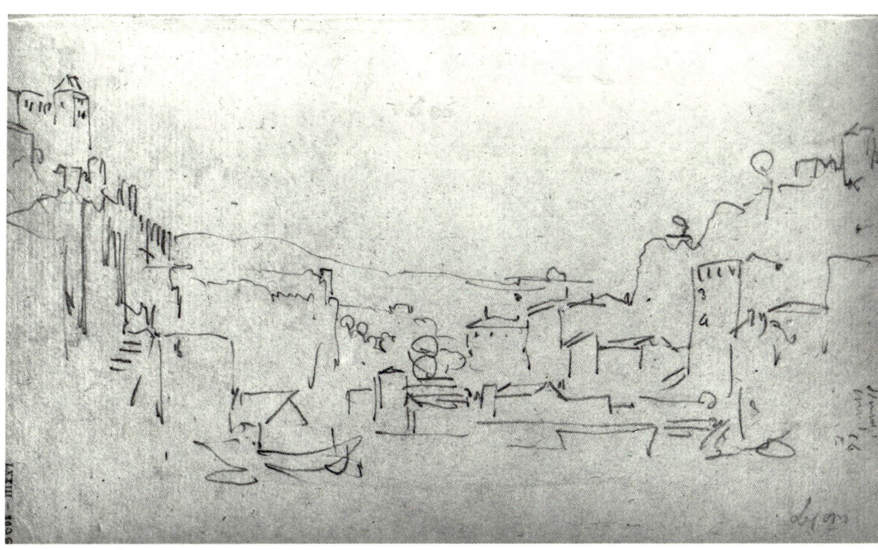

29

29 Lyons 1802

From the *France, Savoy, Piedmont* sketchbook
Paper covered boards with green leather spine
222 × 146 × 22 (8¾ × 5¾ × ⅞)
Page size: 216 × 137 (8½ × 5⅜)

Grand Carré Octavo
Self-coloured light grey-buff laid
Chain lines: 3 cms (1 3/16 in) apart
Laid line frequency: 7 per cm (17 per in)
Watermarked: (partly indecipherable – . . . erene & Raff . . . du Marais . . .'[1]
Made by Jean-Louis Delagarde at Papeteries du Marais, Seine et Marne, France

Pencil

Turner Bequest: LXXIII 36
D04429

29A Composite transmitted light detail of watermarks and look-through.

29B Raking light detail of chalk, fibre and rugged surface. × 7 magnification.

The Papeteries du Marais was one of the mills that had produced paper for Assignats, the paper currency of the Revolution.[2] This book, and probably the rest of the French paper that Turner used in 1802, was purchased in Paris from the stationer, Coiffier. The label in this sketchbook is one of the few pieces of evidence that we have as to where Turner purchased any of his papers.[3]

The contrast between this pencil sketch of Lyons and the much larger work exhibited in cat.no.35 is most instructive. Here we have a swift sure hand, working with considerable variations both in the pressure of the pencil on the paper and in the angle at which the pencil has been held, often all within the same mark. By contrast, in the larger, more formal work, Turner has used a harder pencil on a harder paper, with a smaller vocabulary of marks, but has made a finer and much more discriminating study.

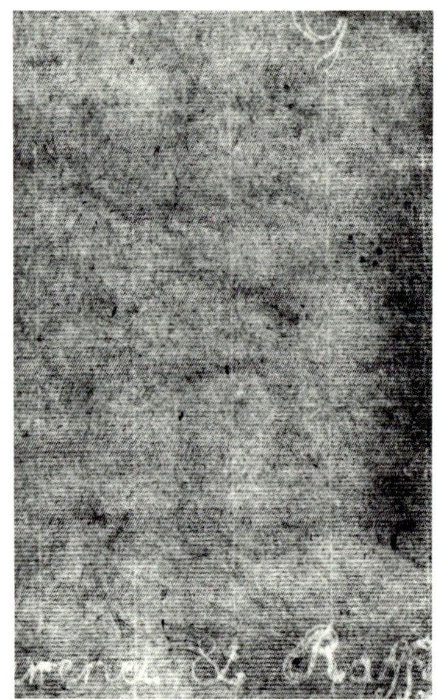

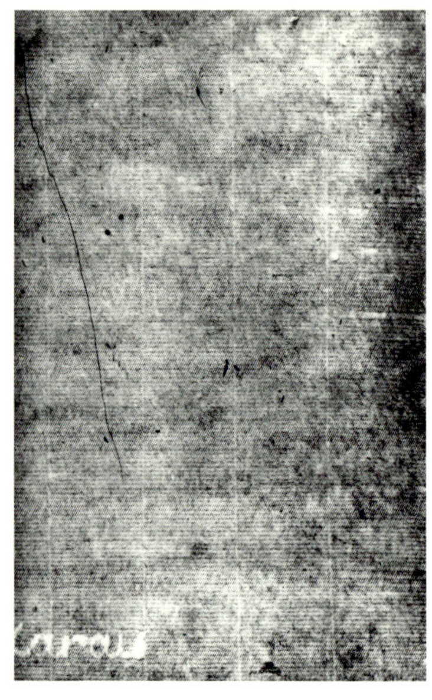

29A

[1] cf. Heawood 3384. *Watermarks mainly of the 17th & 18th Centuries*, 1986.

[2] Lafaurie, 1981, p.23 ff.

[3] English merchants and stationers were only starting to market their papers with advertisements and promotional literature at the beginning of the nineteenth century. In the period under consideration in this exhibition such stationers' labels are found in five other sketchbooks, all dating from 1810 onwards:

(a) TB CXXII, the *Finance* sketchbook
White wove
Watermarked: E&P / 1801
Made by Robert Edmeads and John Pine, Ivy Mill, Maidstone, Kent.
This sketchbook carries the Label:

Thos William's / (late Hall & Co) / Much Approved VELVET PAPER / MEMORANDUM BOOKS with METALLIC PENCILS, the points / of which will never break and the / writing remain ? from erasure. / Keep the point of the Pencil / smoothly *scraped* flat and write / with them in the same direction / as with a pen
Sold Retail by the / Stationers and Vendors / of Pocket books in Town and Country / and wholesale for Fourdrinier / by Thornhill & Son Fish Street Hill London.

Henry and Sealy Fourdrinier were paper merchants and makers, who were at this date already involved in the finance and development of the first production paper machines at Two Waters in Hertfordshire. They also acted as merchants for both Balston and the Hollingworths. Despite the phenomenal success of the new machines they were bankrupted by their involvement, but their name lives on: most modern machines are still known as 'fourdriniers'.

(b) TB CXXIII; see cat.no.38.

(c) TB CXXIX, the *Woodcock Shooting* sketchbook.
White wove
Watermarked J WHATMAN /1805
Made by the Balston and Hollingworth partnership, Turkey Mill, Maidstone, Kent.

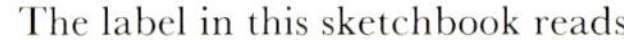

The label in this sketchbook reads:

Mills & Son / BOOKSELLERS, STATIONERS & BINDERS / No 368 OXFORD STREET, near the PANTHEON / Stationary wares Wholesale & Retail on Low Terms / for ready Money / Account Books bound & ruled in an improved manner / No charge for ruling / News Papers served in Town and sent Post Free / to every part of the United Kingdom. / ENGRAVING & PRINTING

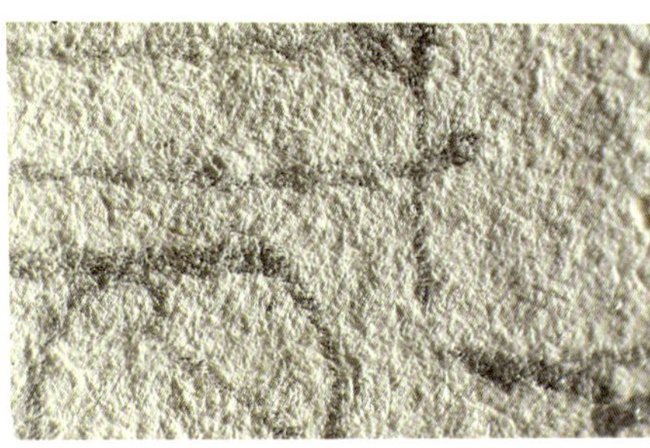

29B

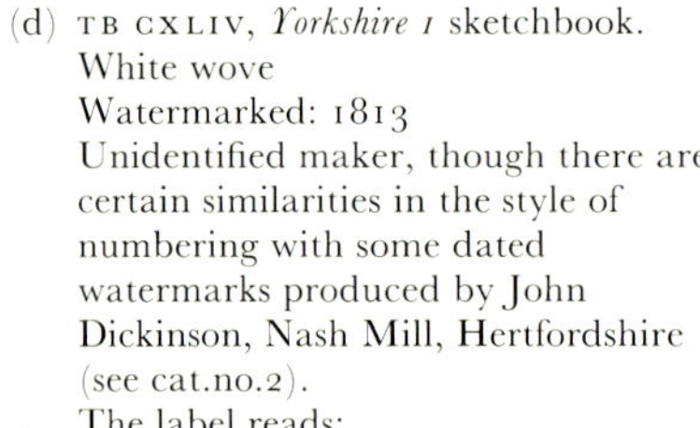

(d) TB CXLIV, *Yorkshire 1* sketchbook.
White wove
Watermarked: 1813
Unidentified maker, though there are certain similarities in the style of numbering with some dated watermarks produced by John Dickinson, Nash Mill, Hertfordshire (see cat.no.2).
The label reads:

GARDINER & SON / No 20 / Princes Street / Cavendish Sq /

(e) TB CXLV, *Yorkshire 2* sketchbook.
White wove
Watermarked: I & E SMITH / 1812
Made by Joseph and Elizabeth Smith, Dursley Mill, Gloucestershire (see cat.no.38).
This sketchbook bears another label from Mills & Sons (see c. above) but the last lines have been altered. Where the TB CXXIX label talks of Account books and News papers, this label reads:

The Greatest variety of Bath, Note and Letter Paper / so much esteemed for their cheapness and good / qualities.

Occasional examples of such Bath letter papers can be found in the Bequest: see TB LXX E

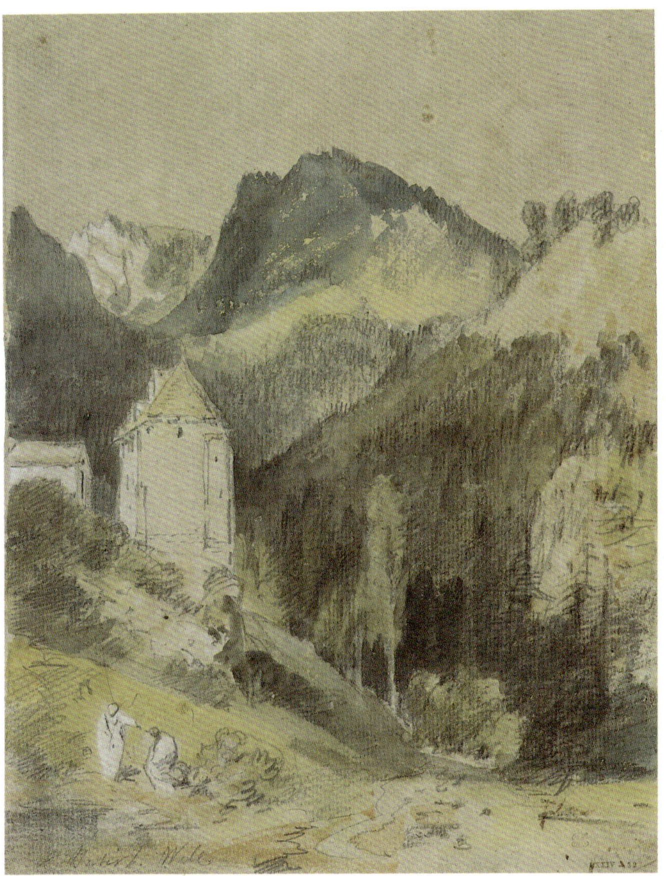

30

30 The Little Church of St. Humber
1802

Unbound sheet from the *Grenoble* sketchbook
Page size: 284 × 216 ($11\frac{3}{16} \times 8\frac{1}{2}$)

Grand Carré Quarto
Self-coloured brown laid
Chain lines: 2.9 – 3cms ($1\frac{3}{16}$ in) apart, variable
Laid line frequency: 7–8 per cm (17–20 per in) variable
Shadows present: single faced mould
Watermarked: Papeterie du Marais
Made by Jean-Louis Delagarde at Papeteries du Marais, Seine et Marne, France

Pencil, watercolour and white bodycolour

Turner Bequest: LXXIV 32
D04525

30A Transmitted light detail of watermark and look-through, reversed.

30B Raking light detail of watercolour, pencil and paper surface. × 7 magnification.

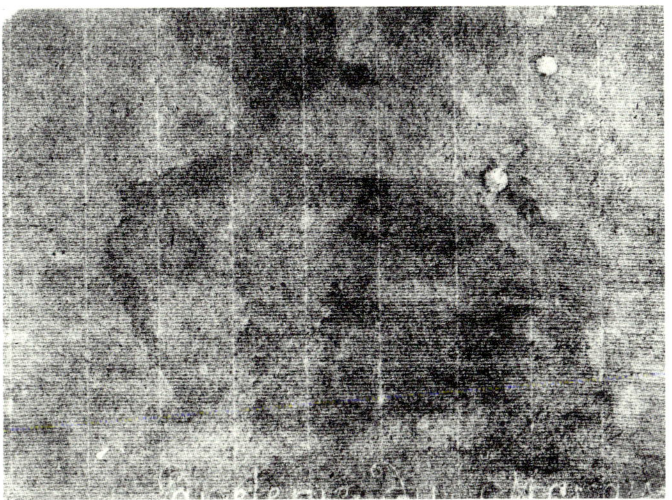

30A

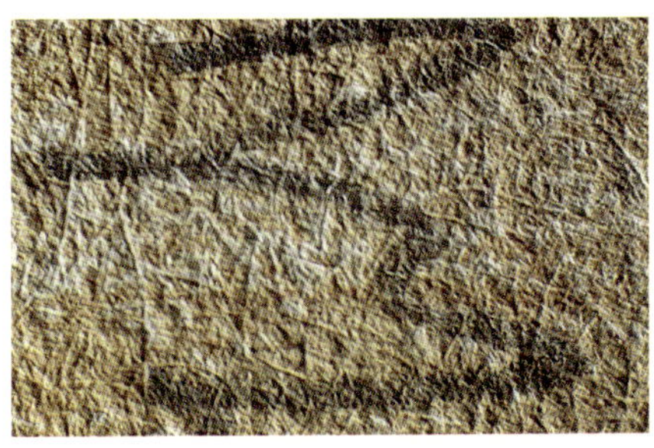

30B

31 Castle of the Ringenberg 1802

Unbound sheet from the *Grenoble* sketchbook
Page size: 216 × 284 ($8\frac{1}{2} \times 11\frac{3}{16}$)

Grand Carré Quarto
Self-coloured brown laid.
Chain lines: 2.9–3 cms ($1\frac{3}{16}$ in) apart, variable.
Laid line frequency: 7–8 per cm (17–20 per in) variable.
Shadow present: single faced mould.
Watermarked: Papeterie du Marais.
Made by Jean-Louis Delagarde at Papeteries du Marais, Seine et Marne, France.

Pencil, black chalk and white bodycolour.

Turner Bequest: LXXIV 46
D04539

31A Raking light detail of chalk and pencil worked together. × 7 magnification.

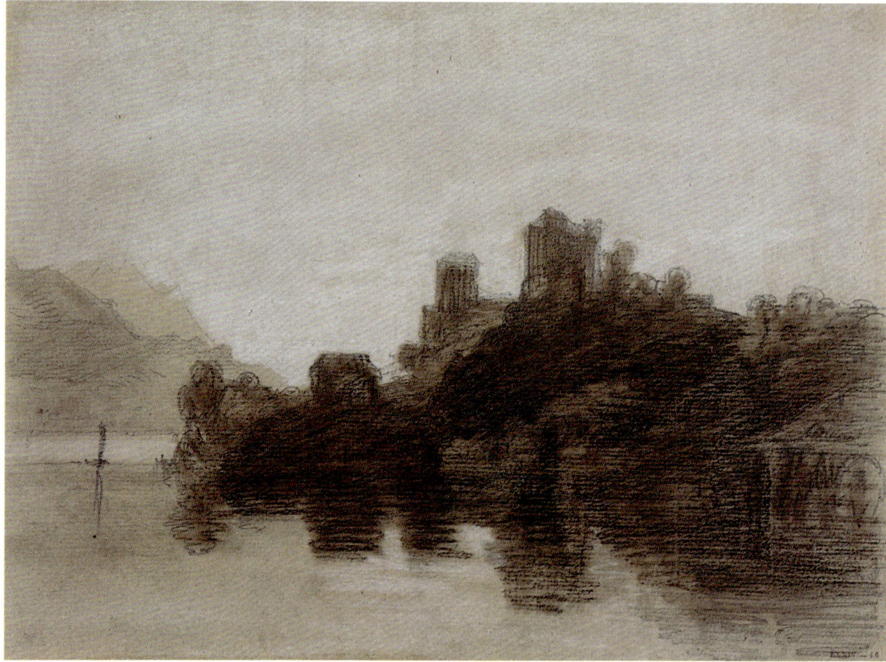

31

Many of these sheets in this sketchbook exhibit considerable colour differences between the wire and felt sides of the paper, with large areas of surface discolouration, flurry marks, probably caused by froth on the surface of the pulp in the vat during the formation of the sheets. Whilst consistent supplies of good rags were becoming increasingly difficult for most mills in Europe during this period, the French mills, in particular, had been having very serious supply problems owing to the chaos, first of the Revolution, and then later under the conditions during the War. The finest materials were almost impossible to obtain. Rags were replaced by hemp fibres from old rope, and by recycling older papers: the trimmings of old books and 'other small pieces cut by the booksellers and stationers'.[1]

There has been considerable discussion as to whether or not these drawings were ever actually in a sketchbook. At present they are all loose sheets. A close examination of all the sheets especially the edges that have not been cut, initially led me to suppose that they were pages from two different sketchbooks. Further examination has shown that the stitch binding, visible in the edges of many of the sheets, falls into several distinct groups, probably corresponding to the sections of one bound book. The variations in the tone and weight of many of the sheets are attributable to the random variation in formation typical of many mills at this time.[2] This sketchbook was bound up so that the chain lines run horizontally across the page, rather than vertically.

Any discussion of the *Grenoble* sketchbook is further complicated by the various other pieces of paper associated with it in the Turner Bequest. The examination of these papers poses more questions than it answers. Many of the drawings had been mounted by Turner, with the titles of the drawings written either on the mounts or on paper slips attached to the mounts. But when these works came to be framed up for exhibition after Turner's death the mounts were all trimmed. A collection of these 'labels', wrapped in another paper, are in the Bequest, and three of them bear watermarks.[3]

Many of the drawings are still backed, but only three of them with papers that could possibly have been used in Turner's lifetime.[4] These have been tipped onto their backing sheets, unlike the others, which have been laid down onto a machine made paper dating from the late 1850s.[5] Unfortunately neither of these backing papers bears any physical relation to the label papers.

One of the drawings is on a completely different paper to the rest of the Marais

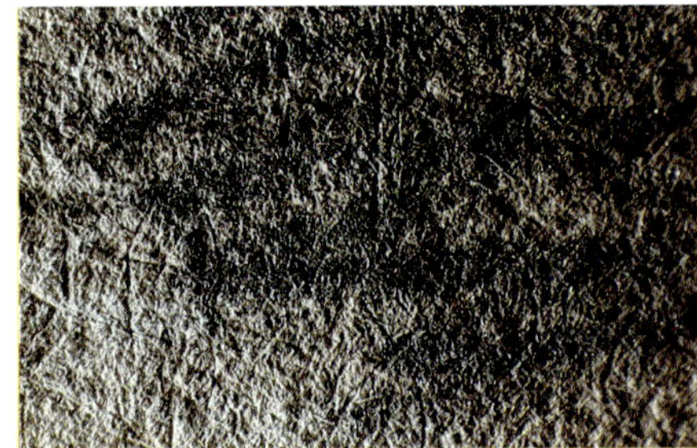

31A

papers. TB LXXIV 1, which Finberg describes as being drawn on a 'flyleaf', is a pale blue laid:

280 × 420 ($11\frac{1}{8} \times 16\frac{9}{16}$)
Chain lines: 28–9 mm ($1\frac{1}{8}$ in) apart, variable.
Laid line frequency: 9 per cm (22 per in)
Double faced mould.
Watermarked: R C
Unidentified maker.
Probable origin: French.

At this date one would expect a paper made on the newly developed double-faced mould to have been a quality product: this type of mould was developed for making the finest papers. But this sheet is very poorly formed. It has a very opaque, wild look-through, and has been made on a mould whose surface was no longer rigid, but sagged in the centre, producing a much greater density of pulp and thickness of the sheet in that area. The size and format of the sheet make it likely that it is precisely what Finberg thought, one of the end-papers of the sketchbook.

1 Reynaud, 1985, p.240.

2 One of the sheets catalogued as belonging to this group, TB LXXIV C, is actually a different paper: a buff toned wove paper, which has yellowed considerably. From its colour, feel and handle, and to some extent the lettering style of its watermark (the hint of a serif and a complete 'W'), in comparison with other papers in my collection, it would appear to date from the late 1830s. This would accord with Andrew Wilton's dating of the drawing to 1843. Wilton and Russell, 1976.

3 The labels are all on a white laid paper.
Chain lines: 28–30 mm ($1\frac{1}{8}$ in) apart, variable.
Laid line frequency: 10 per cm (25 per in)
Unidentified maker.
The labels bearing the following inscriptions are watermarked:

(a) 'Le Pont de Montigny Le Vallais'
Watermarked: IV and another indecipherable mark.
(b) 'Grenoble Mt Blanc' and
(c) 'Untersen(?) de lac de Brentz'
Watermarked: Traces of a mark that might be a '7', perhaps indicating a French origin for the paper. The '7' in that case would be a date mark for Revolutionary year 7 (September 1798 to September 1799).

The labels are all wrapped in a deep blue laid, English made Foolscap Ledger paper, dating from after Turner's death:
Chain lines: 25 mm (1 in) apart
Laid line frequency: 7 per cm (19 per in)
Double faced mould.
Watermarked: Britannia
Countermarked: E TOWGOOD / 1857

4 These are the backing papers to TB LXXIV 35, 94, 96.
White laid rough printing paper
Chain lines: 28–32 mm ($1\frac{1}{8}$–$1\frac{1}{4}$ in) apart, variable.
Laid line frequency: 7 per cm (17 per in)
Shadows present: single faced mould.
Watermarked: Fleur-de-Lys (TB LXXIV 35, 94) Indecipherable lettering (TB LXXIV 96)
Unidentified maker.
The traces of single line lettering in 96 are typical of late eighteenth century French paper.

5 LXXIV 51–82 backing papers:
A heavily sized, off white, machine made wove paper.
No trace of watermark.
A very distinctive wire mark on one side of the sheet.
Unidentified maker.

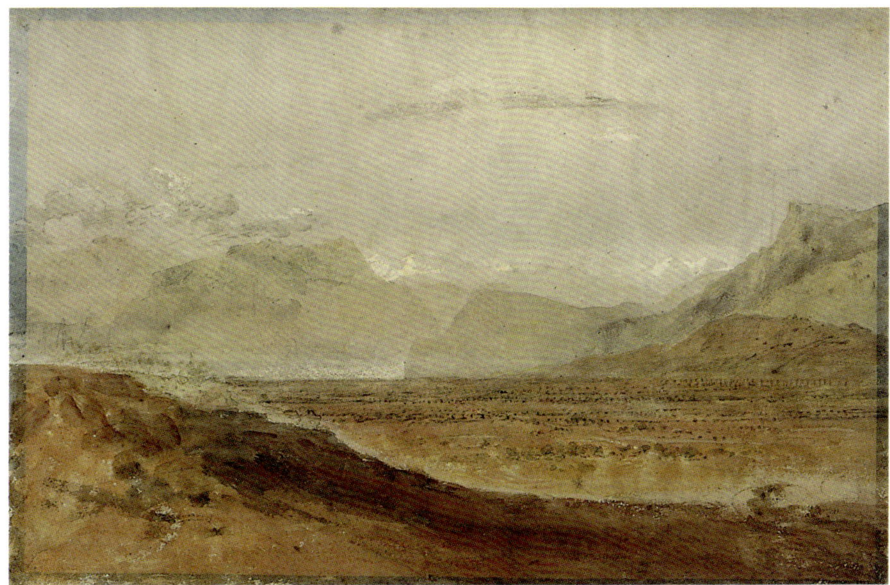

32

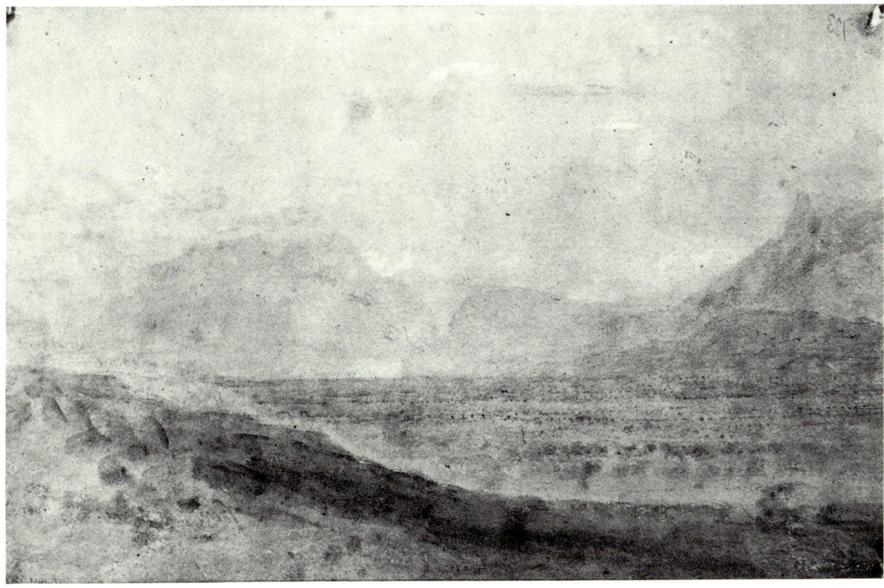

32A

32 The Alps from Grenoble to Chambéry 1802

From the *St Gothard and Mont Blanc* sketchbook
Calfbound with two brass clasps
325 × 584 × 25 ($13\frac{13}{16}$ × $21\frac{7}{8}$ × 1)
Page size: 313 × 473 ($12\frac{3}{8}$ × $18\frac{5}{8}$)

Super Royal Folio
White wove, prepared with a grey wash on both sides of the sheet
Watermarked: 1801 / J WHATMAN
Made by Balston and the Hollingworth Brothers, at Turkey Mill, Maidstone, Kent

Watercolour

Turner Bequest: LXXV 26
D04618

32A Look-through, taken with transmitted light.

32B Raking light detail of paint layer and paper surface. × 7 magnification.

The sketchbook is generally worked in pencil and white chalk, with some drawings coloured. Many of the sheets are no longer in the Bequest.[1] Finberg records that:

> This book has been almost entirely disintegrated – only six leaves remaining in the covers. No record has been kept of the sequence of the pages . . . the order in which the pages are now placed is largely fortuitous.[2]

Owing to the very serious fading of the indigo used in this watercolour, it was withdrawn from exhibition in the 4th Loan Collection in 1906. Despite the increasing stability of various pigments developed during the early years of the nineteenth century many artists continued to use fugitive pigments in their colours, usually because some of the actual tones and depth they required were sometimes only achievable using such pigments. Amongst the Windsor and Newton Archives, at Harrow, is a brief typescript, *A Short History of the House of Winsor & Newton Ltd*, written by W.E. Killick, who worked for the company for many years. Writing in 1925, he records a tale,

> which I think is authentic, and that is, that Mr Winsor during his life was pretty intimate with the great artist Turner, who used to get his colours from us and noticing from time to time the very fugitive colours that Turner bought from us, plucked up courage one day to remonstrate with him for so doing. Turner's answer, in spite of the friendship between the two men, was somewhat uncompromising; he is alleged to have said 'Your business Winsor is to make colours for Artists, mine is to use them.' I am afraid poor Mr Winsor had nothing to say in reply.

32B

The composition and permanence of artists' pigments was to cause increasing concern throughout the nineteenth century to colourmen, artists and conservators. The colourmen were increasingly criticised for selling fugitive pigments. At the end of the century Winsor and Newton became the first colourmen to publish information on the permanence of their colours. At the same time they published a policy statement in which, no doubt with Turner in mind, they insisted that artists must be allowed to decide for themselves whether or not to use fugitive colours, and that they would continue to produce such colours, whilst making every attempt to make them as permanent as possible.

1 e.g. Two works in the Whitworth Art Gallery, Manchester, catalogued as nos. 26 and 27 in Hartley 1984 (W357 and W359). Another work from this sketchbook is in the Fitzwilliam Museum, Cambridge, no. 10, in Cormack 1975 (W360).

2 Finberg 1909, Vol.1, p.201.

33 Lauffenberg 1802

From the *Lake Thun* sketchbook
205 × 165 × 20 ($8\frac{1}{8} \times 6\frac{1}{2} \times \frac{13}{16}$)

Page size: 201 × 156 ($6\frac{1}{4} \times 8$)

White laid writing paper
Chain lines: 2.7 cm ($1\frac{1}{8}$ in) apart
Laid line frequency: 7 per cm (17 per in)
Watermarked: ornamented monogram
Countermark: SE GRUNER
Shadows present: single faced mould
Made by Samuel Emanuel Gruner, working in Berne, Switzerland, between 1796 and 1810[1]

Worked in pencil, on both wire and felt surfaces.

Turner Bequest: LXXVI 25V
D04681

33A Composite transmitted light detail of watermark and look-through.

33B Raking light detail of laid surface, fibre and graphite. × 10 magnification.

During his time in Switzerland Turner purchased three sketchbooks, all containing white writing paper of generally good quality. The *Swiss Figures* sketchbook[2] contains paper from the same Berne papermaker. But the *Rhine, Strasburg and Oxford* sketchbook contains paper made by a different maker at Basle.[3] The paper in all three books has a slight flecking, perhaps due to the bleaching of the blend of linen and cotton fibres used, and some process dirt.

Most of the work in this group of sketchbooks has been done using a relatively soft graphite pencil, admirably suited to the combination of the hard gelatine size with a slightly coarse 'toothed' texture.

Judging by this relatively crisp sizing of the papers, all three books were probably made for writing in, rather than sketching. There are some indications in the *Swiss Figures* sketchbook, where some of the pages have been worked in colour, that the paper was so heavily sized that the colour had difficulty in adhering to the paper's surface.

33B

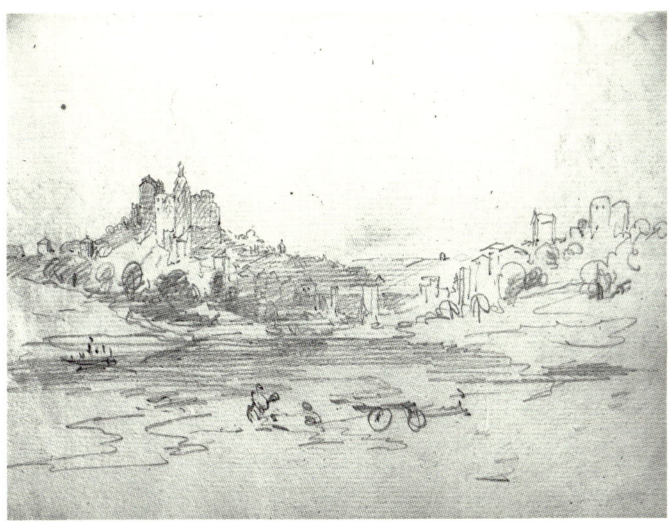

33

33A

[1] Hans B Kälin-Sautter, '*Wappen in Schweizer Wasserzeichen.*', from the *I P H Yearbook 1986.*

[2] TB LXXVIII. A white laid paper, watermarked: SE GRUNER with the same ornamental monogram.

[3] TB LXXVII. A white wove paper, bearing two watermarks: I C de R IMHOF and G R MED in different parts of the sheet. The paper was made by Johann Christoph de Rudolf Im-Hof, who had a mill at Basle between 1778 and 1849. The G R MED mark possibly refers to a paper size slightly larger than English foolscap ($17 \times 13\frac{1}{2}$).

34 Schaffhausen from below the falls 1802

555 × 724 ($21\frac{5}{8} \times 28\frac{1}{2}$)

Trimmed Imperial

White wove, prepared with a grey wash

Watermarked: HAYES & WISE / 1799

Made by John Hayes and John Wise at Padsole Mill, Maidstone, Kent

Pencil and rubbing down to reveal the white of the paper[1]

Turner Bequest: LXXIX D

D04878

34A Transmitted light detail of watermark and look-through.

34B Raking light detail of soft graphite deep in the surface of the sheet and the glistening of the gelatine size. Unfortunately the lighting of this particular image has 'bleached' out the grey preparation of the surface. × 7 magnification.

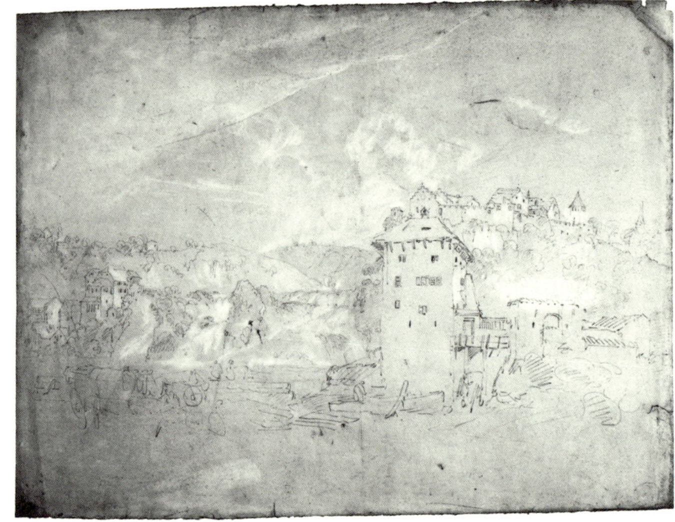

34

34A

The nineteen drawings catalogued by Finberg as the 'Schaffhausen etc. Folio drawings' belong to two distinct categories. Twelve drawings are on English-made white wove paper prepared with a grey wash on both sides of the sheet, of which this is one. These papers are all approximately 22 × 29 in. All these sheets were originally made as Imperial by Hayes and Wise, but have been variously trimmed to slightly different sizes. The second group consists of seven untrimmed French-made sheets, which unlike the English papers are self-coloured. They were not prepared before use; the colour comes from the raw materials used to make them (see cat.-nos. 35 and 36). Each sheet shows signs of having been folded both before use and after.

The toning of such papers 'for designing on' as described in *Rees' Cyclopaedia* of 1819 was very common by the early years of the nineteenth century, particularly for the growing amateur market. This 'bistred paper' was a

> white paper washed with a sponge dipped in soot water. Its use is to save the labour of the crayon, in places which are to be shadowed the same depth with the teint of this paper. For light places, they are made thereon with white chalk.[2]

Turner's use of such dark ground papers is so individual, so distinctive, with its rubbing and scratching out of the ground back to the white, that they cannot have been prepared commercially for the general market. Given the fading of the grey, particularly visible in LXXIX M,[3] I would suggest that this is a ground of Turner's own devising, and whilst it might contain some soot a major component may be the notoriously fugitive pigment indigo.

By the end of Turner's life, the Artists' Colourmen had developed the mass production of such papers. By 1851 Winsor and Newton were selling their 'graduated scraping tinted tablets' and 'prepared vellum tints' describing them as 'a novel and beautiful invention for the assistance of the pencil and watercolour sketcher'. These tints were

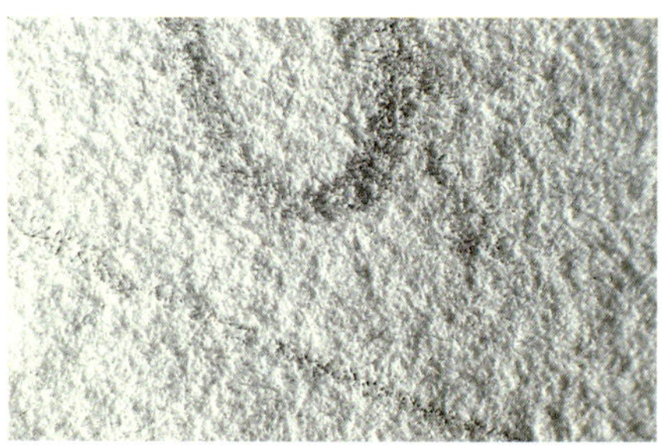

34B

'printed on drawing paper, in lithography . . . produced in a variety of tints, to suit different classes of subjects . . . the lights are obtained by scraping off the colour with a knife, by which means white touches are left where they are required'.[4]

1 Upstone, 1990, and Finberg, 1909, come to different conclusions as to the exact nature of the white in use on this drawing. Upstone favours bodycolour, Finberg white chalk, but the highlights seem in fact to have been produced by rubbing out down to the original white ground of the paper.
2 Besides this reference from 'Paper' in Rees the 1797 *Encyclopaedia Britannica* (p.715) also discusses paper prepared for drawing by passing 'a sponge over it, which has imbibed water impregnated with soot'.
3 The sheet was exhibited in the nineteenth century, no.610.
4 *1851 Winsor and Newton Trade Catalogue* p.39. Windor and Newton Archives.

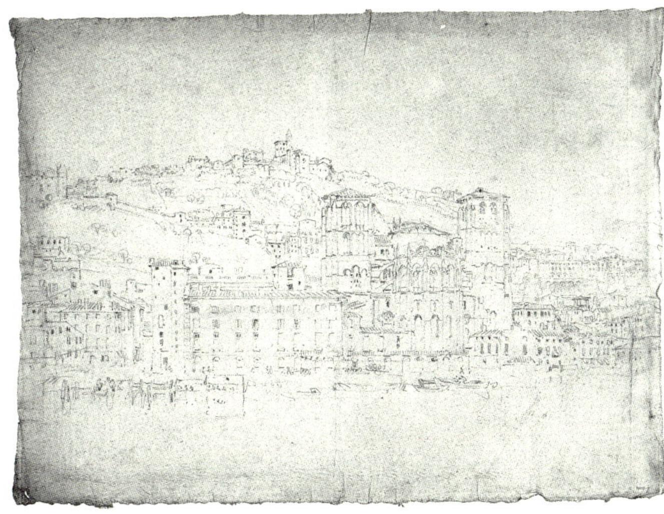

35

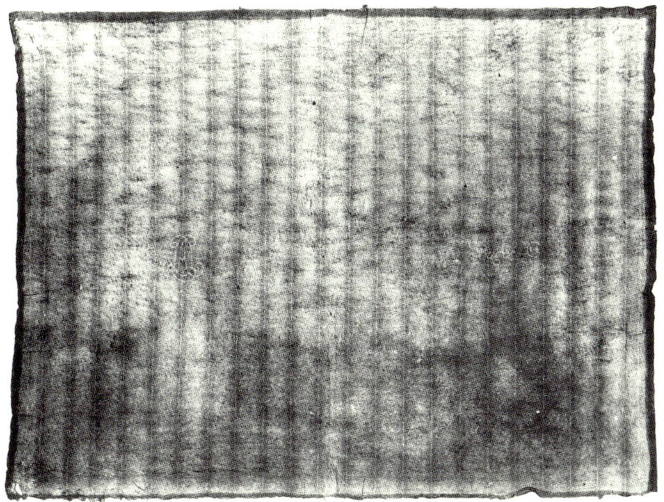

35A

35 Lyons 1802

454 × 661 ($7\frac{3}{4} \times 23\frac{1}{2}$)
Grand Carré
Self coloured flecked pale grey laid
Chain lines: 2.8 cms ($1\frac{1}{8}$ in) apart
Laid line frequency: 9 per cm (22 per in)
Shadows present: single faced mould
Watermark: D L monogram
Countermark: Buges
Made by Leorier Delisle, at the Buges Mill, Montargis, France

Worked in pencil

Turner Bequest: LXXIX P
D04890

35A Transmitted light detail of watermark, countermark and look-through.

35B Raking light detail of pencil, laid texture and fibre. × 7 magnification.

This work is another of the Schaffhausen folio drawings, but executed on paper by a different maker from that of the rest of the French paper that Turner purchased on this tour. The particular grey of this sheet comes from a combination of white linen rags, blue and red rags and some hemp, probably old ropes. The hemp and linen will have been bleached. This bleaching has shown up the many shives that fleck the sheet. Experiments with the chemical bleaching of fibres had begun at the Buges mill, during the Revolution, under the direct control of the National Convention, when the mill, like the Marais mill (see cat.nos.29, 30, 31 and 36), was producing paper for Assignats. Guillot, the Director of Artists on the Comité des Assignats et Monnaies, made frequent journeys to Delisle's mill at Buges from the Autumn of 1793 onwards, to conduct experiments with the ci-devant artistocrat, Claude-Urbain Reth de Servières (who had changed his name to Reth with the Revolution) on the problem of producing fine white papers during a period in which it was difficult to obtain consistent supplies of good rags.[1]

The Revolution had brought chaos and considerable problems to all French industry, and brought the paper mills to a near standstill. Hector Campbell described his view of French papermaking in 1802:

> . . . her coarse foul cotton rags were not made better by separation and assortment; her engines were deficient, and her mills exhibited no mark of prosperity, but every symptom of slovenly neglect.[2]

35B

The French had been using cotton rags for far longer than the English, who still preferred linen. But cotton rags could still be 'brought to an equality with fine linen rags' by bleaching with 'oxygenated muriatic acid', or chlorine gas. Campbell who had patented his own highly successful bleaching process ten years earlier[3] considered that:

> The bleaching gas is much better adapted to coarse cotton rags than coarse linen or hempen rags; because the former is without ligneous particles, and the latter abounds with them, and these particles, called by the papermakers 'sheaves' are made more conspicuous by bleaching[2]

The increasing use of inferior cotton rags in English papermaking in the early years of the nineteenth century, in combination with the over-enthusiastic use of the new chlorine-based bleaching powders, was eventually to cause great problems for both makers and users. John Murray, recorded in 1824:

> I have in my possession a large copy of the Bible printed at Oxford, 1816 (never used,) and issued by the British and Foreign Bible Society, crumbling, literally, into Dust. . . . specimens there are [of paper] that being folded up, crack at the edges and fall asunder: . . . One letter which I forwarded by post, fell to pieces by the way, . . .[4]

[1] Camus, 1941.
[2] Campbell, 1802.
[3] Hector Campbell. Patent No.1922. December 1792.
[4] Murray, 1824, *p.7*.

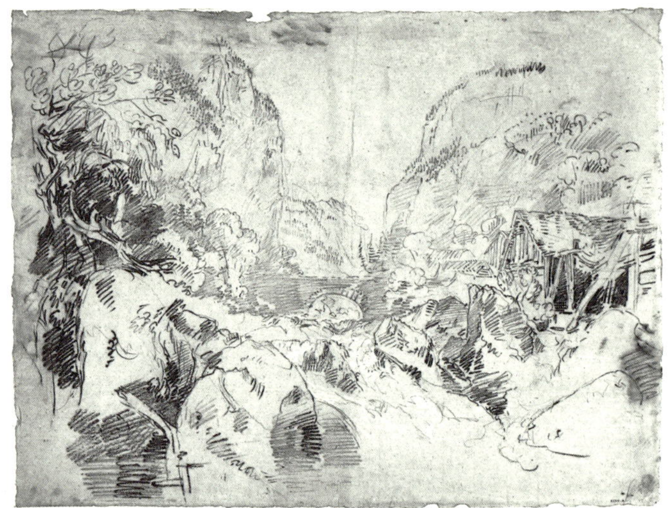

36

36A

36 Bridge among Mountains 1802

454 × 661 ($17\frac{3}{4} \times 23\frac{1}{2}$)
Self-coloured flecked buff laid
Chain lines 2.8–3 cms ($1\frac{1}{8}$–$1\frac{3}{16}$ in) apart, variable
Laid line frequency: 10 per cms (25 per in)
Shadows present: single faced mould
Watermarked: Marais
Made by Jean-Louis Delagarde at Papeteries du Marais, Seine et Marne, France

Black and white chalk and pencil

Turner Bequest: LXXIX O
D04889

36A Transmitted light detail of watermark and look-through, reversed and inverted.

36B Raking light detail of surface texture, fibres, chalk and pencil marks. × 7 magnification.

This work is from the second group of papers in the 'Schaffhausen Folio Drawings' and was purchased in France, probably at the same time as the *France, Savoy, Piedmont* sketchbook and the *Grenoble* sketchbook papers (see cat.nos. 29 and 30).

The prominent fleck in these sheets comes from particles of straw fibre, used to bulk up the pulp in a time of great shortage of rags as a raw material. Each of these sheets, like the English papers which have been catalogued with them in the Bequest, shows evidence of having been folded before and after use.

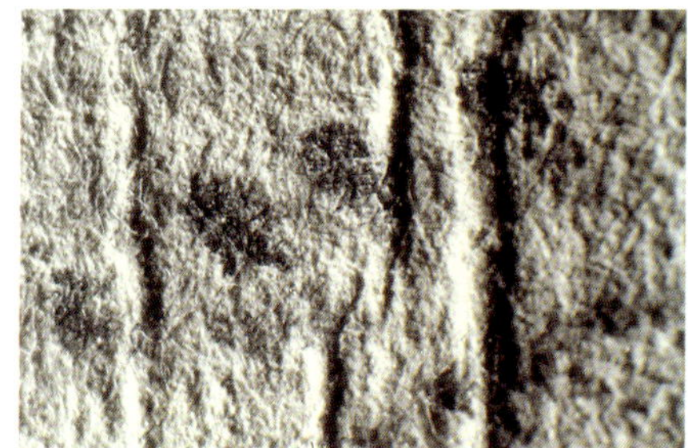

36B

Changing Concerns (cat.nos.37–50)

By the early years of the nineteenth century paper was no longer so rare or precious as it had been in the previous century. More and better paper was being made, and in a much greater variety. Turner's use of paper in the years after his return from the Continent in 1802 reflects this to a certain extent. Some of the individual sheets that he tried out show various technical improvements, particularly in the finishing of their surfaces. But he seems to have been more concerned to develop the potential of those papers that he already knew and trusted.

He does not seem to have been affected to any great extent by the flowering of such artists' suppliers as Ackermann and his imitators, who despite their connections in the professional art world, were largely dependent on the amateur market, persuading people that, with the 'right' equipment and materials, they too could be artists. Much of the contemporary published documentation on drawing paper relates more to this amateur market rather than the professional. One must beware of reading too much into the claims of various entrepreneurs for their products.

Between the 1802 tour to Switzerland and the long tour of Italy in 1819–1820, Turner continued to use a range of Whatman writing and drawing papers, similar to those he had been using before. But at the same time his interests and involvements widened. In 1807 he became Professor of Perspective at The Royal Academy Schools (see cat.nos.49 and 50). Projects such as the engraving and mezzotint of the *Liber Studiorum* involved working in a very different way, on a new range of papers. He was not unfamiliar with these (see cat.no.14), but approached them now with a new vision, and different needs, and with the direct stimulus of his collaboration with engravers, whose experience of papers and their properties was, of necessity, very different to Turner's.[1]

He continued to travel constantly, touring the length and breadth of England, and in 1817 made his second Continental tour, to the Rhineland and the Low Countries (see cat.no.43). New names enter the catalogue of makers whose paper Turner used.[2] Many occur only in sketchbooks worked in pencil but among the drawings catalogued by Finberg as 'Miscellaneous Works 1802–1810'[3] are several loose sheets, either used to try them out, or examples of Turner working on what was to hand (see cat.nos.44 and 45).

In the Bequest there are many examples of papers obviously acquired in the houses of people he was staying with. Some good examples can be found amongst the Farnley material dating from 1816 onwards. The drawing, 'Wharfedale from Chevin' is on a folded letter paper similar to that of a fragment of a letter from Walter Fawkes to Turner, on which there is a drawing of a church.[4] The letter reads:

> By to-morrows coach I shall send you a box containing two Pheasants, a brace of partridges, and a hare, – which I trust you will receive safe and good. We have tormented the poor animals very much lately and now must give them a holiday.
>
> Remember the Wharfedales – everybody is delighted with your Mill – I sit for a long time before it every day.

Farnley Hall, the Fawkes family home near Leeds, was a place of great importance to Turner, almost a home from home. He visited annually from 1808 until Walter Fawkes' death in 1825. Fawkes was perhaps Turner's greatest friend and a substantial patron.[5] Some of the most delightful descriptions of Turner painting come from these visits. The Fawkes girls described Turner's bedroom at Farnley, with

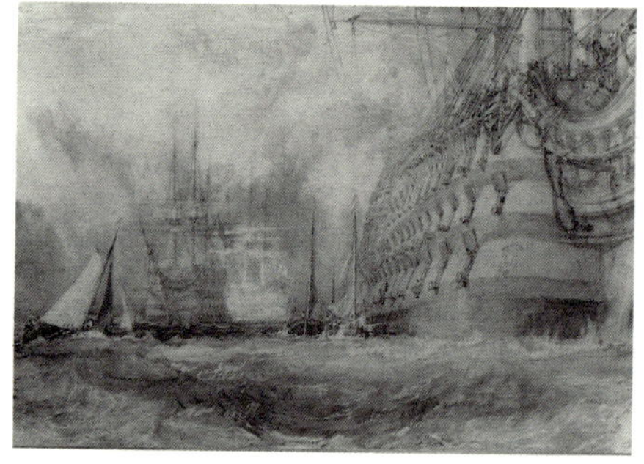

fig.17 *The First Rate Taking on Stores*, Cecil Higgins Art Gallery, Bedford

> Cords spread spread across the room as in that of a washerwoman, and papers tinted with pink and blue and yellow hanging on them to dry.[6]

Perhaps the most famous description of Turner's speed of working also comes from one of his stays at Farnley. Fawkes had suggested, one breakfast time, that Turner might make him

> 'a drawing of the ordinary dimensions that will give some idea of the size of a man of war.' The idea hit Turner's fancy, for with a chuckle he said to Walter Fawkes' eldest son, then a boy of about 15, 'Come along Hawkey, and we will see what we can do for Papa.', and the boy sat by his side the whole morning and witnessed the evolution of 'The First-Rate Taking in Stores'. His descriptions of the way Turner went to work was very extraordinary; he began by pouring wet paint on to the paper till it was saturated, he tore, he scrubbed at it in a kind of frenzy and the whole thing was chaos – but gradually and as if by magic the lovely ship, with all is exquisite minutia, came into being and by luncheon time the drawing was taken down in triumph.[7]

A different and slightly more detailed account, from another occasion, gives a more instructive description:

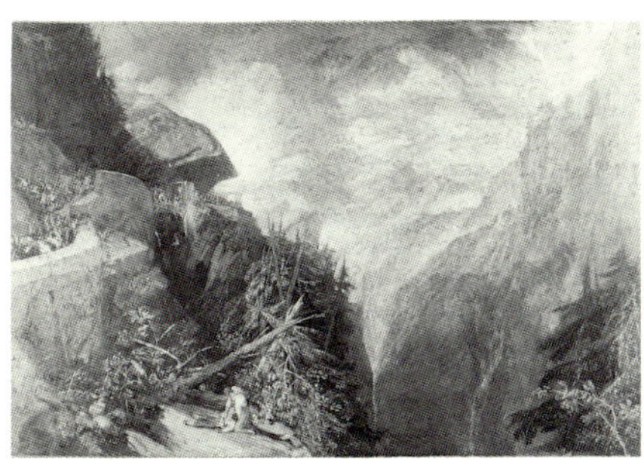

fig.18 *The Battle of Fort Rock.* TB LXXX g

> he stretched the paper on boards and, after plunging them into water, he dropped the colours onto the paper while it was wet making *marblings* and gradations throughout the work. His completing process was marvellously rapid, for he indicated his masses and incidents, took out half lights, scraped out highlights and dragged, hatched and stippled until the design was finished.[8]

It had taken Turner years to find papers he could have confidence in, which could survive such swift and dramatic onslaughts, and to develop his understanding of the paper surface. Works such as *The Battle of Fort Rock, Val d'Aosta, Piedmont, 1796* completed in 1815, have passages of painting of just the beautiful complexity, that is described in the quotations above. This large watercolour has been worked on a smooth surfaced and strongly sized, Double Elephant paper. Though he was turning more to drawing papers for his large-scale works, this sheet appears to be a writing paper. Double Elephant was the largest size writing paper available, but was not often made. Usually the writing surfaces Turner favoured, such as those used for the Fawkes fifty one Rhine Drawings (discussed in cat.no.43), were only made in relatively small sizes.

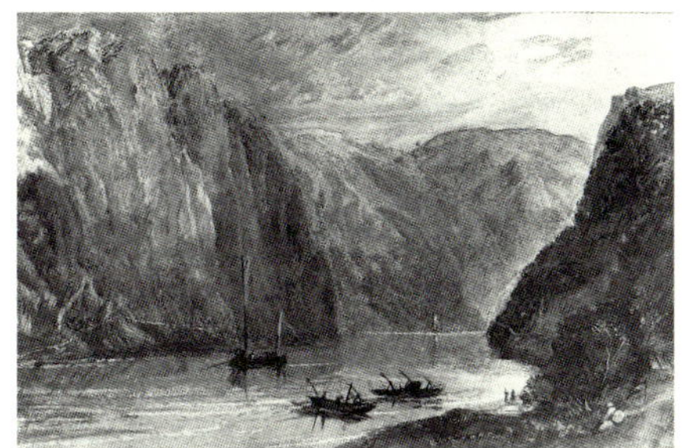

fig.19 *Lurleiberg.* Whitworth Art Gallery, Manchester

The Posts and Large Posts made by Balston, which Turner liked to use (see cat.no.40, 42, and 46) were at one stage only available through the paper merchant Grosvenor, in London, though he would have been supplying other stationers. Balston's partner, William Gaussen, who had begun to look after the London end of the business in 1814[9] wrote to him, in one of his regular reports, discussing what stocks were still held in London. He appears to have wanted Balston to make specific papers to order, rather than making ream after ream and having stocks build up which could not be sold quickly:

> In much sorrow I write to show in what manner you engage our money, which only happens for want of a little system. First I will give an account of what is in London not sold:

12 rms of Drawing Columbier		£123
12 rms of Drawing Atlas		123
58 rms Thin Post Large	34/-	98
71 rms Thin Post	28/-	99
32 rms Super Royal		150
Hollingworths' Printing Demy		1,000
Do. at Mill		300
		£1,893

> Trifles I do not mention.
> How long do you think the Atlas and Columbier will remain on hand? A year, at least, but more likely two years. The Posts I dare not offer at a lower price, but then we must keep them for Grosvenor; no one else ever has or will take them.[10]

Gaussen's estimate of how long it would take them to sell their drawing papers, possibly two years to sell 11,500 sheets, is an interesting reflection on the amounts of papers used by artists. Even the finest of drawing papers were a slow moving product. The Post writing papers were also much cheaper: 28/- rather than £10 5/- for 480 sheets: three farthings a sheet as compared to just over 5d for the drawing papers. Cost may well have played a significant part in many of Turner's purchases of paper. Much of the paper in the Bequest could not be said to be of the highest quality, despite their illustrious maker's names (see cat.nos. 25, 26, 27, 49 and 50). But, despite their imperfections, close examination shows that they are generally sound, particularly as regards the sizing of the sheet. What deficiencies they have are never serious enough to inhibit working on them. Turner bought his paper carefully, he knew exactly what he was buying, and he got very good value for his money.

1 Finberg, 1924, pp.lxvii-lxxx, gives a breakdown of the papers used in its printing:

Parts I–IV, published between 1807 and 1809, were produced on a white laid Columbier (609 × 876 mm (24 × 34½ in) made by Dupuy of Moulin de la Grande Rive, Marsac, Auvergne, France, and designed specifically for such work. These sheets were quartered before working. Judging by its high quality, this must have been old stock, made and imported well before the revolution. Parts V–X, published in 1811 and 1812, were produced on two different white wove Columbier engraving papers, watermarked J WHATMAN and H SMITH, respectively (see cat.no.38 for some discussion of papermakers called Smith).

Parts XI and XII, published in 1816, and Part XIII, published in 1819, were produced on another French white laid Columbier printing paper from the Auvergne, but of a far inferior quality to the original Dupuy paper. It was made by Richard of Moulin du Prat, La Forie.

Part XIV, published in 1819, contained paper from Dupuy, but of an inferior quality. The French paper industry had suffered greatly during the Revolution and the resulting wars.

2 Besides makers already mentioned elsewhere, these makers include:

Austen Stace: Seabrook Mill, Cheriton, Kent. TB CXX L

John Fellows: Eynsford Mill, Kent. TB CXXV, CXXXIII CLI

John Dickinson: Nash Mill, Hertfordshire. TB CLXV

Henry Salmon: Langcliffe Mill, Yorkshire. TB CXXVII

T W & B Botfield: Hopton Wafers Mill, Shropshire. TB CIV

Some sheets bear watermarks from as yet unidentified makers:

TB CXX W	Watermarked: unidentified Coat of Arms. Countermarked: MAM (possibly French)
TB CXX F	Watermarked: Britannia Countermarked: CARRON, (possibly Carrongrove Mill, Scotland.)
TB CXX R	Watermarked: Britannia Countermarked: CLARENCE MILL
TB XCVI	Watermarked: Britannia Countermarked: GS / 1806
TB XCVIII	Watermarked: Crowned Fleur-de-Lys Countermarked: HH monogram (possibly French)
TB CLXIII	Watermarked: BATH / 1815.

3 TB CXX and TB CXXI

4 TB CLIV F 'Wharfedale from Chevin'

White wove letter paper
222 × 362 (8$\frac{3}{4}$ × 14$\frac{1}{4}$)
Watermarked: HOOKE & SON / 180(3?)
Made by Thomas Hooke, Tile Mill, near Reading, Berkshire.
Though this work is mounted and backed, it has been possible to read most of the traces of the watermark, using a raking light.
TB CLIV Y is from the same batch of paper, watermarked: HOOKE & S../1803
Another drawing in the same group, TB CLIV A, inscribed 'Subject for Mr Fawkes', is drawn on the back of a letter to Fawkes, and bears a postmark: LANGHOLME/321/C

5 By the time of his death in 1825, Walter Fawkes had purchased six oils and some 250 watercolours by his friend.

6 Lietch, 1894.

7 'Memoire of Edith Mary Fawkes', quoted by Gage, 1987, pp.159–160.

8 James Orrock, quoted by Gage, 1969, p.32.

9 The financial troubles which were beginning to afflict many manufacturing industries towards the end of the Napoleonic Wars, and which were to get much worse during the years following England's victory, had led to Balston taking two partners in 1814. The two men, William Gaussen and Richard Bosanquet, were both relatives of Susanna Whatman. This partnership was to last thirty-five years.

10 William Gaussen to William Balston, 9th June 1815, quoted by Balston, 1954, p.120.
The listing of 'Hollingworths' Printing Demy is another intriguing glimpse into the connections between the two 'Whatman' mills, Turkey Mill and Springfield Mill. At this date at least, Balston must have been marketing Hollingworth papers for them in London. It is important to realise how much the two separate companies were tied together by their common 'trade name'.

37 Studies for *'Sun rising through Vapour'* and *'Hero and Leander'*

1800–1805

From the *Calais Pier* sketchbook
Sketchbook, bound in boards, covered in marbled paper, with two brass claps
282 × 442 × 23 (11$\frac{1}{8}$ × 17$\frac{2}{5}$ × $\frac{9}{10}$)
Page size: 270 × 435 (10$\frac{3}{5}$ × 17$\frac{3}{20}$)

Large Double Loaf Folio
Blue laid wrapping paper
Chain lines: 25 mm (1 in) apart, variable
Laid line frequency: 7–8 per cm (18–20 per in) variable
Watermarked: Fleur de Lys / 1794
Countermarked: IV / 1794[1]
Shadows present: Single faced mould
Unidentified maker

Black and white chalk

Turner Bequest: LXXXI 56,57
D04958, D04959

37A Composite transmitted light detail of watermark, dates and look-through of LXXXI 7, 55.

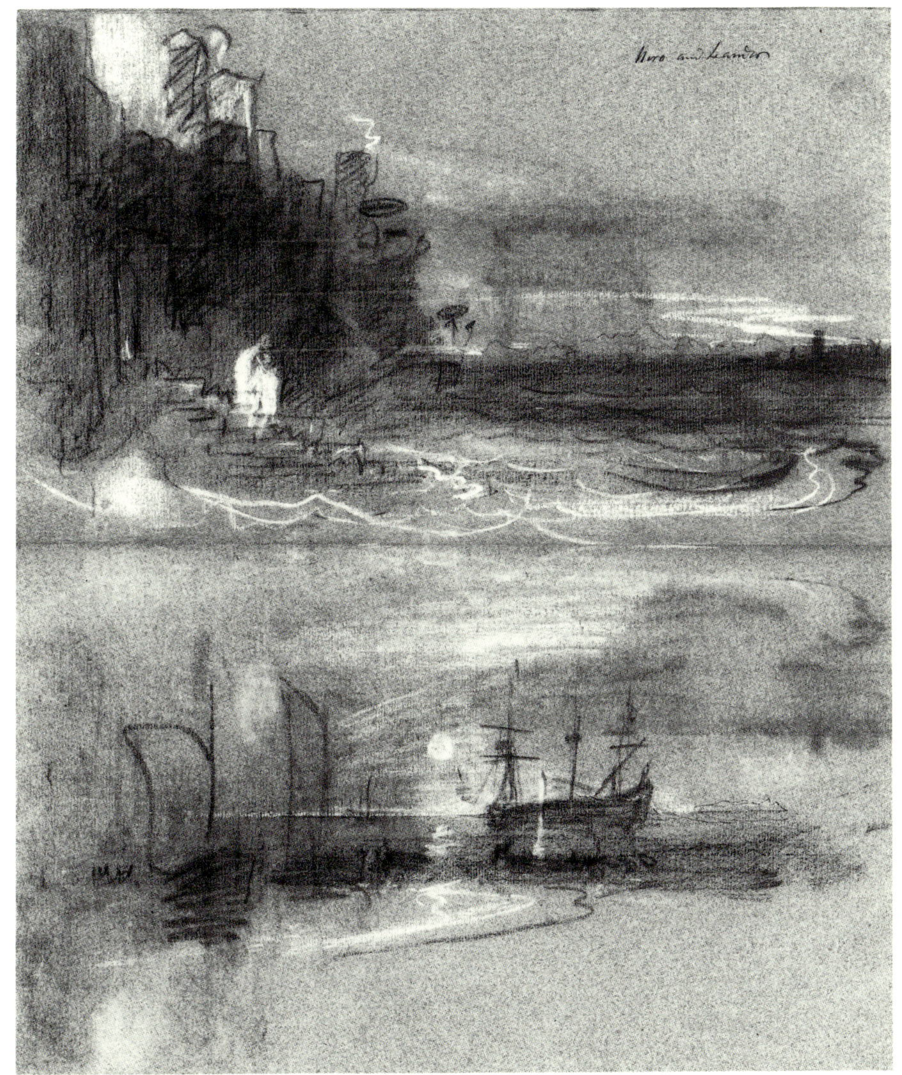

37

The decoration of the brass clasps would suggest that this sketchbook was bound up by William Dickie, the same binder responsible for many of Turner's sketchbooks at this period (see cat.no.38).

Turner used the sketchbook over a period of some five years. It is worked in a variety of ways. The original rich blue of the paper acts as a resonant ground for a whole range of techniques: black and white chalk, some pen and ink, some pencil and some wash. It contains a wide range of sketches and studies for many of his most celebrated oil paintings of this period.

This deep mottled blue paper is typical of many mid to late eighteenth-century wrapping papers, often made from blends of blue rags, old hemp rope, bagging and sailcloth, and often with a proportion of wool fibres. The considerable yellowing and colour loss, visible in those pages which have been exhibited, suggest the presence, either in the original coloured rags, or as an additional dye, of the fugitive indigo.

Many of the details of the paper would suggest a French origin, particularly the combination of a certain crisp softness in its surface and the presence of the Fleur de Lys watermark and IV countermark. But a relatively small detail tells us that this paper is of English manufacture: the presence, in both halves of the sheet, of the date 1794, as a single line wire mark in a different lettering style, suggesting that the dates were attached to the mould some time after it had come into use. The date in the countermark half of the sheet has been attached to the mould, upside down and reversed in relation to the countermark, which would suggest it was applied rather hurriedly.[2]

The use of a date in the mould suggests that this paper is no ordinary wrapping paper, but was designed specifically for artists as a 'fine' paper, despite its apparent lack of quality. English fine papers began to be dated in the watermark in 1794, in response to an Act of Parliament[3] regulating the duty payable on papers. Papermakers producing papers destined for export would receive a rebate if the paper was watermarked with the year of manufacture. Dickie advertised '. . . books . . . for Exportation, or Home consumption, . . .'.[4] The combination of such a rich toned paper, the size of the sketchbook, one of the largest in the Bequest, and the presence of the date[5] would all suggest that this could be a relatively early example of such a coloured Artist's paper, rather than a wrapping.

Despite this, the actual formation of the sheets is not particularly good, with noticeable variations in both bulk and weight between different sheets. Many of the sheets also exhibit 'tears', small circular thin areas in the sheet, which become visible when the paper is held up

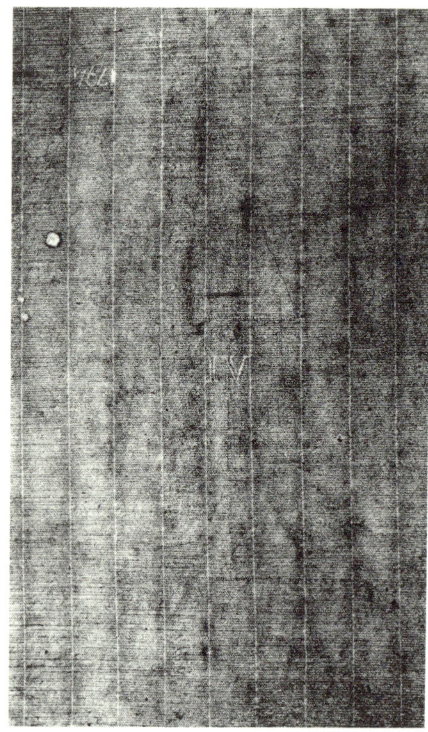

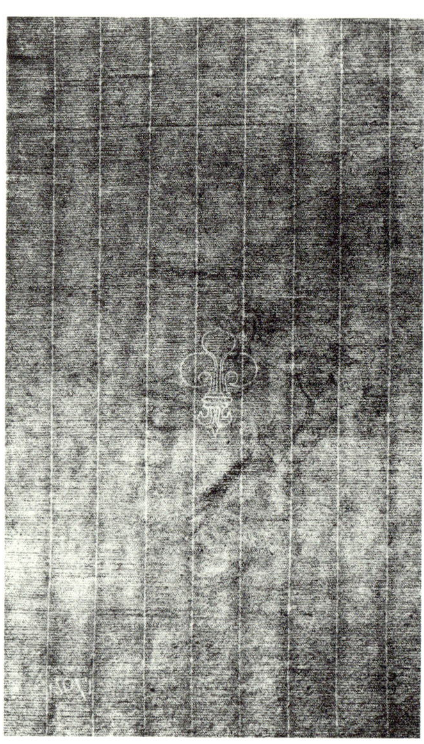

37A

to the light. These are caused by drops of water falling onto the newly formed sheet when the deckle is removed, immediately after the formation of the sheet. Such 'tears' and the variations between the sheets are probably the result of either an inexperienced vatman, or of working too hastily. Many of the smaller mills would have let such paper go for sale without a qualm, but makers such as Whatman, with a reputation to sustain, were generally more conscious of the quality of their products.[6]

1 The IV countermark was originally the initials of the French papermaker Jean Villedary, who worked the Vraichamp, Beauvais and La Couronne mills in the Angoumois, from 1688 onwards. Most of his paper was produced for the Dutch factors, Abraham Janssen, Francois van Tongeren, Pierre van Tongeren and Gilis van Hoven, who exported it all over Europe: much of it came to Britain. The excellence of Villedary's paper led to his IV countermark being appropriated by makers throughout western Europe as a mark of quality. From the middle of the eighteenth century it is often found in conjunction with the LVG mark, again the initials of a particular maker which had come to mean quality; in this case, those of the Dutchman, Lubertus van Gerrevinck, who worked the Phoenix Mill. Both these marks were appropriated during the eighteenth century by many English mills, particularly those making the finer grades of paper, including the two makers who were to do most to establish the enduring quality of English paper: Henry Portal and James Whatman.

2 The addition of such dates was very common: another example can be found in the Bequest: TB LXXXII A, 'Battersea Bridge', where a 1770s Crown/GR watermark has had the 1794 date added underneath it, again reversed in relation to the other lettering. One other curiosity about that particular mark is that the '4' has been added later than the rest of the date, perhaps because the original '4' became loose. Finberg (vol.I, p.64) has catalogued this watermark as 'E.R. 179–', only one of many instances where his readings are somewhat inaccurate.

3 34 Geo. III, c. 20.

4 See cat.no.32, The *Devonshire Coast No 1* sketchbook, for a printed prospectus from William Dickie.

5 Any French paper made in 1794 and dated in the watermark, would not have borne that date, but either 2 or 3, for the Revolutionary Year it fell in (Year 2 if produced before September 1794, or Year 3 after September). The Revolutionary Calendar introduced by Fabre d'Eglantine was finally officially abandoned under Napoleon in 1805, though most people had ceased to use it many years before. Papers can be found dated up to Revolutionary Year II.

6 Whatman papers with such defects can be found in the Bequest, usually amongst the sketchbooks, where they are much less

obvious than in a loose sheet. See TB XXXIV 89 and TB XCI 39 and 40, for traces of very large air bubbles, formed during couching. Formation faults can be seen in TB XL and process dirt, possibly a button, crushed during pulping, can be found in TB XLVI. It is possible that these particular papers, perhaps all from the same batch, were produced around the time the ownership of the business was being transferred from James Whatman the younger to the Balston and Hollingworth partnership in 1794.

38 William Dickie's Prospectus

1811

From the *Devonshire Coast No 1* sketchbook
A calfbound copy of the 'The British Itinerary' by Nathaniel Coltman, bound with interleaved blank paper, and having one brass clasp
122 × 84 × 27 ($4\frac{13}{16} \times 3\frac{5}{16} \times 1\frac{1}{16}$)
Page size: 119 × 75 ($4\frac{7}{10} \times 2\frac{15}{16}$)

Imperial 32mo
White wove printing paper
Watermarked: W DICKIE
Unidentified maker[1]

Turner Bequest: CXXIII 20
D08399

38A Transmitted light detail of watermark and look-through of CXXIII 1.

38B Composite transmitted light detail of watermark and look-through of CXXIII 46,47.

38C Composite transmitted light detail of CXXIII 13,23.

This book bears the printed information:

'Stationary & Account books ruled and annotated for Exportation, or Home Consumption, wholesale and Retail ENGRAVING & PRINTING in all its branches.

The most compleat and Improved Travelling Desks, Copying machines, & Portable cases, for writing, Drawing, or Dressing.

Books Bound in Elegant, or Plain Binding, by Wm Dickie, No.120 Strand: opposite Exeter Change.'

Besides the text paper described above this book contains two other papers:
(a) The endpapers:
Chain lines: 25–27 mm ($1–1\frac{1}{16}$ in) apart, variable.

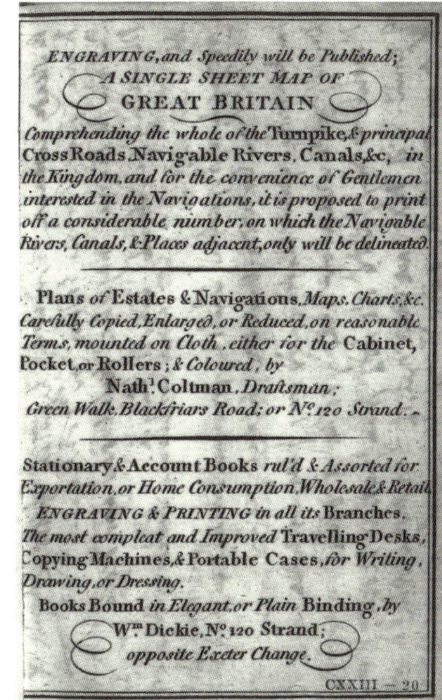

ENGRAVING, and Speedily will be Published;
A SINGLE SHEET MAP OF
GREAT BRITAIN
Comprehending the whole of the Turnpike, & principal Cross Roads, Navigable Rivers, Canals, &c, in the Kingdom, and for the convenience of Gentlemen interested in the Navigations, it is proposed to print off a considerable number, on which the Navigable Rivers, Canals, & Places adjacent, only will be delineated.

Plans of Estates & Navigations, Maps, Charts, &c. Carefully Copied, Enlarged, or Reduced, on reasonable Terms, mounted on Cloth, either for the Cabinet, Pocket, or Rollers; & Coloured, by
Nathl. Coltman, Draftsman;
Green Walk, Blackfriars Road; or N°.120 Strand.

Stationary & Account Books rul'd & Assorted for Exportation, or Home Consumption, Wholesale & Retail.
ENGRAVING & PRINTING in all its Branches.
The most compleat and Improved Travelling Desks, Copying Machines, & Portable Cases, for Writing, Drawing, or Dressing.
Books Bound in Elegant, or Plain Binding, by
W^m. Dickie, N°.120 Strand;
opposite Exeter Change.

CXXIII – 20

38

38A

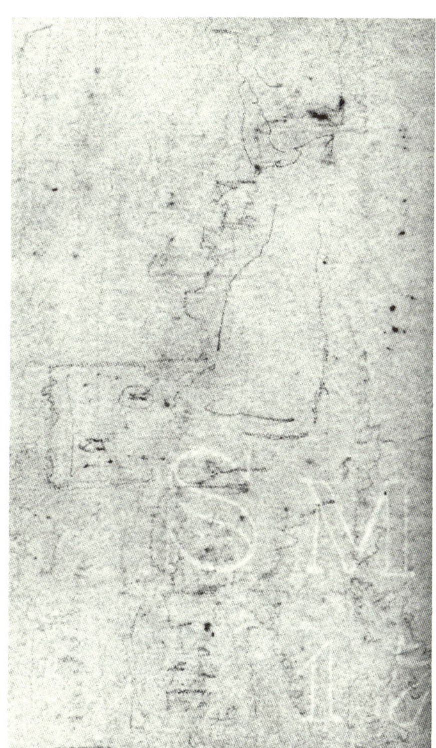

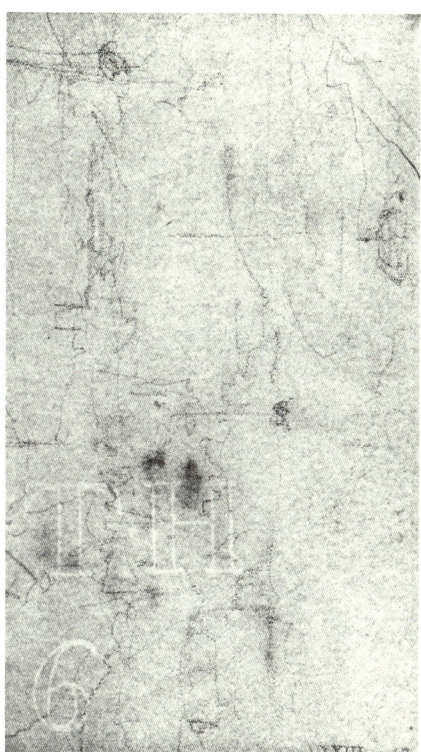

38B

Laid line frequency: 9 per cm (22 per in) variable.
Shadows present: single faced mould.
Watermarked: 1798 & 17 8, where the watermark has been damaged.
Unidentified maker.

(b) The blank interleaved sheets:
White wove writing paper.
Watermarked: SMITH / 1796
Unidentified maker.

Without an initial it is difficult to ascertain which particular papermaking Smith this might be. The only other Smiths occuring amongst Turner's papers are in TB CXLV, watermarked I & E Smith 1812 : the mark of Joseph and Elizabeth Smith who worked Dursley Mill, Gloucestershire. Another Smith watermark found in the Bequest is that of Thomas Smith of Pine, Smith & Allnutt, later Smith & Allnutt, who worked Ivy Mill and other mills in Kent, and provided the paper for various sketchbooks from 1816 onwards. Paper from this same mill, but by different makers, had been used by Turner from as early as 1795 in the *South Wales* sketchbook, where paper watermarked E & P / 1794 is found in combination with both dated and undated Whatman marks from the 'broken H' batch of Large Post paper. The binding details of the *South Wales* sketchbook suggests that it is from William Dickie's bindery.

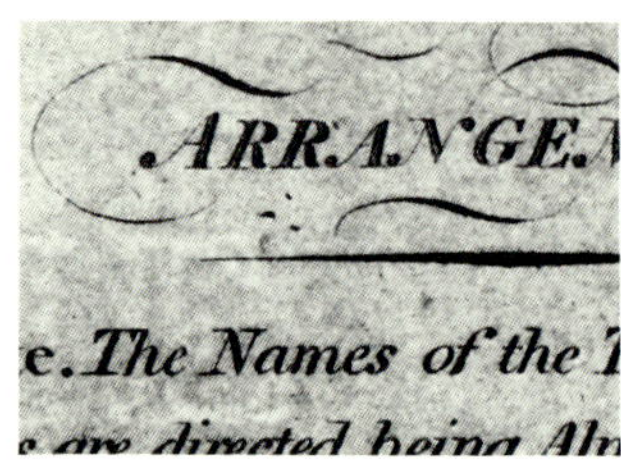

38C

[1] This watermark is an early example of a stationer's or merchant's watermark. Dickie operated no papermills himself, so he must have had a mill make up this paper with his own mark in it. As yet there is no evidence as to which mill this would have been. Judging by the range of makers' marks found in the various books whose binding details correspond with the details of this one, it could have been any of a number of makers. The majority of sketchbooks used by Turner prior to 1807 appear to have been bound up by Dickie.

The makers found in the books bound by Dickie include Robert Edmeads and John Pine, of Ivy Mill, Maidstone, Kent; William Gater of West End Mill, South Stoneham, Hampshire (TB XLIX); John Hayes and John Wise, Padsole Mill, Maidstone, Kent, (TB LXVII, LXXII); and the Balston and Hollingworth partnership, Turkey Mill, Maidstone, Kent.

39 Bridge with cottage and trees
1813
165 × 260 ($6\frac{1}{2}$ × $10\frac{1}{4}$)
Blue wove wrapping paper
Watermarked: none visible
Unidentified maker
Oil over black chalk on prepared paper
Turner Bequest: CXXX F
D09212
B&J 218

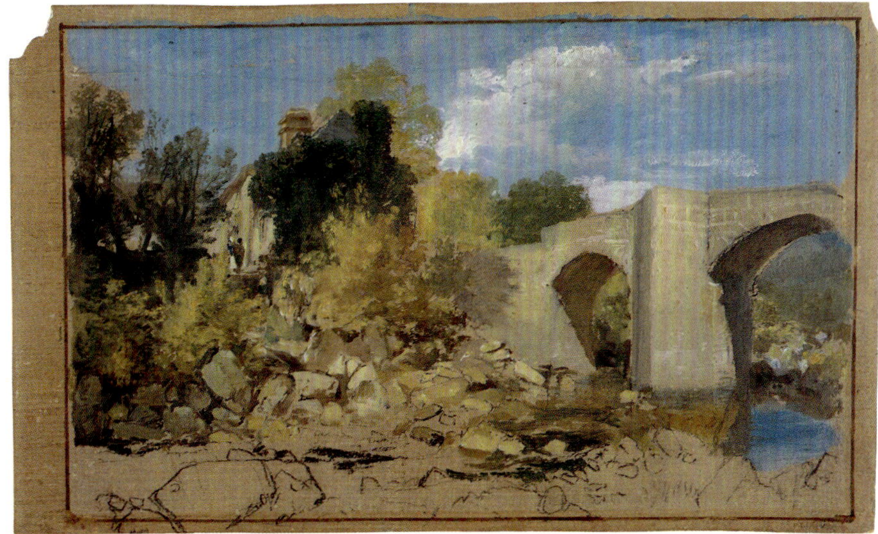

39

The sequence of oils on paper executed by Turner on his tour of Devon in the summer of 1813 is a relatively rare example of his use of this medium.[1] Though Finberg describes all the papers used for these Devonshire oil sketches as being on prepared board, only one of them is strictly a board, being a laminate of at least two sheets, either couched directly together when wet or pasted together afterwards. The others are ordinary papers, possibly of two different types. This sequence of works is unusual also in that the papers were neither prepared nor specifically chosen by Turner, having been provided for him by the landscape painter Ambrose Johns:

> Mr Johns fitted up a small portable painting-box, containing some prepared paper for oil sketches, as well as the other necessary materials. When Turner halted at a scene and seemed inclined to sketch it, Johns produced the inviting box, and the great artist, finding everything ready to his hand, immediately began to work.[2]

Some fifteen or so of these sketches are known to exist, but by all accounts there were many more. Turner is reputed to have said, in answer to a later inquiry about them.

> that they were worthless, in consequence, as he supposed of some defect in the preparation of the paper; all the grey tints, he observed had nearly disappeared.[2]

Whilst it is certainly true that some deterioration has taken place in one or two instances, particularly in TB CCCX H which has been painted on the unprepared side of the paper, one wonders if Turner is here talking of deterioration of the greys in the paint or in the ground.

The particular preparation used for these papers may well have been originally a grey ground containing a proportion of indigo which would, over time, have changed to the buff-grey that we now see. In this example one can see by the different tones where the edges of the sheet have been masked during previous exhibitions, that the ground has continued to lighten. The papers themselves were probably light blue wrappings, changed to a buff by the oils used in the preparation of the surface for oil painting.

One of the studies, TB CXXX A, painted on the back of a printed prospectus for *The British Gallery of Pictures*, by William Young Ottley and Henry Tresham, published in 1808. It is this work that is on the laminated paper mentioned above. The other papers seem to have been prepared using ordinary strong wrappings. The dense, opaque nature of the ground used by Johns makes it almost irrelevant what colour they were originally. Having seen the effect of linseed oil on blue-grey paper over a period of time, I am inclined to think that two different blue-grey papers were used, one of them originally of a darker, richer blue that the other.

1 A few other oil studies on paper exist, notably a group of works done at Knockholt, Kent, TB XCV(a) A–G, dating from *c.*1801.

2 Thornbury, 1866 pp.219–20.

40 Egglestone Abbey and Henry Cooke's Paper Mill 1816

From the *Yorkshire 4* sketchbook
Paper covered boards
$212 \times 128 \times 10$ ($8\frac{3}{8} \times 5 \times \frac{3}{8}$)
Page Size: 204×122 ($8 \times 4 \times \frac{13}{16}$)

Large Post Quarto
White woven writing paper
Watermarked: J WHATMAN /1814
Made by William Balston at Springfield Mill, Maidstone, Kent

Worked in pencil on both wire and felt sides of the sheet

Turner Bequest: CXLVII 31V
D11491

40A Watermark and look-through of TB CXLVII 31 and 15, in transmitted light.

40B Raking light detail of pencil and paper surface. × 7 magnification.

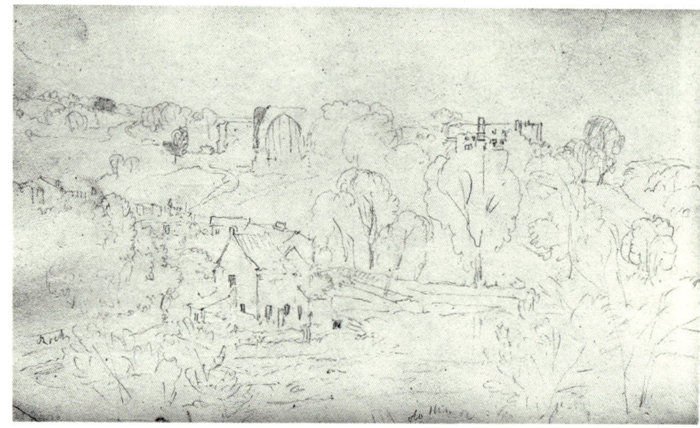

40

40A

The paper used in this sketchbook is a very typical Balston writing paper, made as Large Post, with a good 'nap' and a relatively hard sized surface. It is quite different in quality from the earlier Whatman paper, used in the *North of England* sketchbook (and discussed under cat.no.15), which contains Turner's original drawing of this subject, being both better formed, better sized, and with a very consistent bulk and opacity. There seems to have been a problem with quality at various stages of the Whatman development. 1794, with the changeover to the new partnership had been one such period. The years just prior to the making of this paper had been another, when paper was actually being returned to the mill because of deficiencies:

> there is a letter from Morgan [a London merchant] . . . complaining of the Retree Thick Post being size stained, which they mean to return together with the Medium, but you may probably have seen them, and settled about it.[1]

Egglestone Abbey Mill was for several years run by a woman, Elizabeth Cooke (see cat.no.41). Women were very important in the running of many mills and Springfield Mill was no exception. While William Balston was away selling paper in London, the day-to-day running of the mill fell on his wife Catharine's shoulders. They regularly corresponded when he was travelling, the following being a typical example of her grasp of the working of the mill:

> I have sent for Metcalf [the beaterman], who says that he has been endeavouring to get the engines in proper order, and he hopes tomorrow to accomplish it. If so, he shall then write to you. He brought up some sample sheets and desires me to tell you that the stuff [a papermaker's term for pulp in the beater] for the thin post is some of the best he ever saw, and as firm as cloth, but it is still a long while off: the last engine was five hours. I mentioned the paper for Keys [a London merchant who had placed an order for 15 reams] would be wanted in a hurry, and they will be ready to begin whenever you direct. The six vats are working very steadily, and the paper appears to me generally to look well: the stuff is longer than

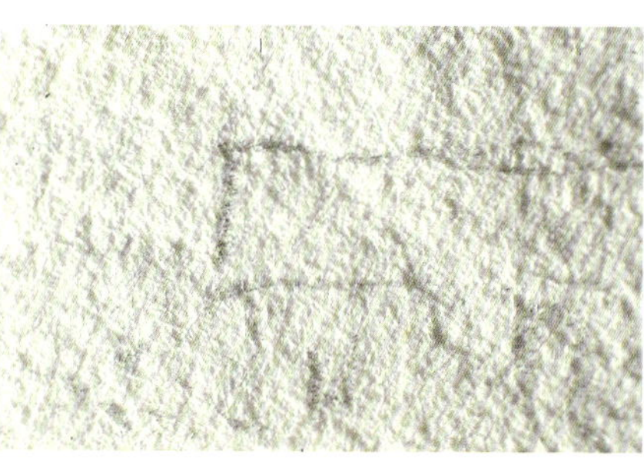

40B

what you saw, and that you may judge how it is I have sent a little piece of the paper.[2]

The Thin Post paper discussed in this letter would be a paper very similar to that used in this sketchbook. Trying to achieve real consistency in the papers they produced was a never-ending struggle for many mills. Supplies of rags were never constant, either in their quality or in their obtainability. The papers wanted by clients were always changing: one order would be for a lighter weight than before, or for slightly heavier sizing, or something a little whiter, crisper, or smoother. The large mills such as Springfield, which could call on years of experience amongst their workforce, were much better placed to deal with all these variables. Smaller mills, such as Egglestone Abbey Mill, with probably one, possibly two vats, and a very small workforce, would have found such quality control especially difficult.

[1] Catherine Balston to William Balston, 31st March 1813. The Whatman and Balston Archives, Kent County Archives. U2161/Z1/2.
Catharine Balston went on in her letter to say that she thought that Morgans, the paper merchants, were 'no better than cheats' for having returned Retree for the very reason that the paper had been graded Retree in the first place, and advised Balston to 'deal with them as little as possible'.

[2] Catharine Balston to William Balston, 19th February 1812. The Whatman and Balston Archives, Kent County Archives. U2161Z1/2.

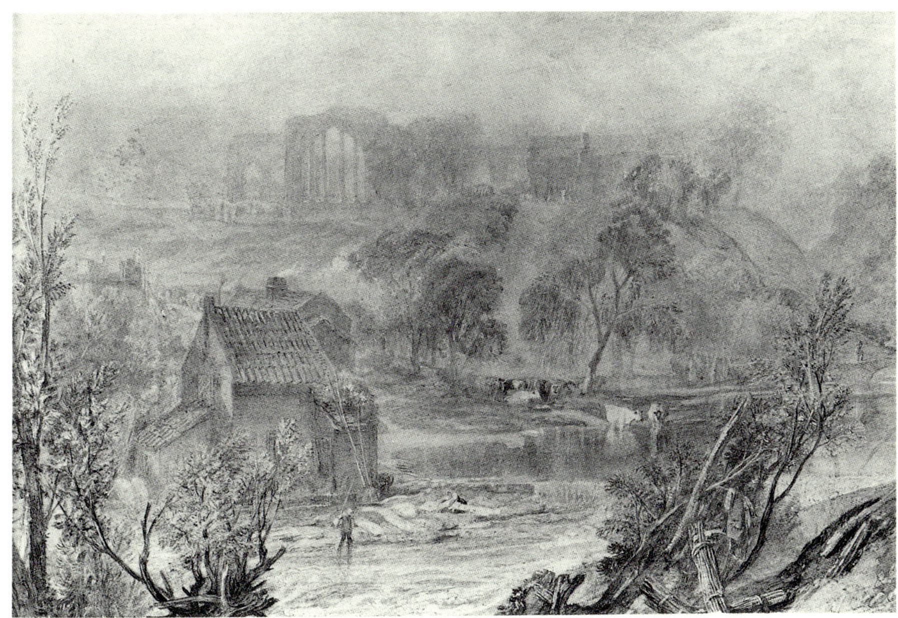

41

41 **Egglestone Abbey, near Barnard Castle** 1818

286 × 419 ($11\frac{1}{4} \times 16\frac{1}{2}$)

Watercolour

W 565

Private Collection

This drawing and the other works relating to it (see cat.nos. 15 and 40) are so far the only views by Turner definitely identified as being of a paper mill.[1] When Turner had first visited the mill in 1797 it was worked by James Cooke. His widow, Elizabeth, continued to run it after his death, until her own in 1809, when Henry Cooke, her second son took over.[2] She must have been a remarkable woman to have both run the mill and brought up her seven children at the same time. In 1809 there had been a fire in the drying loft, a real hazard in papermills at this date.[3] It is possible that the two figures working in front of the mill buildings are Henry Cooke and his first wife Hannah.

The activity of the woman in the centre of the picture has been described as 'washing and laying out paper to dry'.[4] The drying of paper on grass outside mills had been common practice in earlier times, leading to place names such as Paper Mill Mead and Paper Meadow in different parts of England, but by the nineteenth century it had all but died out. I am inclined to think that, rather than handling paper, she is cutting or tearing down felts to the right size for couching. No European hand-made paper has ever been made as large as these long thin sheets. Paper made on the earliest paper machines was not dried on the machine but reeled up wet, cut from the reel and then dried and sized in the same way as hand-made paper. But the sheets shown are not machine-made paper either for Henry Cooke did not acquire a paper machine until 1823 and when he did it was not installed at the Egglestone Abbey Mill but at Whitcliffe Mill, Richmond, eighteen miles away. Cooke had decided on the acqusition of a machine when he realised that

> the term of the patent, granted to Mr Fourdrinier for inventing a machine for making paper, had just expired and learning that the principal part of the papers I made by Hand were amongst those made to most advantage by the machine, and also that such a machine paper had a decided preference in the market, I at once determined on having a machine.[5]

The Egglestone Abbey Mill continued to make paper by hand until 1830, when the Cooke family moved to Richmond, and the mill was converted to a corn mill. Hill suggests that the building work that can be seen behind the mill, and originally drawn by Turner in 1816 (see cat.no.40), is connected with the repair of fire damage.[6] I feel this is unlikely as the mill fire had occured some seven years before Turner's 1816 visit and the building shown is not part of the mill, being the house in which Cooke and his growing family lived until their move to Richmond. The cows on the river bank were probably Cooke's. He rented 42 acres around the mill at an annual rent of £190, keeping six fields for grazing and three others for growing wheat, oats and clover.[7]

[1] This work was also engraved by T. Higham in 1822 for Whitaker's *History of Richmondshire* (R 174). It is possible that

some of the buildings sketched in and around Amalifi in the *Pompeii, Amalfi etc.* sketchbook (TB CLXXXV) are paper mills. But further work needs to be done on such identifications.

2 *Henry Cooke, Papermaker, 1773–1973*, 1973.

3 *Bath Chronicle*, 29th July 1809.

4 Hill, 1984, p.107.

5 Letter from Henry Cooke, quoted in *Henry Cooke, Papermaker, 1773–1973*, 1973. p.7.

6 Hill, 1984, p.107.

7 *Henry Cooke, Papermaker, 1773–1973*, 1973. p.5.

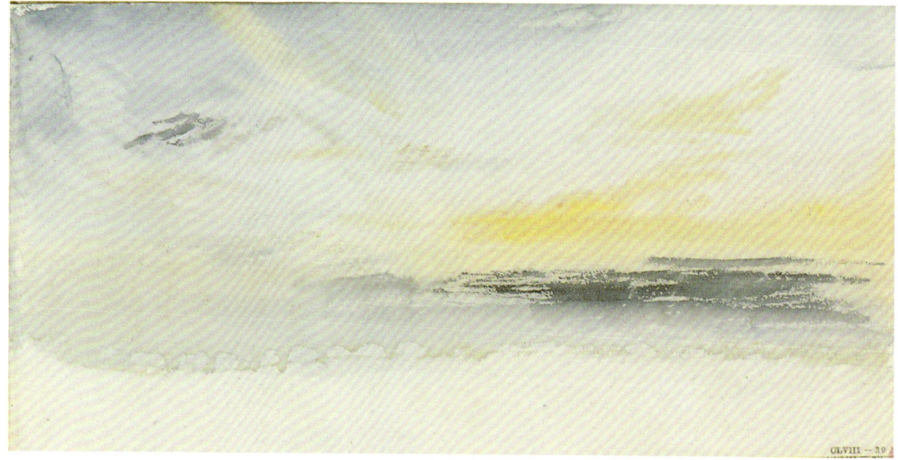

42

42 Study of Sky *c*.1818

From the *Skies* sketchbook
Vellum-bound sketchbook
128 × 255 × 18 ($5\frac{1}{16} \times 10\frac{1}{16} \times \frac{3}{4}$)
Page size: 125 × 247 ($4\frac{7}{8} \times 9\frac{3}{4}$)

Large Post 6mo
White wove
Watermarked: J WHATMAN / 1814[1]
Made by William Balston at Springfield Mill, Maidstone, Kent

Watercolour
Turner Bequest: CLVIII 39
D12487

42A Transmitted light detail of watermark and look-through of CLVIII 3, reversed & inverted.

42B Raking light detail of watercolour and surface. × 7 magnification.

42C Raking light detail of ghostmark of CLVIII 12.

42A

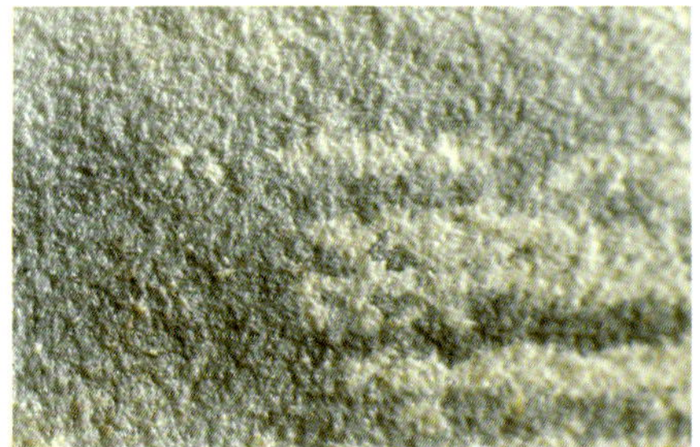

42B

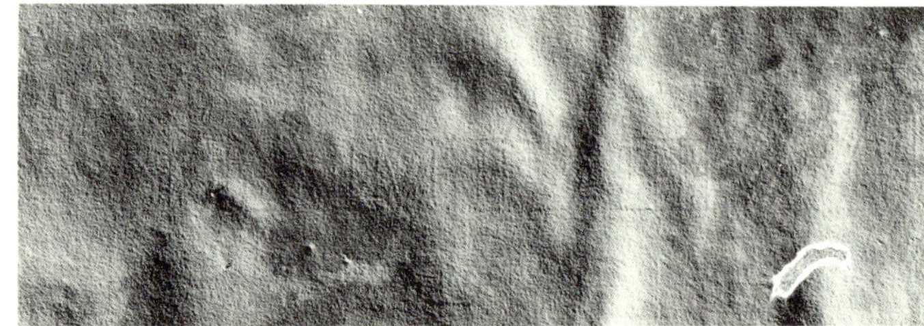

42C

This sketchbook contains a rich variety of observations on skies, both sunsets and sunrises, and the effect of light upon cloud masses. Turner has worked on both the wire and felt sides of the sheet, sometimes in pencil but more usually in watercolour.

An important feature of this book is the variation in tone, weight, opacity and, to some extent, finish, of its leaves. It would appear that several different papers, each made to fulfill different functions: writing, printing and drawing, have been bound together in the same sketchbook. All the papers have the same J WHATMAN / 1814 watermark, and were probably made as large Post, before being bound 6mo.[2] When Balston began operations at his new mill, Springfield, he had concentrated on the production of writing and printing papers, but he soon began to develop an interest in the drawing papers that were to bring the Whatman name world renown. The Whatmans and the Balston and Hollingworth partnership had always produced papers which artists liked to work on, but gradually, as the market became more sophisticated, the mills began to develop very specific properties in some of their papers, related to particular media: watercolour, pencil, chalks and the newly developed crayons. Many people in the paper industry could not conceive that drawing papers would be of any real interest to a mill, because the mills would never be able to sell enough to make it worth their while.[3]

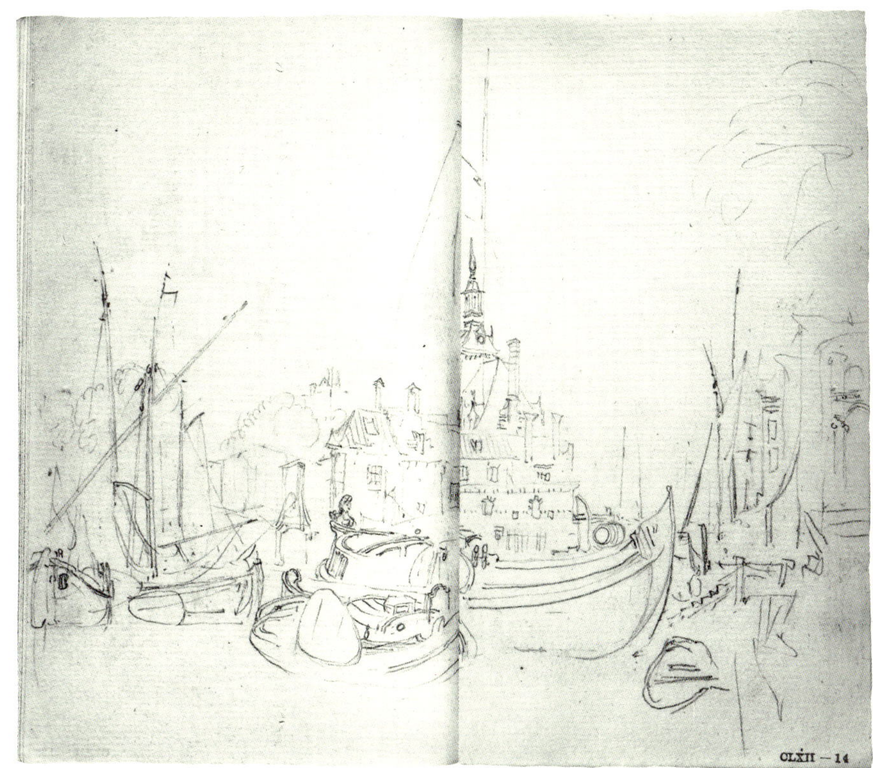

43

1 Besides the normal watermarks, pages 5, 6, and 12 in this sketchmarks also show 'ghost' marks, where the impression of a watermark has tranferred to another piece of paper, either in pressing at the mill, during the making of the paper, or, more rarely, from the pressure exerted during the binding of the book. Occasionally one finds in books the ghostmark of one maker transferred from a sheet of his paper to the surface of another watermarked sheet from a different maker used in the same book.

2 That is to say folded in such a way as to give six leaves out of the sheet when it is bound, rather than the more usual Folio (2 leaves), Quarto (4 leaves) or Octavo 8 (leaves).

3 Susanna Whatman wrote to Balston from London in 1813 regarding drawing papers:

> I have been in town for two days and procured a bit of paper from Smith and Warner Piccadilly. It is called Cartridge paper, and is said to be the discovery of Messrs Edmeads and Pine, very ingenious men who had labour'd hard and tried many experiments before they could succeed in bringing it to its present perfection. . . . The Dutch cartridge is prefer'd to Mr Pine's for drawings but it is not to be had now. But I don't conceive that merely drawing paper could be any object to you.

Susanna Whatman to William Balston, 10th February 1813. Balston and Whatman Archives, Kent County Archives. U2161/Z1/2.

43 **Oude Hoofdpoort, Rotterdam, seen from Oude Haven** 1817

From the *Dort* sketchbook
Bound in blue boards, with green parchment spine
161 × 104 × 17 ($6\frac{3}{8} \times 4\frac{1}{8} \times \frac{13}{16}$)
Page size: 156 × 95 ($6\frac{1}{8} \times 3\frac{3}{4}$)

Foolscap Octavo
'Blue' laid writing paper
Chain lines: 27–9 mm ($1\frac{1}{8}$ in approx.) apart, variable
Laid line frequency: 8 per cm (20 per in)
Watermarked: Unclear, possibly the Arms of Orange-Nassau
Countermark: J K(O . . .).
Shadows present: single faced mould
Made by Jan Kool and Company, Holland[1]
Pencil

Turner Bequest: CLXII 13V, 14
D13020, D13021

43A Composite transmitted light detail of Van der Ley Pro Patria watermark and look-through.

43B Composite transmitted light detail of Jan Kool Arms watermark and look-through.

43C Raking light detail of pencil and surface. × 7 magnification.

When the endpapers are included, this sketchbook contains three distinctly different papers, all of Dutch manufacture. Two of which were made as 'corrected' white papers, where a blue tint has been added to the pulp to whiten otherwise drab rags.

(a) Endpapers:
White laid writing paper.
Chain lines: 24–6 mm (1 in approx.) apart, variable
Laid line frequency: 10 per cm (25 per in).
Double faced mould.
Watermarked: Vryheit Lion / PRO PATRIA

(b) 'Blue' laid writing paper.
Chain lines: 22–6 mm ($\frac{9}{10}$ – 1 in) apart, variable.
Laid line frequency: 9 per cm (22 per in).
Watermarked: 'Pro Patria'
Countermarked: VDL
Shadows present: single faced mould
Made by Van der Ley, Fortuyn Mill, Zaandyk, Holland[2]

The wars in Europe had kept Turner in Britain since his tour of France and Switzerland in 1802. But in the August and September of 1817 he again travelled on the Continent, touring Holland and Belgium and making the first of many visits to the Rhine. He took with him three sketchbooks[3] and some folded sheets of loose paper. During this continental tour he apparently only purchased one sketchbook, containing Dutch-made papers.

Turner has filled this book with pencil drawings, working on both the wire and felt sides of the paper. This particularly calm and precise sketch is drawn with a sharp hard pencil, well suited to the crisp gelatine size of the paper. Many of the other, more hasty, sketches in the book have been worked with at least one other, softer, pencil.

Dutch paper had a very good reputation throughout the eighteenth century, particularly for writing, the intended use of the two papers that make up the bulk of the *Dort* sketchbook: the Frenchman Lalande writing in 1761 considered that

> . . . although Dutch paper is finer than the French, it lacks the finish of the latter. Dutch paper has a finer, smoother and more transparent appearance than ours. This is due to the uniform fineness of their linen rags, which are carefully selected and not mixed. Dutch paper is thicker and better prepared than ours because their moulds are deeper, and because pulping by Dutch Cylinders is superior to that by stampers. Moreover Dutch workmen work with more care and deliberation than our workmen are accustomed to. The wealth of their papermakers, the thrift of their inhabitants and the power of their finances combine to make their mills more efficient than ours. What has been said, however, concerning the properties of Dutch paper applies only to the superfine qualities, such as: large horn, Pro Patria and the Arms of England and Venice. There are many sorts that are inferior to our paper of the Auvergne, such as the double fine crown and double fine ecu made at Thiers, Ambert and Annonay.[4]

The Dutch papers named are all writing paper sizes, whereas the French named papers are all printing papers. One would expect considerable differences in character and behaviour in papers designed for such different uses.

One important feature of this tour was to be the creation of the fifty one Rhine drawings, all executed on paper which Turner had taken with him from England, and none of which are in the Bequest.[5] This group which was to be purchased for £500 by Walter Fawkes, of Farnley, on Turner's return to England would eventually be scattered across the world. From the works in this group that I have been able to examine there are indications that more than one paper was used. Most were executed on a very lightweight, heavily sized, white wove paper, prepared with grey washes of varying intensity. With the exception of w671, 674, 675 and 683, they are half sheets of writing Foolscap, watermarked, in at least one case (w682) J WHATMAN / 1816. Various mills made Foolscap writings to approximately the same size: 432 × 343 (17 × $13\frac{1}{2}$), which would give an approximate Foolscap folio size of 343 × 216 ($13\frac{1}{2}$ × $8\frac{1}{2}$), bearing in mind the variations between makings and between mills. It has been suggested in the past that these drawings were originally part of a roll sketchbook, but the works I have examined would suggest that the majority of the paper comes from a quire of loose writing paper. This paper was sold, folded, in quires of 24 sheets, which would give 48 working surfaces. The remaining drawings in the series appear to have been executed on a slightly heavier paper. Further research must wait

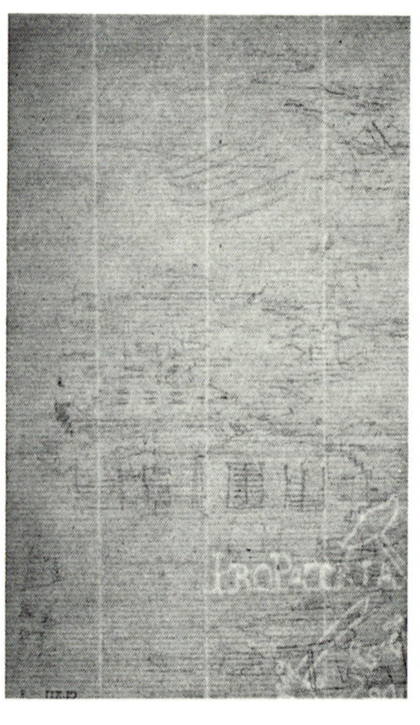

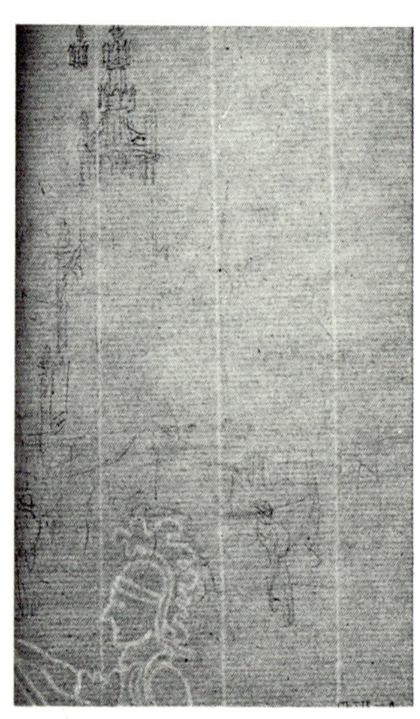

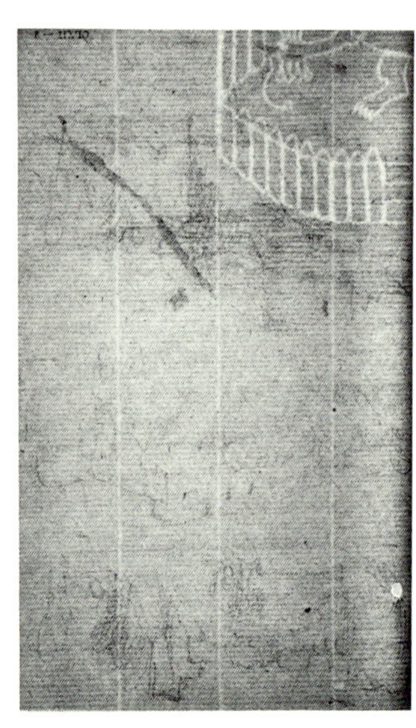

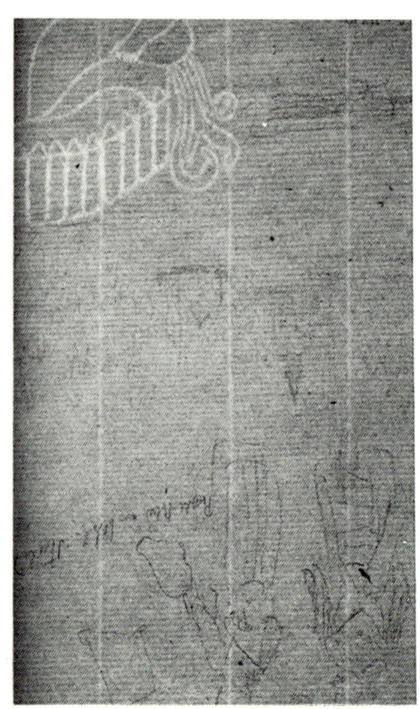

43A

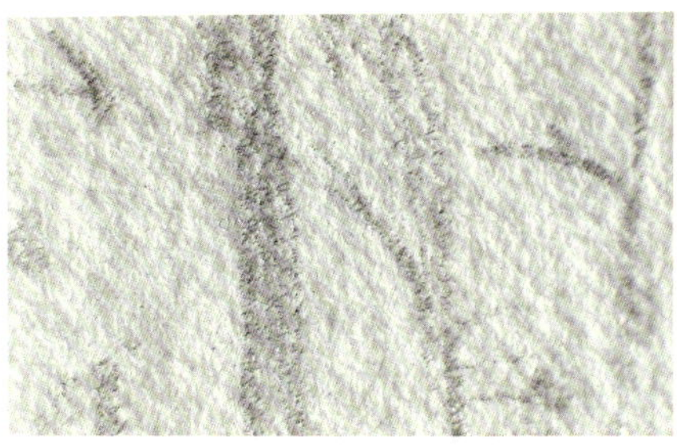

43C

until more of the drawings can be examined.

Given the qualities and characteristics of the French and Swiss-made papers Turner had bought and used in 1802, and the paper in this sketchbook, it is perhaps surprising that he did not buy more European made papers on his increasingly frequent travels on the Continent. Though he did make use of various French, Italian, German and Austrian papers in sketchbooks purchased on his later travels he appears not to have purchased any foreign made paper on his next continental tour, of Italy in 1819 and 1820 (see cat.nos. 51, 52, 53 and 54).[6]

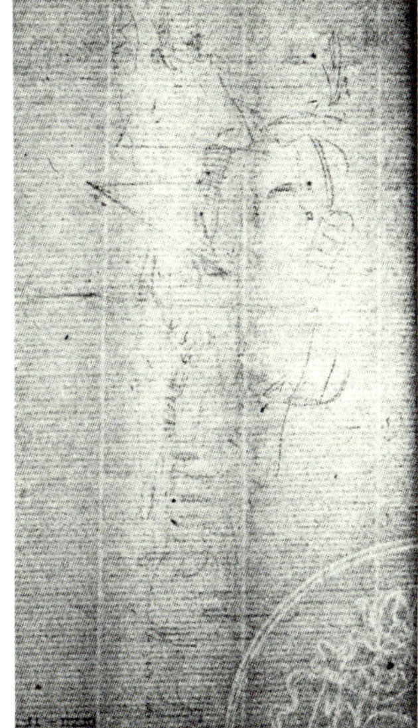

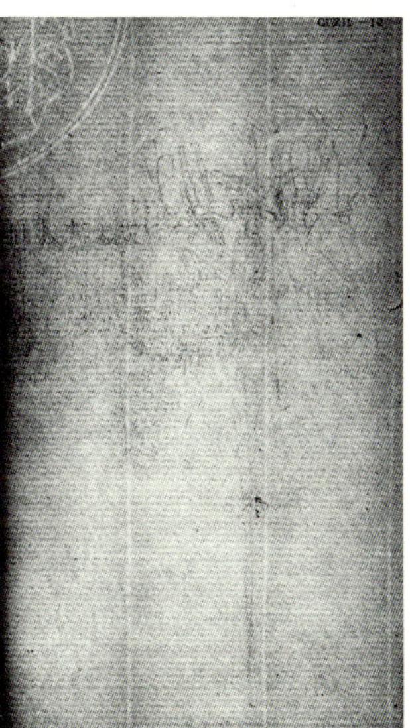

43B

1 Jan Kool and his descendants made fine papers of all descriptions from 1728 until at the least 1820s.

2 The 'Pro Patria' watermark, also known as the 'Garden of Holland' or the 'Maid of Dort', (very appropriate given the name of this sketchbook), was in use in Holland from the 1680s onwards, until well into the nineteenth century. It was also copied considerably by makers in other countries, including England, where it is commonly found with the DURHAM countermark of Postlip Mill, Gloucestershire, and even, in one instance, from the 1770s, with a JW, possibly from James Whatman, the younger. Other Continental makers who used this mark include Johan Lorch of Wachtesmühle, Bavaria and the Gransholm Mill in Sweden, soon after its foundation in the 1790s.
A similar Dutch-made 'Pro Patria' mark can be found in the *Rotterdam* sketchbook, of the late 1830s. (TBCCCXXI).
Pieter van der Ley founded the family fortunes with a paper mill in 1665 and the company continued in operation until the end of the nineteenth century.

3 TB CLIX *Itinerary Rhine Tour* sketchbook
Demy 16mo
57 × 113 ($2\frac{1}{4} \times 4\frac{7}{16}$)
White wove
Watermarked: RUSE & TURNERS / 1817
Made by Joseph Ruse and Richard Turner, Upper Tovil Mill, Maidstone, Kent.

TB CLX *Waterloo and Rhine* sketchbook
Super Royal 16mo, heavily trimmed
96 × 147 ($3\frac{3}{4} \times 5\frac{7}{8}$)
White wove
Watermarked: J WHATMAN /1816
Made by William Balston, Springfield Mill, Maidstone, Kent.

TB CLXI *The Rhine* sketchbook
Medium Octavo
202 × 266 ($7\frac{15}{16} \times 10\frac{1}{2}$)
White wove
Watermarked: J WHATMAN / 1816 and J WHATMAN/1817
Made by William Balston, Springfield Mill, Maidstone, Kent.

4 Joseph Jerome Le Francais de Lalande, *L'Art de faire le papier*, vol.4 of *Des Arts et Metiers* of the Academie des Sciences, Paris, 1761. This translation from Churchill, 1935, p.8.
All the paper sizes mentioned get their names from the watermarks the sheets carry: the 'large horn' is more commonly known, in England, as Large Post, from the Posthorn watermark, 'Ecu' is the Arms of France.

5 w636–686.

6 One very interesting sketchbook, though lying outside the remit of this exhibition, is the *Danube and Graz* sketchbook, (TB CCXCIX) dating from the late 1830s. It contains a hot-pressed cream wove paper, with a very fine wire texture easily visible in a raking light, but with a curious mottled look-through. It bears the watermark that we have seen so many times throughout Turner's work: J.WHATMAN, but with one

very significant difference: the full stop. No genuine Whatman mark ever has a full stop. This is in fact an Austrian-made forgery of Whatman Paper. The pirating of well known makers' names was very common in the eighteenth century, but it is surprising to see it in the nineteenth. Another example of the Whatman name being used on the Continent, can be found in France. The Canson et Montgolfier paper mill at Annonay still have French-made moulds, dating from the early years of the nineteenth century, two of which bear the names of English makers: Whatman and J Green.

John Green, of Hayle Mill, Maidstone, Kent, produced paper used in two of Turner's sketchbooks:

TB CXLIII *Liber Notes* sketchbook.
100 × 160 ($3\frac{3}{4} \times 6\frac{5}{16}$)
White wove
Watermarked: J GREEN / 1814

TB CLXVI *Edinburgh 1818* sketchbook.
Large Post 16mo
89 × 114 ($3\frac{1}{2} \times 4\frac{1}{2}$)
White wove writing paper
Watermarked: J GREEN / 1817

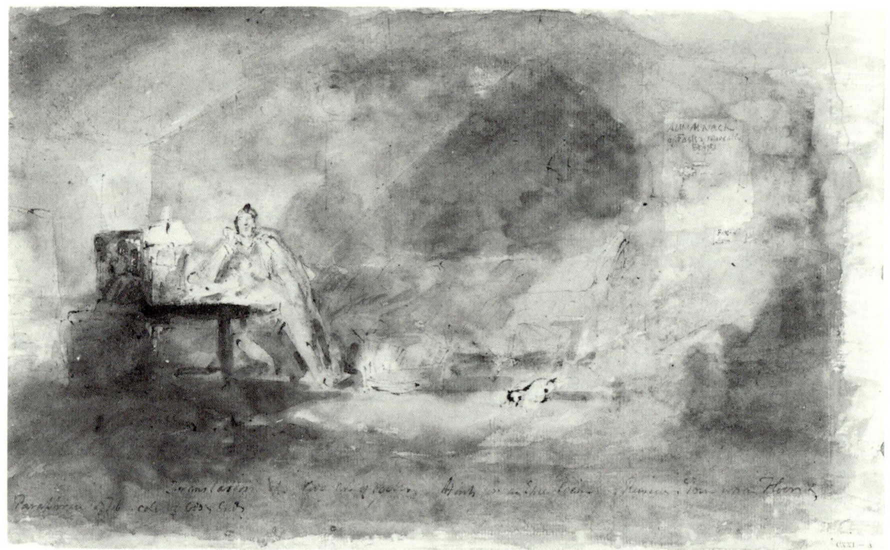

44

44 A Study for the Garreteer's Petition 1809
183 × 302 ($11\frac{15}{16} \times 7\frac{1}{4}$)

White laid writing paper
Chain lines: 10 per cm (25 per in)
Laid line frequency: 26–7 mm ($1\frac{1}{8}$ in) apart, variable
Watermarked: Hanoverian Royal Arms
Shadows present: single faced mould
Made by Thomas Hyde at Cheddar Mill, Somerset

Pen and ink and wash, worked on the felt side

This sheet is the half sheet to cat.no.45

Turner Bequest: CXXI A
D08256

44A Verso, showing how visible watermarks can be under ordinary lighting conditions.

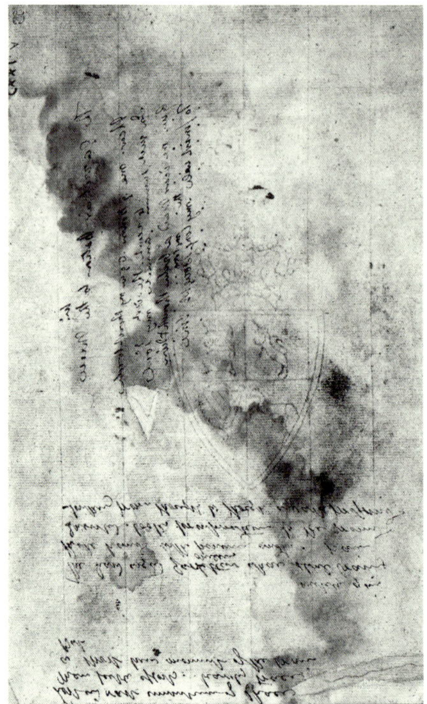

44A

45 The Amateur Artist 1809

183 × 302 ($11\frac{15}{16} \times 7\frac{1}{4}$)

White laid writing paper.
Chain lines: 10 per cm (25 per in)
Laid line frequency: 26–7 mm ($1\frac{1}{8}$ in) apart, variable.
Countermarked: T HYDE & CO /1806
Shadows present: single faced mould.
Made by Thomas Hyde at Cheddar Mill, Somerset.

Pen and ink and wash, worked on the wire side

This sheet is the half sheet to cat.no.44

Turner Bequest CXXI B
D08257

45A Verso, showing the countermark easily visible under normal lighting conditions.

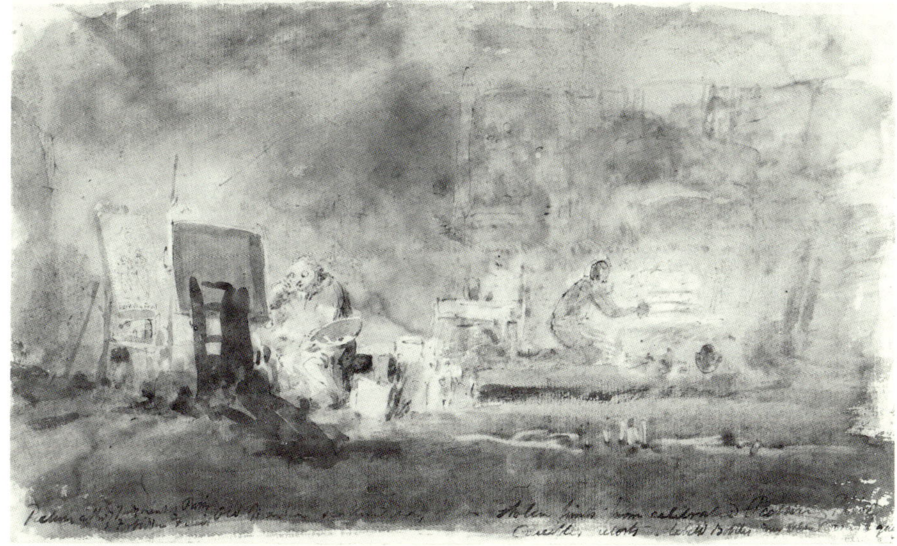

45

There are several examples in the Bequest of papers similar to this: essentially local or provincial writing papers, produced by small mills and usually sold within a relatively small area of the mill, perhaps only in the nearest big towns. Like any artist Turner would often use what was to hand, but judging by his general use of papers throughout his career, he must have been well aware of the limitations or qualities of most of the papers that he would have found around him: of any paper he might have to work on. Whilst he might not have chosen to work on such a low quality paper as this, the imperative of his vision, of the work in hand would probably have meant that he would work with whatever was to hand. In the case of these two works, he has instinctively used the kind of materials which would have given the best results: pen and ink.

This paper was apparently damaged by water at some early period in its history. Some of the background colour described by Finberg as wash seems to be colour spread and bled from the line drawing due to the soaking that the sheet has received. Given that Finberg catalogued it as wash in 1909, the Thames flood of 1928 cannot have been responsible.

The continued use of the Hanoverian Royal arms in the paper is something of an anachronism at this date. Most mills had long since stopped using such a mark, but there does seem to have been a slight resurgence of its use during the early part of the Revolutionary Wars, which in some of the smaller and more old fashioned mills continued into the early years of the nineteenth century.

There were three mills operating at Cheddar at this date:

> where nine small springs, pure as crystal, burst from the foot of the cliffs, all within the space of about thirty feet, and joining together within forty yards of their source formed a broad rapid river of the clearest and finest water in the world.[1]

It is possible that Thomas Hyde was working this mill as early as 1800 but the first definite date we have for him is 1805, when a fire insurance policy describes some of the details of the mill.[2] Judging by the details of this policy, it was a relatively small operation. The Upper Paper Millhouse, the machinery and fixed utensils were insured for £150, with moveable utensils and stock in trade at £200. His second mill was even smaller: fixed machinery and utensils were insured for £100 and the moveable utensils and stock in trade at £100 also.[3]

Such small mills as this had been the mainstay of European papermaking for centuries, but the increasing industrialisation, both in the newly developing machine-made paper industry, and in the hand-made mills, as they responded to the competition of the new technology, would soon lead to the gradual demise of most of these small provincial mills, by the end of the nineteenth century. It is difficult to determine how long Hyde was in business, but he had definitely ceased trading by 1816, when the mill was given the excise number 9, in the name of John Gillings.[4]

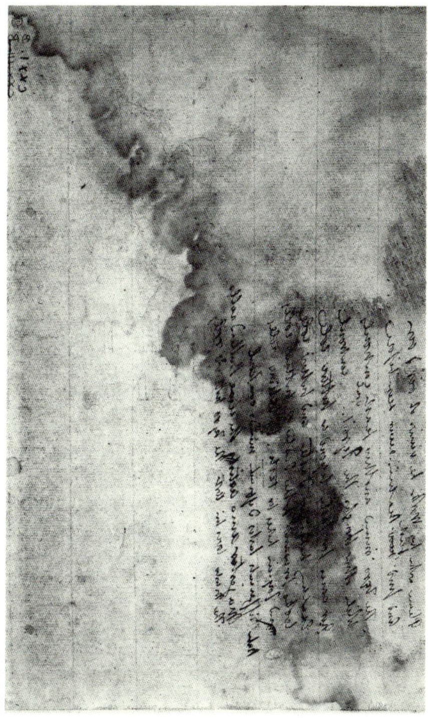

45A

1 Collinson, 1791.
2 Royal Exchange Fire Insurance Policy No.217128 for 18th July 1805.
3 To give some idea of the difference in operation and scale between a mill such as this and the Whatman concern when The Whatman business was valued in 1794 prior to the retirement of James Whatman the younger, the eight vats of Turkey, Loose and Poll Mills had been valued at some £20,000. An individual working vat was valued at £125 per annum at that date, Coleman, *1958*.
4 *General Excise Letter, October 8th 1816, quoted in Watermills of Somerset*, in the unpublished Simmons Collection at the Science Museum Library Archives, London.

46

46 Landscape with Trees *c*.1814

214 × 269 ($8\frac{7}{16}$ × $10\frac{5}{8}$)

White wove writing paper
Watermarked: none
Made by William Balston, Springfield Mill, Maidstone, Kent

Monochrome watercolour, worked on the felt side of the sheet

Turner Bequest: CXCVI J
D17174

46A Transmitted light image of watermark and look-through of CXVI K.

46B Raking light detail, x7 magnification

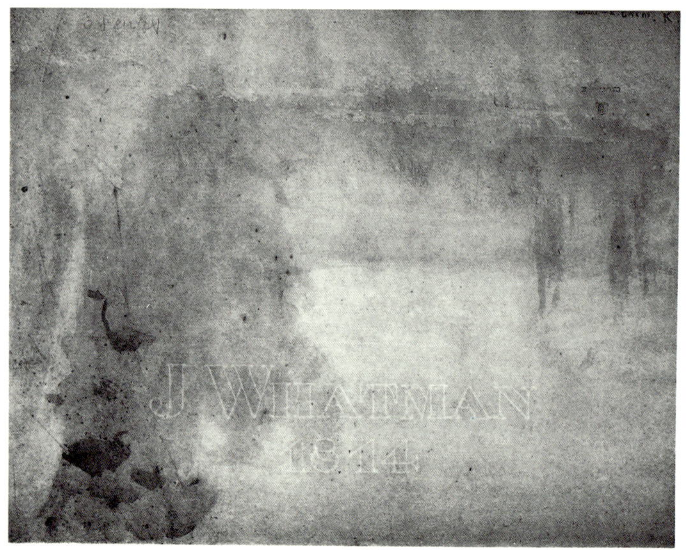

46A

This drawing forms one quarter of a Large Post sheet, watermarked J WHATMAN / 1814.[1] The other three quarters of the sheet are TB CXCVI I, K and L. The different treatment of these four monochrome drawings during their lifetime has led to significant changes in the size and, to a very slight extent, the proportions of each of them. Both K and L are unmounted, J is unmounted, but has been backed, I has been window-mounted. At some point in their history, they have also been exposed to a great deal of water, probably the Thames Flood of 1928, which will have caused some dimensional change, as well as perhaps washing some of the colour out of the images. Their different mounting and conservation histories have also contributed to these dimensional changes.

The original sheet was torn into four irregular shaped pieces. Their present measurements are:

TB CXCVI I 200 × 263 × 207 × 260
TB CXCVI J 212 × 264 × 214 × 269
TB CXCVI K 209 × 260 × 207 × 260
TB CXCVI L 219 × 264 × 211 × 267

Analysis of the tear marks reveals that whilst they have all come from the same sheet of paper, their present dimensions are no longer original. The tears correspond but the pieces have expanded or contracted under different influences.

46B

The work exhibited, which was backed, is now larger in relation to both K and L than it should be. K and L have probably contracted in drying out after the flood. I, which is window mounted, has expanded during cleaning and window-mounting.

Another area of interest in this group of works lies in the combination of two things: the paper used is similar to, if not from the same batch as the grey-washed 1814 Whatman used in many of the 1819–20 Italian Tour sketchbooks;[2] and the subject matter of the four drawings which never formed part of a sketchbook, is possibly Italian.[3] If Turner worked on these drawings, which have never been part of a sketchbook, in Italy, then he must have taken some loose paper with him on the tour, as indeed he had done on his earlier tour to Switzerland in 1802. If so, it would be unlikely that this sheet was the only one.

1 This sheet bears two watermarks, side by side, each at the bottom of the half sheet. Such double watermarks most usually occur in papers destined for the legal profession and, by this date, designed for use with the newly popular steel nibs produced by Gillott and others in Birmingham. This is yet another instance of Turner using a paper for something other than the use it was originally designed for.

2 See cat.nos.50 and 51. The sketchbooks used on the Italian Tour which contain this paper are as follows:
TB CLXXXIII *Tivoli*
TB CLXXXVII *Naples, Rome C. Studies*
TB CLXXXIX *Rome C. Studies*
TB CXC *Small Roman C. Studies*
TB CXCII *Return from Italy*
TB CXCIII *Remarks (Italy)*
TB CXCIV *Passge of the Simplon*

3 Finberg suggests that TB CXCVI I is 'possibly a study for an Italian Subject.'

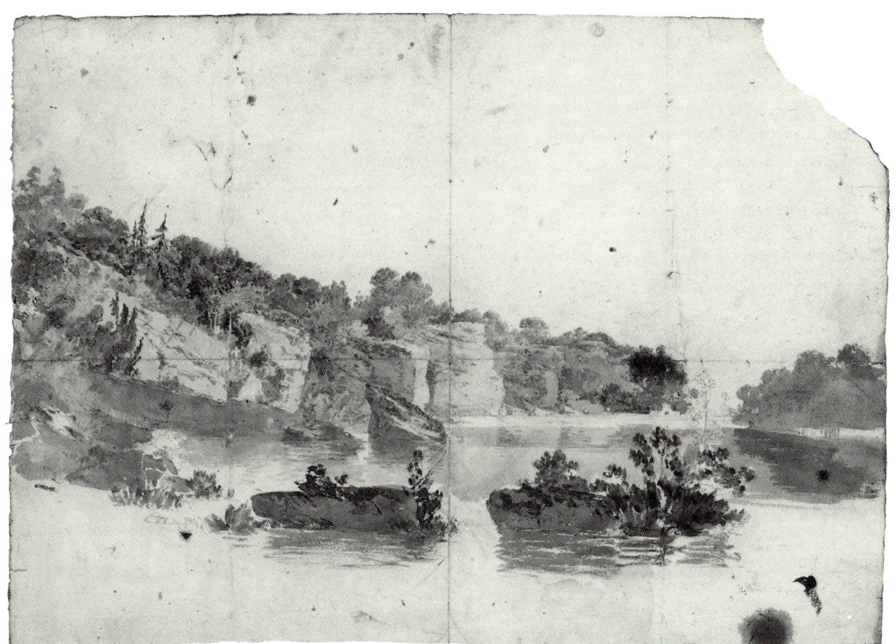

47

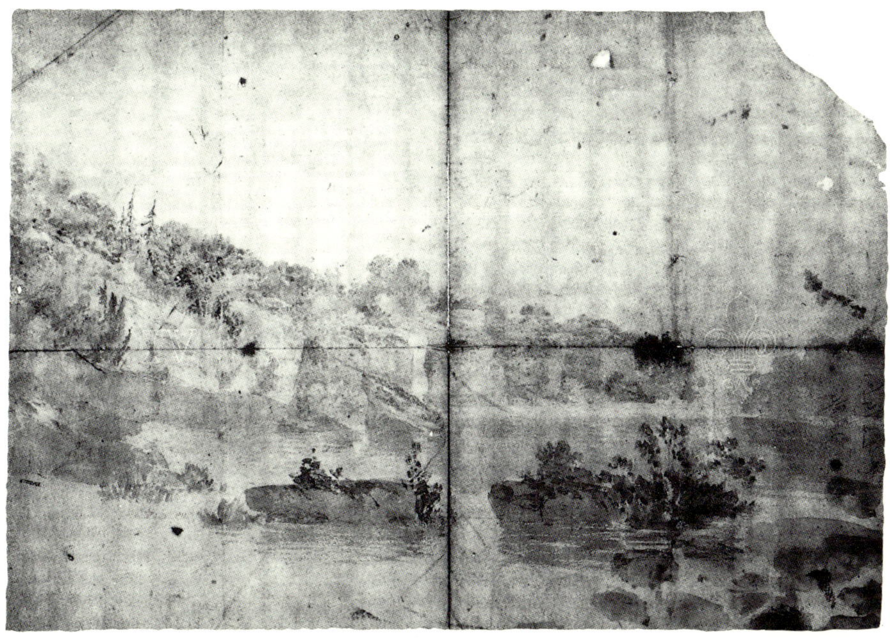

47A

47 Plumpton Rocks near Harrogate *c.*1798

365 × 510 ($14\frac{3}{8} \times 20\frac{1}{8}$)

White wove
Watermarked: 'Fleur-de-Lys'
Countermarked: IV
Unknown maker

Worked in watercolour on the wire-side of the sheet

Turner Bequest: CXCVII L
D17202

47A Transmitted light details of watermark, countermark and look-through.

47B Raking light detail of surface texture and paint layer. × 7 magnification.

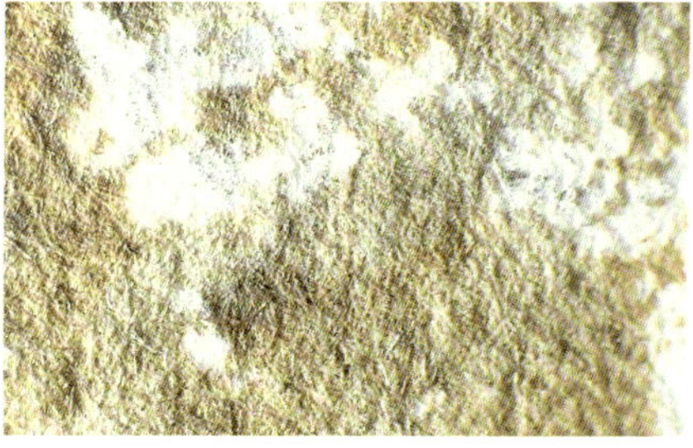

47B

This drawing is an unfinished watercolour study for one of a pair of oil paintings of 'Plumpton Rocks' (B&J 27) executed for the Earl of Harewood; perhaps Turner's earliest commissioned oils. Like all artists, Turner would sometimes work on a sheet or two of a paper that he had come across, either to try them out or because they were to hand.[1] This was just such a sheet, typical of the range of papers he was exploring in the 1790s. Several features of this sheet give us pause for thought. Watermarks in hand-made wove papers are usually found in the bottom right or left corners of the sheet. The placing of the watermark and countermark, each in the centre of the half sheet, was a feature of some wove papers, both here in England[2] and in France, but only in the earliest years of their manufacture. This paper was probably made sometime around 1780, not long after Turner was born.

Identifying the origin of this paper has so far proved impossible. The fleur-de-lys watermark and a countermark of the initials of the French maker Jean Villedary, would suggest a continental origin, but there is no trace of Villedary making wove at this early date. The first French wove papers were only made by the Johannots and Montgolfiers in 1779.[3] Though this sheet has been cut down on one of the long edges, the position of the watermark and countermark in relation to the remaining deckle edges, combined with the folds in the sheet allows one to make some judgements as to its original size, probably $20\frac{1}{4} \times 15\frac{3}{4}$. This size does not correspond with any continental sizes but is approximately the English writing paper size Small Demy.[6]

[1] Another sheet of the same paper can be found in the Bequest: TB LI U 'A Mansion seen from the Grounds' and TB LI T 'Landscape with Trees' are the two halves of a white wove sheet watermarked with a fleur-de-lys and countermarked IV, each centred in the half sheet.

[2] see cat.no.19, a white wove watermarked JW in the centre of the half sheet.

[3] see cat.no.37, and especially footnote 1 to that entry, for a discussion of the IV countermark and Jean Villedary.

[3] For a discussion of European paper sizes in relation to their designed use, see Labarre, 1952, p.251 ff.

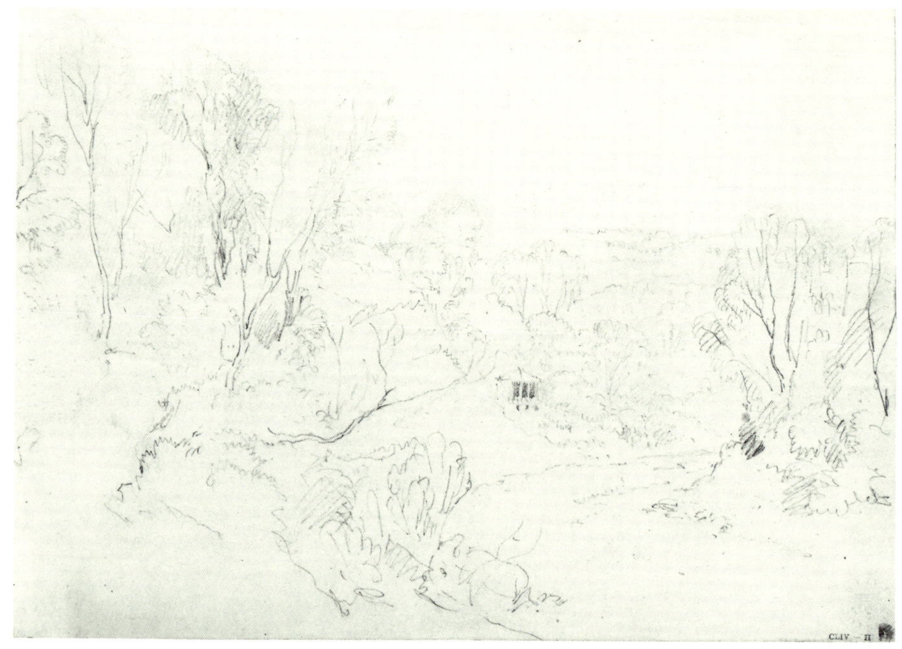

48

48 On the Banks of The Wharfe *c.*1816

187 × 263 ($7\frac{3}{8} \times 10\frac{3}{8}$)

White wove board

Watermarked: none visible

Stamped: BRISTOL PAPER with a Crown

Unidentified maker

Worked in Pencil

Turner Bequest: CLIV H

D12106

48A Raking light detail showing BRISTOL PAPER stamp.

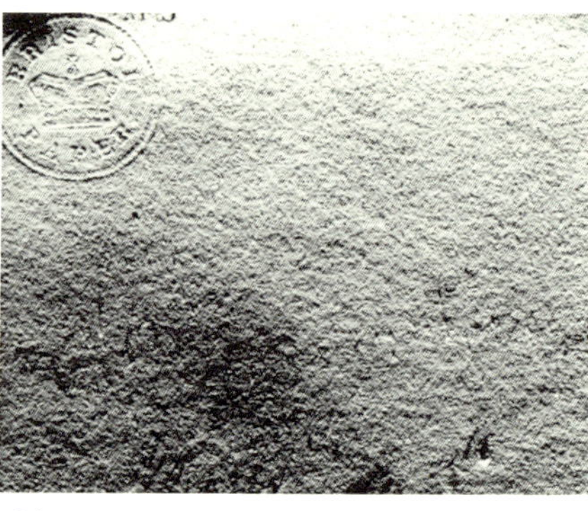

48A

This drawing and the two other scenes from the Wharfe Valley catalogued with it in the Bequest and also on Bristol Paper,[1] were done on one of Turner's visits to Walter Fawkes at Farnley in Yorkshire between 1809 and 1825 and cannot be dated with any accuracy.

Bristol Paper, or Boards, as they came to be known, were laminated and glazed drawing papers. No watermarks are visible in this work or in the two associated drawings, but it is possible that the missing quarter of the sheet would have contained a watermark. The marks of several different makers have been found in various Bristol Boards. Originally produced at the beginning of the nineteenth century, by an as yet unidentified London stationer for playing cards, and later commonly used for visiting cards, they were named after Frederick Hervey, Earl of Bristol and soon became popular with some artists, for the particular qualities of mark achievable on the highly glazed surface.

A similar, but higher quality, board was developed some years later. Called London Board, it was made exclusively of two, three or even four Whatman drawing papers, pasted together and then highly glazed. The best known of these London boards were made by Turnbulls, and sold by Reeves, Winsor and Newton, and other artists' colourmen by the early 1830s.[2]

Much later in the century, papermakers were to develop their own version of such manufactured boards, where they couched two or three newly formed sheets of paper directly onto each other, without the intervening felts. The first pressing of the wet sheets turned them into solid pieces of paper. Such papers were known as 'pasteless boards' and designed specifically for watercolour work. Laminating the sheets during their formation gave the paper a rigidity which meant it did not have to be stretched.

Despite Turner's preference for hard sized relatively smooth papers in much of his watercolour work, he does not appear to have liked to work on these highly glazed surfaces. The only examples of such boards in the Bequest can usually be traced to occasions when he was staying with someone, as here, when he was at Farnley, and the card was available. There are similar occasional uses of what was then almost a household name in terms of paper, the famous 'Bath Wove Post'. This was in general not a particularly well-made letter paper, though some examples, from Bally, Ellen and Steart's De Montalt Mill, near Bristol, were of very high quality indeed.[3]

[1] TB CLIV G, 215 × 260 ($8\frac{7}{16} \times 10\frac{1}{4}$) and I, 203 × 258 ($8 \times 10\frac{3}{16}$). Given the sizes of these two works, and that of the work exhibited, it is likely that they are from the same sheet of board; there should be one other piece to make up the complete board, Bristol Boards were usually sold as Foolscap, Demy, Medium, Royal or Imperial. This sheet would have been made as a Medium, 394 × 520 ($15\frac{1}{2} \times 20\frac{1}{2}$).

[2] See various colourmen's catalogues in the Winsor and Newton Archives, Harrow.

[3] For example: TB LXX E, white wove, stamped 'BATH SUPERFINE with a Fleur-de-lys' in an oval. An excellent account of some of the deficiencies of this paper can be found in Murray, 1824.

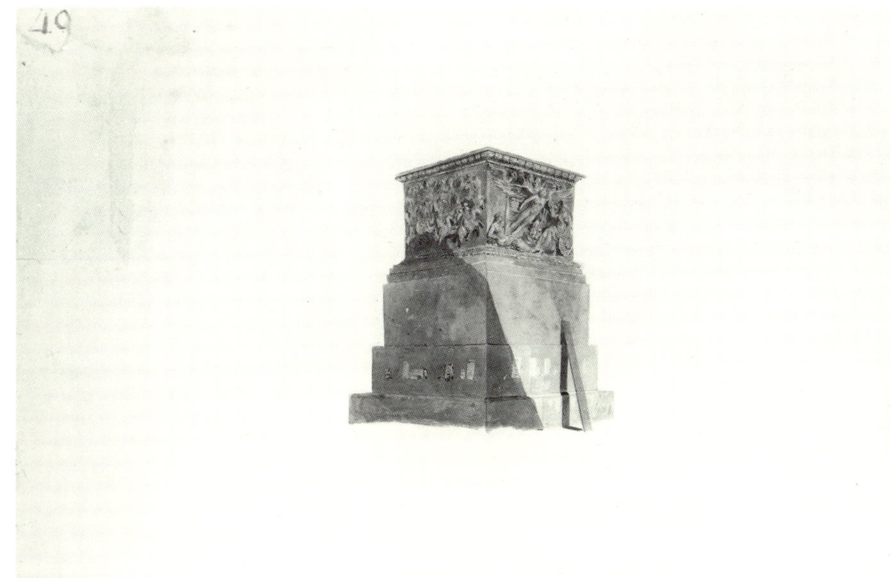

49

49A

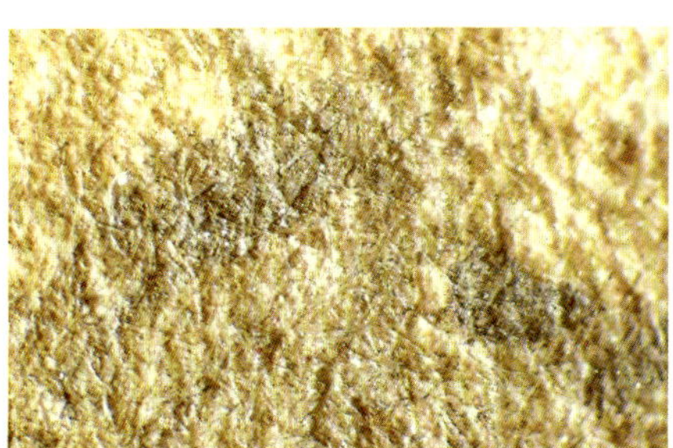

49B

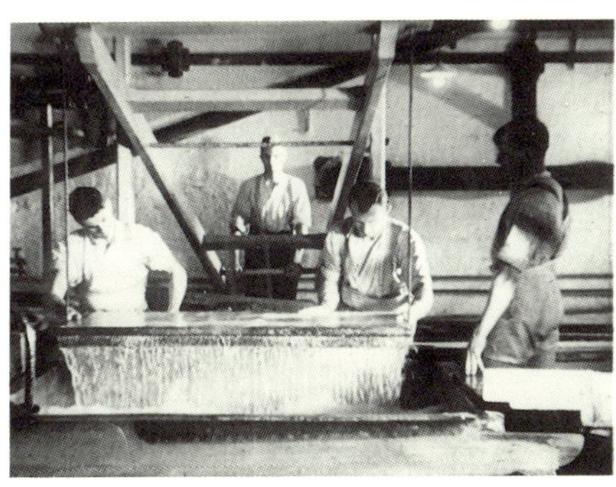

49C

49 A View of the pedestal of the Column of Antoninus Pius

635 × 984 ($25 \times 38\frac{3}{4}$)

White wove drawing paper
Watermarked: JAMES WHATMAN TURKEY MILL KENT 1794
Made by the Balston and Hollingworth Partnership at Turkey Mill, Maidstone, Kent

Watercolour and pencil

Turner Bequest: CXCV 96
D17066

49A Transmitted light detail of watermark and look-through.

49B Raking light detail of paint layer and surface. × 20 magnification.

49C Still from a 1930s film of one of the last makings of Antiquarian paper at Springfield Mill, showing the Bellows man operating the 'contrivance', two vatmen forming a sheet and the 'pig in the pound' whose job was to take the weight of the mould when the vatman on the right disengaged the mould from the 'bellows' after the formation of the sheet. *Whatman Ltd.*

Given the size of this sheet and its four cut edges, one might assume that, like several sheets in this group of essentially large scale works, it was made as a Double Elephant (27 × 40 in). But this paper is a cut down Antiquarian (31 × 53 in) which has been radically trimmed, mainly along the top edge and the two sides. Antiquarian was the only size of paper made by any of the various makers of Whatman paper which was ever watermarked with JAMES rather than J, and with the word KENT added to TURKEY MILL.[1]

Antiquarian paper, sometimes called Double Atlas, was the largest paper made by hand in Europe. James Whatman the younger was originally commissioned to produce it by the Society of Antiquaries in 1772, for the printing of James Basire's engraving of 'The Field of the Cloth of Gold'. Owing to the size of the projected engraving, Basire required a paper at least 49¼ × 27 ins, but no paper of that size was made in Europe at the time. The nearest was a Dutch plate paper measuring 48 × 27½ ins.[2] English copperplate prints at that date were mostly produced on Dutch or French-made paper. The Council of the Society of Antiquaries directed Basire 'to secure an estimate of the expense of such a paper, sufficient for taking off 500 impressions. Mr Whatman, Paper-maker, was directed to be consulted.' James Whatman replied in November 1772:

> The Double Elephant which I at present make is 3ft 4in by 2ft 2in, and is as large as any paper I have ever seen manufactured in Europe. Two sheets of that pasted together would be large enough, but I suppose the bad consequences of that method is what they wish to avoid, if a single sheet could be made. My present conveniences will not permit of my making any larger than the Double Elephant without alterations of most of the Utensils, and even then it cannot be made by hand, but I have no doubt but a contrivance I have thought of will enable me to make it, although that will draw on a certain expense of at least Fifty pounds for things which cannot be of use to me on any other occasion. Of this Paper I suppose the quantity wanted will be but small. I don't wish to get any more than the usual profit for the work done at the Vatt in the same time, notwithstanding the very great Trouble I must necessarily have; the Credit such a Work would do me being all the inducement I can have to undertake it. But I should think I had bought such an Addition to my Reputation rather too dear if I was to be out of pocket by the attempt. If therefore the Society think it worth their while to allow this extra Expense, I will endeavour to accommodate them.[3]

The Society were agreeable to the extra charge for making up the 'contrivance', and in fact ordered four reams, rather than the original commission for one. Whatman was quite wrong in thinking that such a making would be a one-off event. He and his successors continued to produce Antiquarian plate and drawing papers until the 1930s. Basire was very specific about all the requirements for this paper:

> That it not be sized with Parchment, nor any Allum used for whitening it. That the sizing be made of Kid-Leather, and the outward surface of the Paper to approach, as near as may be, to that of the French. It is recommended that an Experiment be made of the effects of the Kid-Leather size on a few Sheets of Paper of a smaller sort before sizing the larger Paper.[4]

Whatman's 'contrivance', or 'bellows', as it came to be called, needed a crew of eleven men working at the vat, rather than the more usual crew of three or four. The bellows man controlled the wooden frame from which the large mould was suspended. Two vatmen guided and controlled the mould during the formation of the sheet. Two deckle men removed the deckle. The pig in the pound helped move the mould with its newly formed sheet to one side, before couching. The ass boy raised one side of it to help the mould drain before couching. Two couchers were responsible for the transfer of the wet sheet from the mould to the felts. Finally two layers separated the wet sheets and felts after pressing.[5]

The drawing on this sheet was one of the Perspective Diagrams prepared by Turner for his lectures as Professor of Perspective at the Royal Academy. They are a large group of very different works, executed over a period of some years, and on several different batches of paper, from various sources, as well as several individual sheets of paper used nowhere else in the Bequest. It is difficult to be certain as to when many of these works were done. Turner had been appointed to the Professorship in 1807, but did not give his first Lecture until 1811. The lectures themselves continued until 1828. The papers used must have been worked over a considerable period. Turner continually reworked his lectures in the face of criticism of his confused, sometimes chaotic delivery and as his own increasing involvement with the subject grew. Preparing these diagrams for the lectures had an effect on his own work; his researches into colour theory provided an important stimulus to his own creativity.

There are several distinct groups of papers amongst the Perspective Diagrams. Most (137 out of the 179) bear a range of different Whatman marks: twenty-two variants in ten different sizes and ranging from papers made by James Whatman the younger, through the period of the Balston Hollingworth partnership (1794–1805) to papers from both William Balston at Springfield Mill and the Hollingworth Brothers, who continued to work Turkey Mill. The remainder come from several makers, with the largest group made by Joseph Ruse (see cat.no.50). Of the papers not made by Whatman or his heirs, none in fact date from after 1800, and one wonders if they were in fact odd sheets, or groups of sheets, that had been sitting around Turner's studio for some time.[6] Judging by the condition of many of them they were not particularly good sheets, and in some cases had not been carefully looked after.[7]

Given the generally very high quality of paper leaving the Whatman mill, these three sheets may well be 'outside' sheets. All three sheets contain much process dirt and No.95 shows some size spotting. They were made on a mould that has been left to sit after use without being properly cleaned: pulp has dried between the wire and the struts, acting as a block to the drainage of the pulp during the formation of the sheet. This produces a kind of accidental watermark, where the pulp lies thinner above the struts, particularly visible in this sheet as 'white' lines running through it.

There are occasional large sheets which if judged solely on their measurements would lead one to suppose that they were again Double Elephants, but in fact they have been made by pasting two Imperial sheets together and trimming them down slightly.[8]

[1] Two other similarly heavily trimmed Whatman Antiquarian papers can be found amongst the Perspective Diagrams: TB CXCV 95 and TB CXCV 176. One complete Antiquarian sheet can be found: TB CXCV 146, watermarked JAMES WHATMAN TURKEY MILL KENT 1809, produced long after James Whatman had died, and surprisingly, given the watermark, probably made by Balston at Springfield Mill rather than the Hollingworths at Turkey Mill. There is considerable uncertainty over the production of Antiquarian papers at this date. We know that Balston was producing them, but have no evidence that the Hollingworths continued to make them after Balston moved to Springfield Mill. But all Antiquarian papers, and some of the Balston produced Double Elephants seem to have carried the Turkey Mill name in their watermarks. It seems most likely that Balston took the moulds with him when he moved and did not change the wording on the moulds. After Springfield Mill started production in 1807 all papers made by the Hollingworths carried the words TURKEY MILL in their watermarks but, with the above exceptions, none of the Balston produced papers did. The confusion of having two separate companies, at two different mills, producing papers under the same name was finally resolved in 1859, when the Hollingworths turned their production over completely to the manufacture of the highest quality machine-made papers and the Whatman name finally returned to the control of one company, the Balstons.

[2] The maximum size of a hand-made sheet was determined by the reach of the vatman's arms. The largest size possible to make, without some mechanical aid was Double Elephant. It is likely that the Dutch paper mentioned was produced with the aid of pulleys which took the weight of the mould. The earliest description of such aids in making large sheets comes in Father Jean Imberdis' poem *Papyrus, seu Ars Conficiendae Papyri* written in 1693, and describing the work of the Auvergne papermaker, Colombier:

> There is one large, impressive sheet
> That caps the craft with scale and skill.
> A frame so vast and cumbersome
> A single man could scarcely move. . . .
> At rest, this heavy framework hangs.
> At every corner well secured,
> Four cords on pulleys raise the frame,
> Counterweighted four-corner-wise,
> Whose swing must be controlled by skill.
> The slightest finger touch will raise
> Or oscillate this wire meshed frame
> Which lumbers like a pendulum

Translated from the Latin by Oliver Bayldon.

[3] Minutes of the Society of Antiquaries: meeting on 7th December 1772.

[4] Minutes of the Society of Antiquaries: meeting on 3rd April 1773.

[5] A full description of making Antiquarian paper, at Springfield Mill, in the 1930's, based on information from Jack Bailey and Mr Spry, who made the paper, can be found in Balston, 1957, p.152–155.

[6] Besides the papers made by Joseph Ruse the other sheets in this group that can be identified with particular makers are as follows:
John Hayes and John Wise: Padsole Mill, Maidstone, Kent. TB CXCV 81,112,128
John Portal and William Bridges: Laverstoke Mill, Hampshire. TB CXCV 98
William Lepard: Hamper Mill, Hertfordshire. TB CXCV 150 and 154
Thomas Budgen: Dartford Mill, Kent. TB CXCV 155 and 157

[7] For example TB CXCV 3, quite a badly made 'second' quality sheet from the Hollingworths, has several cats paw prints on the back probaly from Turner's own cats.

[8] TB CXCV 105, 137 and 138.

50 Entablature

407 × 654 (16 × $25\frac{3}{4}$)

White wove writing paper
Watermarked: J RUSE / 1800
Made by Joseph Ruse, Upper Tovil Mill, Maidstone, Kent[1]

Watercolour and pencil

Turner Bequest: CXCV 129
D17100

50A Transmitted light detail of watermark and look-through.

50B Raking light detail of paint layers. × 7 magnification.

None of the Ruse papers used for the Perspective Drawings, are particularly well made sheets. Indeed the majority of these generally large and heavy weight papers were probably sold as 'outsides'. This drawing is on a cut-down sheet, originally made in a size of paper hardly ever found after this date: Pott Quad, nominally 32 × 25 in and most commonly made for printing, sometimes for writing, and never, as far as I can ascertain, for drawing. Given the way the colour has worked on this particular surface I would judge that this batch of Ruse Pott Quad had been made as a writing paper.[2]

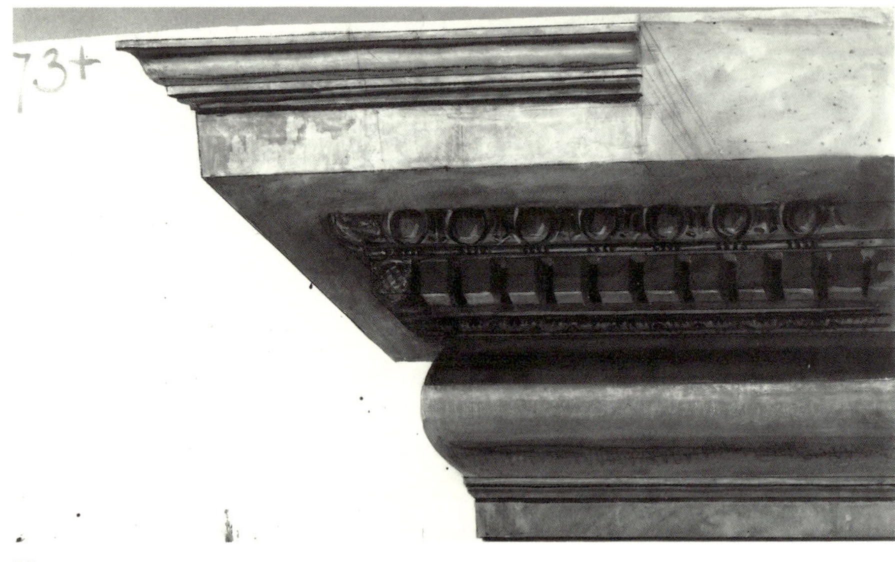

50

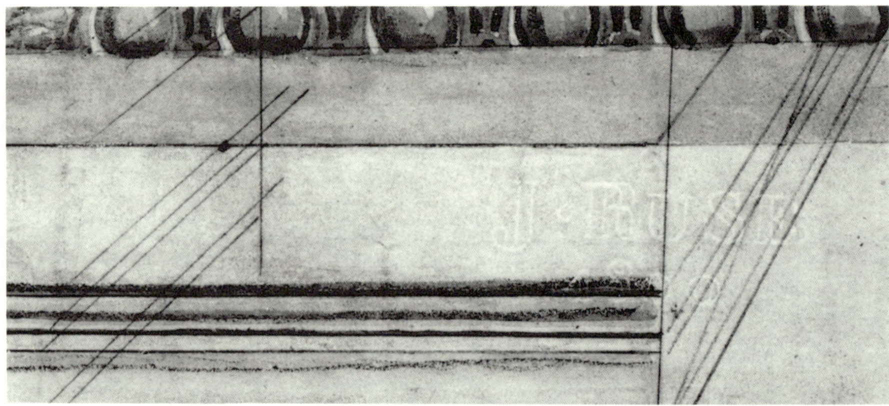
50A

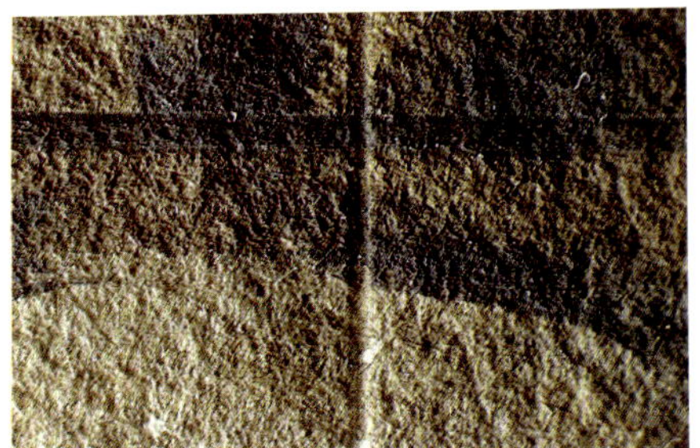
50B

[1] Joseph Ruse began working Upper Tovil Mill in 1798 and continued to work it until 1819, either on his own or in various partnerships with Richard Turner and others, see *Watermills of Kent*, unpublished researches from The Simmons Collection, Science Museum Library Archives, London.

Other papers from this maker can be found in the Bequest:
TB CXVIII K, watermarked : J RUSE / 1799.
TB CXVIII f, watermarked : TOVIL MILL / 1813.
TB CLIX. The *Itinerary Rhine Tour* sketchbook, in use in 1817, watermarked : RUSE & TURNERS / 1817.

There are other Turner watermarks in the Bequest, but they refer to different papermakers of the same name, working other mills:

TB CXX J and TB CLIV B,C,D and E, all with the watermark : G & R TURNER. These Turners worked Aller Mill, Devon.

TB CLXXXVIV, The *Gandolfo to Naples* sketchbook in use in 1819, watermarked: W TURNER & SON. TB CXCV(a) L, with a part mark: . . . ER & SON, William Turner worked Chafford Mill, Kent from 1796 until at least 1816.

[2] The Pott Quad Joseph Ruse papers in the Perspective drawings are TB CXCV-100,101,106,107,109,131,142,164 and 165, (164 has been cut down and 165 is another half sheet). They show considerable variations in the whole sheet size, from 25–26 × $32\frac{1}{2}$–33 in, though details of the watermark, and those elements of the mould surface that can be seen, indicate that they were all made on the same pair of moulds as part of one batch of paper, though probably by different vatmen. The 'shake': the action with which the vatman forms the sheet, varies from person to person, and can lead to considerable differences in shrinkage during the drying of the sheets.

The Italian Tour, 1819–20 (cat.nos.51–54)

The twenty-three sketchbooks which Turner used on his long Tour of Italy from August 1819 to January 1820 contain several curiosities in terms of paper. They are all of British-made paper, from eight different makers. This fact and the various details of these books described below suggest that they were all taken out to Italy by Turner, rather than being bought there. The export of British-made paper had become a flourishing trade to continental Europe, but the bulk of this business was in printing papers. Four of the sketchbooks (including cat.nos.50–53), contain paper from two makers. Although in these cases the papers are of very similar types, there are considerable differences between them in tone, weight, texture and behaviour.

By 1819 the sizes and formats of artists' sketchbooks had generally settled into a particular range of sizes, based on five sizes of drawing papers: 16mo, 8vo, 4to and folio variants of Demy, Medium, Royal, Super Royal and Imperial.[1] With four exceptions, the particular group of sketchbooks that Turner took with him on this tour do not conform to these specifications. In fact they fall into three groups, indicated in the following short catalogue by letters in square brackets: [A] those that conform to the standard that had evolved (and even among them, one, TB CLXXXIX, shows some curious features). [B] Bound up sketchbooks, most of which were made up using a Thin Post writing paper and were probably bought already made up, but which had been designed as notebooks rather than sketchbooks: Turner seems to have appreciated the fact that many gelatine sized writing papers also take the pencil very well. [C] Books containing either prepared papers or combinations of paper or both. It should be noted that the bulk of the grey-washed papers in all these sketchbooks, regardless of their bound up page size, is from one batch of paper: a Large Post Whatman, watermarked 1814, which had been washed with colour before binding. This would indicate that this group of sketchbooks were bound up on Turner's instructions.

It is sometimes difficult to ascertain exactly what the original size of the sheet was, when working with books such as these. But a combination of details can give one the details: the size and format of the book itself; the weight, bulk and texture of the paper; the number of pages in the book in relation to the number, and position in the sheet, of any watermarks present; the presence of the trace or remains of the deckle edge of the sheet, particularly if such traces fall in the same page as a watermark. It is the combination of all such details that allows certain deductions to be made. For example, the group of Post Octavo sketchbooks with papers made by Smith & Allnutt and William Allee might at first sight be assumed to be all Imperial 16mo, a very common sketchbook size; but the slight difference in size in the short dimension (some ½ inch in the case of these books) and the positions of the watermarks in relation to the overall shape of the book, show that they are Post Octavo. To my knowledge neither Post nor Large Post, so often used by Turner, was ever made as a drawing paper in Turner's lifetime.

One indication that the small sketchbooks made up from the Smith and Allnutt and the Allee papers, were mass produced comes from the way they have been cut and bound together. Rather than individual sheets, or pairs of sheets, being folded, bound as sections and then trimmed, the papers have been treated somewhat differently: piles of sheets have been trimmed to double the size, in this case approximately 114 × 360 (4½ × 14¼), folded into sections and then bound. In the case of the Smith and Allnutt sketchbooks the papers appear to be grouped and trimmed in sixes; the Allee papers show a similar grouping but a little less clearly.

Of the nearly 2,000 drawings produced on this tour, most are in pencil, remarkable for their swift precision: but some are in fascinating blends of watercolour and bodycolour. They were to provide Turner with a library of references for the future, joining all his other carefully labelled and kept sketchbooks. In the years after his return from Italy Turner's use of paper was to become more complex. There is a greater variety of paper types, from a wider range of makers, including more European makers. His criteria for choosing particular papers appear to change. The papers themselves change too, under the influence of new raw materials and production methods.

The complete list of sketchbooks taken to Italy in 1819 by Turner and their specifications are listed opposite:

[1] English-made artists' drawing papers were generally manufactured in the following sizes, with some slight variations, depending on the maker and the mill:

Demy	20 × 15 in
Medium	22 × 17 in
Royal	24 × 19 in
Super Royal	27 × 19 in
Imperial	30 × 21 in
Colombier	34 × 23 in
Atlas	33 × 26 in
Double Elephant	40 × 26 in
Antiquarian	52 × 31 in

Bristol and London Boards (made by laminating quality sheets together) were also available in Foolscap (16½–17 × 13½ in).

See various colourmen's catalogues, from Winsor and Newton, Newman, Reeves etc, in Winsor & Newton Archives, Harrow.

TB CLXXI: *Route to Rome* sketchbook. [B]
Post 16mo
88 × 114 ($3\frac{7}{16}$ × $4\frac{1}{2}$)
White wove writing paper
Watermarked: ALLEE /1813
Made by William Allee, Hurstbourne Prior Mill, Hampshire.

Worked in pen and inks, and in pencil, on both wire and felt sides of the sheet.

TB CLXXII: *Italian Guide Book* sketchbook. [B]
Foolscap Octavo
156 × 101 ($6\frac{1}{8}$ × 4)
White wove printing paper
Watermarked: (a) JA / 1811 (b) J
(a) Made by James Ansell, Carshalton Mill, Surrey.

TB CLXXIII: *Paris, France, Savoy 2* sketchbook. [B]
Post Octavo
114 × 179 ($4\frac{1}{2}$ × $7\frac{1}{16}$)
White wove writing paper
Watermarked: J WHATMAN / 1814
Made by William Balston, Springfield Mill, Maidstone, Kent.

Worked in pencil on both wire and felt sides of the sheet.

TB CLXXIV: *Turin, Como, Lugarno, Maggiore* sketchbook. [B]
Post Octavo
111 × 186 ($4\frac{3}{8}$ × $7\frac{3}{8}$)
White wove writing paper
Watermarked: SMITH & (. . .) / 18(. .)
Made by Thomas Smith and Henry Allnutt, Ivy Mill, Maidstone, Kent.

TB CLXXV: *Milan to Venice* sketchbook. [B]
Post Octavo
111 × 189 ($4\frac{3}{8}$ × $7\frac{7}{16}$)
White wove writing paper
Watermarked: ALLEE /1813
Made by William Allee, Hurstbourne Prior Mill, Hampshire.

Worked in pencil on both wire and felt sides of the sheet

TB CLXXVI: *Venice to Ancona* sketchbook. [B]
Post Octavo
111 × 186 ($4\frac{3}{8}$ × $7\frac{3}{8}$)
White wove writing paper
Watermarked: (. . .) & ALLNUTT / (. . .)18
Made by Thomas Smith and Henry Allnutt, Ivy Mill, Maidstone, Kent.

TB CLXXVII: *Ancona to Rome* sketchbook. [B]
Post Octavo
111 × 186 ($4\frac{3}{8}$ × $7\frac{3}{8}$)
White wove writing paper
Watermarked: ALLEE /1813
Made by William Allee, Hurstbourne Prior Mill, Hampshire.

Worked in pencil on both wire and felt sides of the sheet.

TB CLXXIX: *Tivoli and Rome* sketchbook. [B]
Post Octavo
111 × 186 ($4\frac{3}{8}$ × $7\frac{3}{8}$)
White wove writing paper
Watermarked: ALLEE /1813
Made by William Allee, Hurstbourne Prior Mill, Hampshire.

Worked in pencil on both wire and felt sides of the sheet.

TB CLXXX: *Vatican Fragments* sketchbook. [C]
Double Foolscap 16mo
101 × 161 ($6\frac{5}{16}$ × 4)
The bulk of this sketchbook consists of the paper described below, but bound in with it is a single sheet of trimmed white wove Large Post which has been prepared with a grey wash.
Watermarked: J WHATMAN / 1816

White wove writing paper
Watermarked: Prince of Wales Feathers / JM monogram / 1816
Made by John Jones and John Mather, Afonwen Mill, Denbigh, North Wales.
Worked in pencil on both wire and felt sides of the sheet. Only one side of one of the eight grey washed leaves has been worked on.

TB CLXXXI: *Como and Venice* sketchbook. [A]
Royal Quarto
225 × 289 ($8\frac{7}{8}$ × $11\frac{3}{8}$)
White wove drawing paper
Watermarked: J WHATMAN / 1816
Made by William Balston, Springfield Mill, Maidstone, Kent.

Worked in watercolour, and some pencil.

TB CLXXXII: *Albano, Nemi, Rome* sketchbook. [B]
Post Octavo
111 × 191 ($4\frac{3}{8}$ × $7\frac{1}{2}$)
White wove writing paper
Watermarked: (. . .) & ALLNUTT / (. .)18
Made by Thomas Smith and Henry Allnutt, Ivy Mill, Maidstone, Kent.

Worked in pencil on both wire and felt sides of the sheet.

TB CLXXXIII: *Tivoli* sketchbook. [C]
Large Post Octavo
253 × 200 (10 × $7\frac{15}{16}$)
White wove writing paper, prepared with a grey wash
Watermarked: J WHATMAN / 1814
Made by William Balston, Springfield Mill, Kent.

Worked in pencil.

TB CLXXXIV: *Gandolfo to Naples* sketchbook. [B]
Large Post Octavo
122 × 197 ($4\frac{13}{16}$ × $7\frac{3}{4}$)
White wove drawing paper
Watermarked: W TURNER & SON
Made by William Turner, Chafford Mill, Kent.

Worked in pencil on both wire and felt sides of the sheet.

TB CLXXXV: *Pompeii, Amalfi, Sorrento, Herculaneum* sketchbook. [B]
Post Octavo
113 × 189 ($4\frac{7}{16}$ × $7\frac{7}{16}$)
White wove writing paper
Watermarked: (. . .) & ALLNUTT / (. .)18
Made by Thomas Smith and Henry Allnutt, Ivy Mill, Maidstone, Kent.

Worked in pencil on both wire and felt sides of the sheet.

TB CLXXXVI: *Naples, Paestum and Rome* sketchbook. [B]
Post Octavo
113 × 189 ($4\frac{7}{16}$ × $7\frac{7}{16}$)
White wove writing paper
Watermarked: ALLEE /1813
Made by William Allee, Hurstbourne Prior Mill, Hampshire.

TB CLXXXVII: see cat.nos.51 and 52. [C]
Large Post Folio
406 × 255 (16 × $10\frac{1}{16}$)

TB CLXXXVIII: *St Peter's* sketchbook. [B]
Post Octavo
114 × 189 ($4\frac{1}{2}$ × $7\frac{7}{16}$)
White wove writing paper
Watermarked: SMITH & (. . .) / 18(. .)
Made by Thomas Smith and Henry Allnutt, Ivy Mill, Maidstone, Kent.

Worked in pencil on both wire and felt sides of the sheet.

TB CLXXXIX: see cat.nos.53 and 54 [A]
Imperial quarto
368 × 229 ($14\frac{1}{2} \times 9$)

TB CXC: *Small Roman C. Studies* sketchbook. [C]
Large Post 6mo
132 × 206 ($5\frac{3}{16} \times 10\frac{1}{8}$)
White wove writing paper, prepared with grey wash
Watermarked: J WHATMAN / 1814
Made by William Balston, Springfield Mill, Maidstone, Kent.
The grey wash has been mostly applied to the wireside, both sides have been worked, mostly in pencil, but some watercolour and body colour.

TB CXCI: *Rome and Florence* sketchbook. [B]
Post Octavo
111 × 191 ($4\frac{3}{8} \times 7\frac{1}{2}$)
White wove writing paper
Watermarked: (. . .) & ALLNUTT / (. .)18
Made by Thomas Smith and Henry Allnutt, Ivy Mill, Maidstone, Kent.

Worked in pencil on both wire and felt sides of the sheet.

TB CXCII: *Return from Italy* sketchbook. [C]
Large Post 16mo
126 × 96 ($5\frac{3}{8} \times 3\frac{13}{16}$)
White wove writing paper, prepared with a grey wash
Watermarked: J WHATMAN / 1814
This sketchbook also contains paper watermarked J WHATMAN / 1818 which has not been prepared with a grey wash.
Made by William Balston, Springfield Mill, Maidstone, Kent.

Worked in pencil on both wire and felt sides of the sheet.

TB CXCIII: *Remarks (Italy)* sketchbook. [C]
Post 16mo
114 × 90 ($4\frac{1}{2} \times 3\frac{9}{16}$)
This sketchbook contains two different papers:
(a) White wove writing paper
Watermarked: SMITH & ALLNUTT / 1818
Made by Thomas Smith and Henry Allnutt, Ivy Mill, Maidstone, Kent.
(b) White wove writing paper, heavily trimmed Large Post, prepared, on both sides of the sheet, with various grey washes
Watermarked: J WHATMAN / 1814
Made by William Balston, Springfield Mill, Maidstone, Kent.

Worked in pencil on both wire and felt sides of the sheet. But none of the grey washed Whatman has been worked on at all.

TB CXCIV: *Passage of the Simplon* sketchbook. [C]
Large Post Octavo
195 × 120 ($7\frac{11}{16} \times 4\frac{3}{4}$)
White wove writing paper, prepared with various grey washes
Watermarked: J WHATMAN / 1814
Made by William Balston, Springfield Mill, Maidstone, Kent.

51 **Vesuvius** 1819

Unbound sheet from the *Naples, Rome C. Studies* sketchbook

Large Post Folio
255 × 406 ($10\frac{1}{16}$ × 16)

White wove Double Foolscap writing paper
Watermarked: Prince of Wales Feathers / JM monogram / 1816
Made by John Jones and John Mather, Afonwen Mill, Flintshire, North Wales[1]
This paper has been heavily trimmed in order to accommodate the other paper in the sketchbook[2]

Pencil and watercolour

Turner Bequest: CLXXXVII 18
D16106

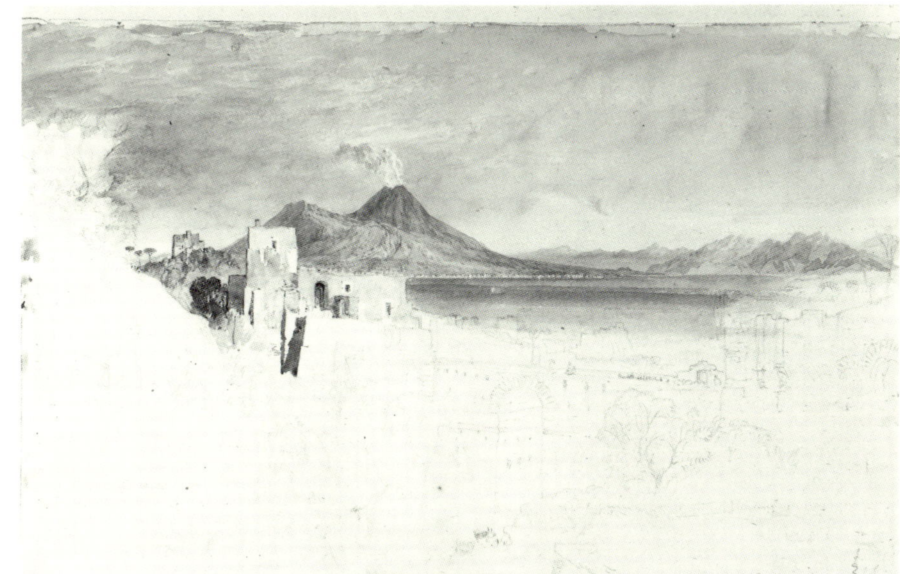

51

52 **Naples** 1819

Unbound sheet from the *Naples, Rome C. Studies* sketchbook

257 × 368 ($10\frac{1}{8}$ × $14\frac{1}{2}$)

White wove writing paper
Watermarked: Prince of Wales Feathers / JM monogram / 1816
Made by John Jones and John Mather, Afonwen Mill, Flintshire, North Wales[1]

Worked in watercolour on the wire-side of the sheet

Turner Bequest: CXVII E
D17195

52A Transmitted light detail of watermark and look-through, reversed.

52B Raking light detail of surface and paint film. × 7 magnification.

52C Raking light detail of watermark.

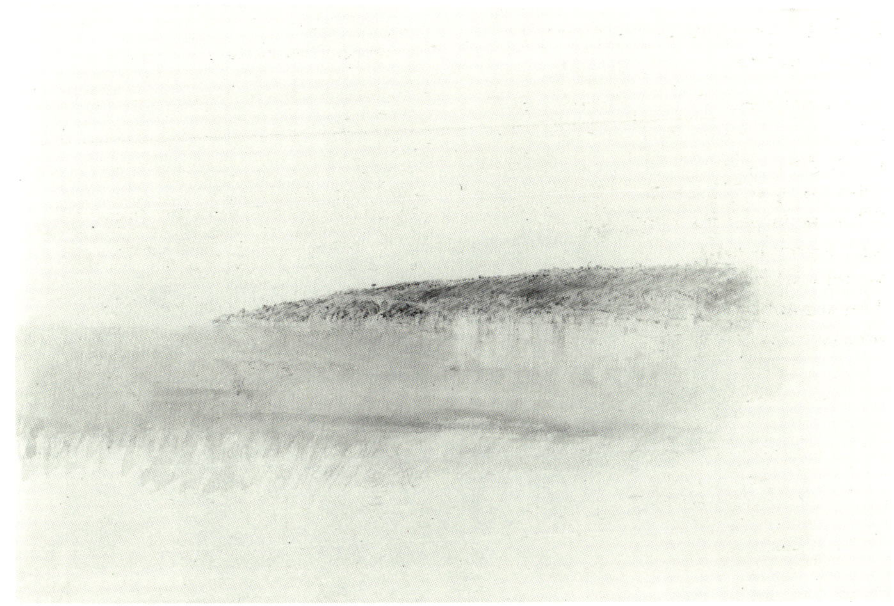

52

This single loose sheet, with cut edges bearing the Jones and Mather 'Prince of Wales' watermark which has been catalogued amongst the 'Colour Beginnings', originally formed part of the *Naples, Rome C. Studies* sketchbook. The trimming would probably have occurred when it was originally mounted up for exhibition the first time. It has been remounted at least three times, judging by the overlapping areas of more or less fading, which can be seen at the edges of the sheet.

The only other example of Turner using Jones and Mather paper is the Double Foolscap 16mo sketchbook, *Vatican Fragments*.[3]

The rest of this sketchbook is made up of a white wove Large Post writing paper prepared with a dark grey wash on both sides of the sheet.
Watermarked: J WHATMAN / 1814.
Made by William Balston, Springfield Mill, Maidstone, Kent.
Both papers have been worked on both felt and wire sides of the sheet.

This size, Large Post Folio, is unusual in a sketchbook. It is more usually found as a large Ledger size. The combination of the size and format and the presence of two distinct papers, one of them prepared before binding, suggest that the book was bound up to Turner's specifications.

The light, strong Jones and Mather paper, with its relatively hard size surface and slight tooth, designed for steel nibs, has taken the watercolour well, allowing both wash and drier brush-strokes to adhere strongly to the surface, and providing an excellent light-reflecting surface, keeping the colours bright.

1 The beginnings of papermaking in Wales are relatively unknown. The earliest mill seems to have been Halghton, in Flintshire, at some date around 1706. By 1750 there were at least three mills, and by 1800, ten. By the 1820s the number had grown to twenty, mostly producing common or coarse wrappings. But both Samuel Price of Hope Mill, Flint and Jones and Mather at Afonwen (sometimes called Wheeler Mill) were producing fine writings, see Shorter, 1971, p184–7.

2 A Double Foolscap Folio would actually produce a page size of $13\frac{1}{2} \times 17$ in, the normal Foolscap sheet size.

3 TB CLXXX.

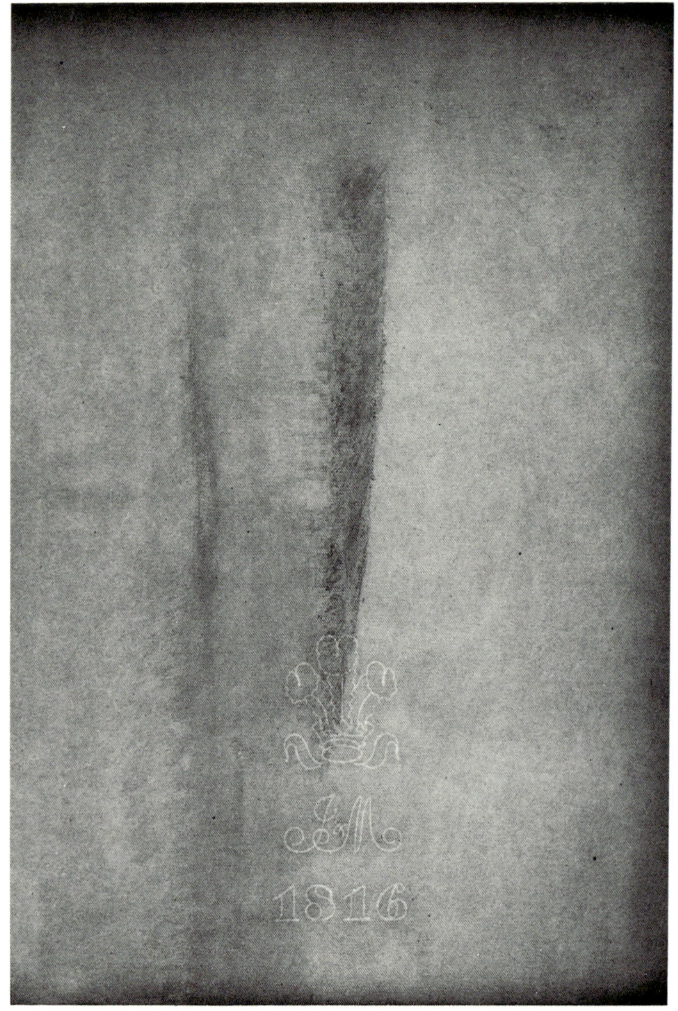

52A

52B

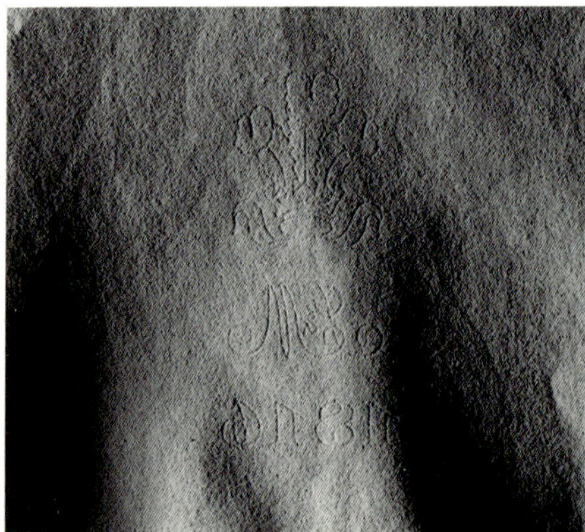

52C

53 The Temple of Minerva Medica 1819

Unbound sheet from the *Rome: C. Studies* sketchbook

Imperial Quarto
368 × 229 ($14\frac{1}{2}$ × 9)

White wove drawing paper, prepared with a grey wash on one side of the sheet
Watermarked: J WHATMAN / 1814
Made by William Balston at Springfield Mill, Maidstone, Kent

Pencil, watercolour and bodycolour

Turner Bequest: CLXXXIX 35
D16362

53A Transmitted light detail of watermark and look-through, reversed.

53B Raking light detail of watercolour, bodycolour and surface. × 7 magnification.

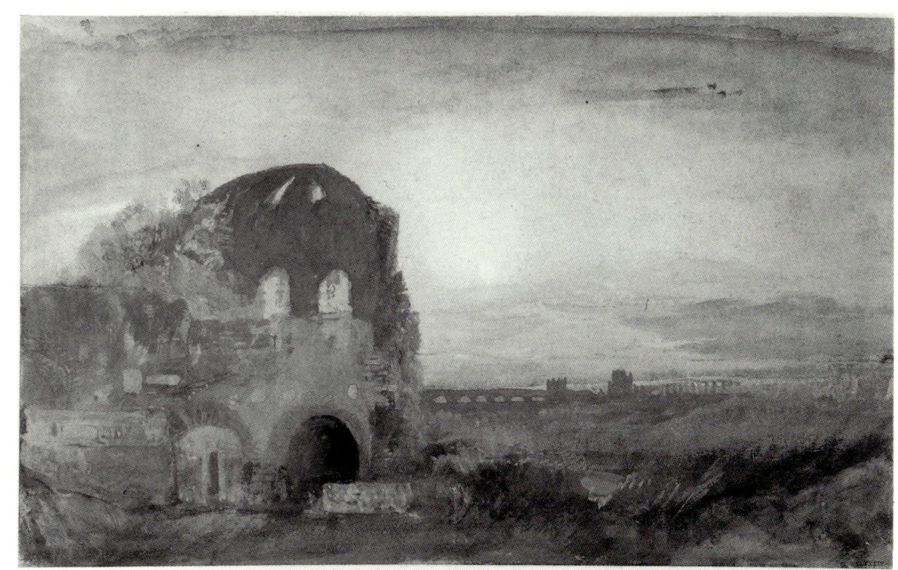

53

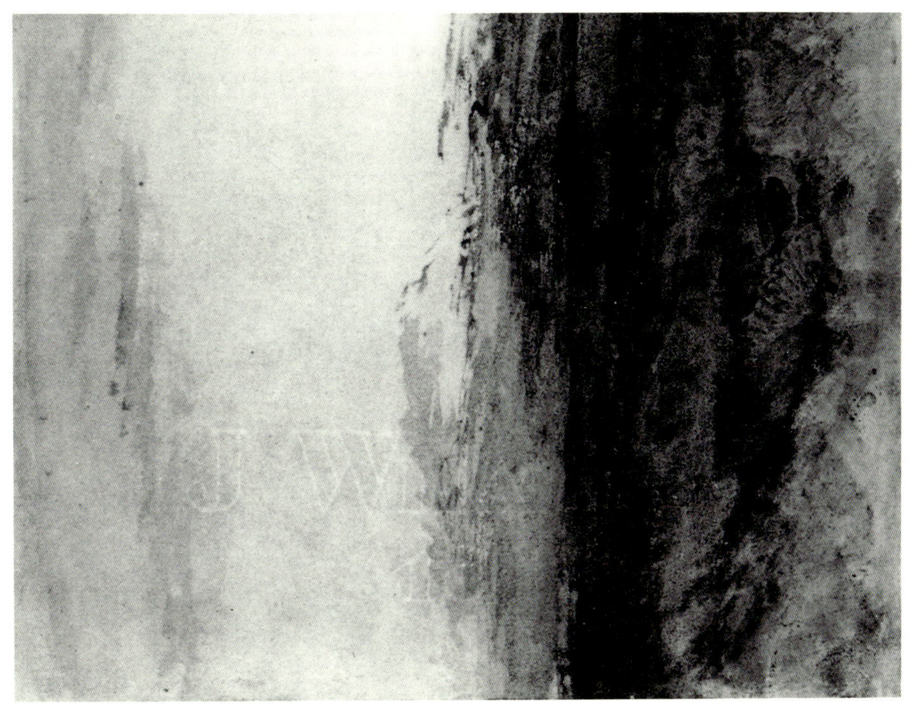

53A

53B

54 The Basilica of Constantine

1819

Unbound sheet from the *Rome: C. Studies* sketchbook

Imperial Quarto.
368 × 229 ($14\frac{1}{2}$ × 9)

White wove printing paper, prepared with a grey wash on one side of the sheet
Watermarked: VALLEYFIELD / 1816
Made by Alexander Cowan, Valleyfield Mill, Pennycuik, near Edinburgh, Scotland[1]

Pencil, watercolour and bodycolour, with pen and brown ink

Turner Bequest: CLXXXIX 38
D16365

54A Transmitted light detail of watermark and look-through.

54B Raking light detail of watercolour, bodycolour and surface. × 7 magnification.

This sketchbook, which is made up of two separate papers, was reassembled and rebound in 1935. Finberg records that 'The book was broken up and the leaves distributed without any record being kept of their relative positions.' Many of the works, including these, are now amongst the mounted drawings.

The 'C' in Turner's title for this sketchbook, and both the related *Small Roman C. Studies* sketchbook (TB CXC), and *Naples, Rome C. Studies* sketchbook (see cat.nos.50 and 51) has been variously interpreted as 'Colour' or 'Chiar-ascuro' in the past, but Cecilia Powell's interpretation of the initial as meaning 'Composition' would appear to cover more of the nature of the works in the sketchbooks than either of those earlier interpretations.[2]

There is considerable variation in the depth of the grey tones used to prepare these sheets, but generally the Whatman papers appear to be darker than the Valleyfield papers. The considerable yellowing and discolouration in many of the works which have been exhibited is probably more the product of the preparation than the paper: like many of the earlier grey washes used by Turner, this probably contains a large proportion of indigo.

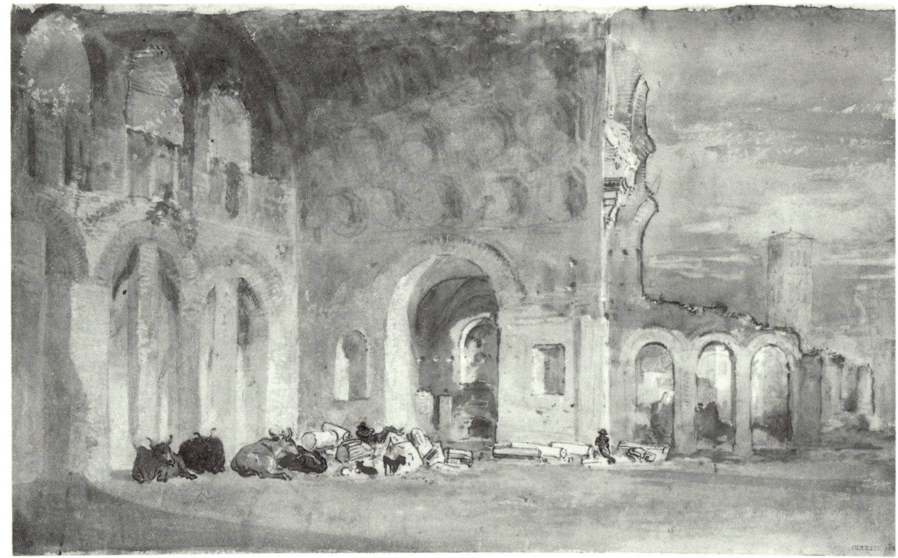

54

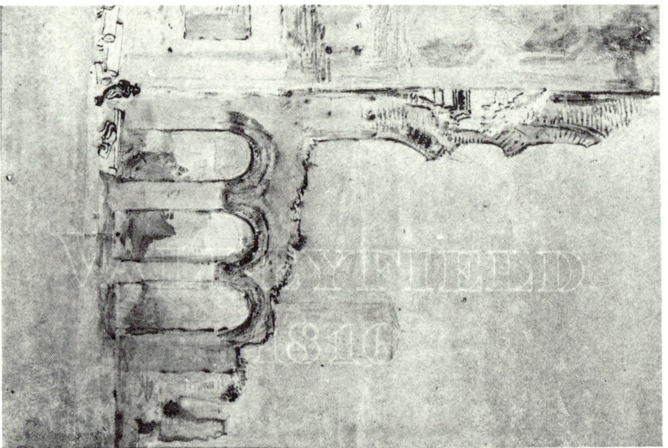

54A

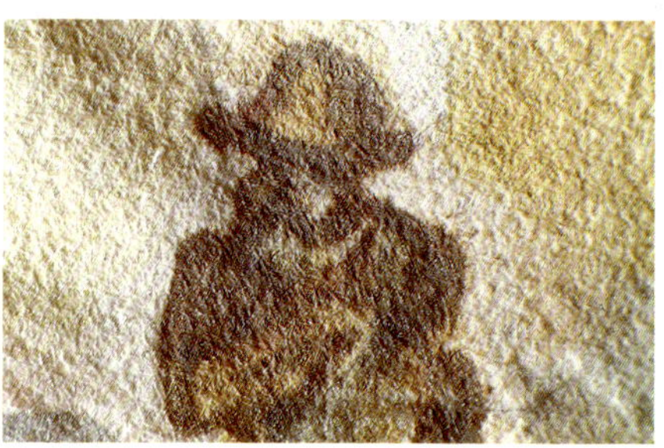

54B

[1] Papermaking in Scotland had begun in 1590, a hundred years after its beginnings in England. Two German papermakers, Pieter Gryther and Michael Keysar, were appointed papermakers to the King for a period of nineteen years. They set up their first mill at West Mill, Dalry, near Edinburgh, in conjunction with two Scots, Mungo Russell and his son Gideon. By the year 1700, possibly as many as thirteen mills were operating in Scotland, most engaged in the manufacture of the lower grades of paper. By 1800, the situation was very different, with 32 mills in operation, of which 18, including Valleyfield, were clustered around Edinburgh, and sending 'vast quantities of printing paper to London, from whence it used formerly to be brought.' see Shorter, 1971, p.192–198.

[2] Powell, 1987, p.44.

Turner and Machine-made Paper (cat.nos.55 and 56)

The first working paper machine had been invented in 1798 by Nicholas-Louis Robert, who worked at Leger Didot's paper mill at Essones, near Paris. Despite the popular belief that it was the rapidly increasing demand for paper that led to the invention of the paper machine, Robert himself gave the reason that the quarrelsome attitudes and restrictive practices of the papermakers themselves, 'influenced and made truculent by the Revolution' led him to make a machine, that would obviate their services.[1]

The early development of the machine was not without some difficulties. A combination of circumstances; differences in temperament and disagreements over money and rights led to ill-will between Didot and Robert. Didot approached his English brother-in-law, John Gamble, who despite the War with France was living and working in Paris, in the hope that the machine could be developed to more effect and more profitably in England. Robert was to gain very little from his remarkable invention.

Gamble took out his first patent in England on April 20th 1801.[2] This was simply a translation of Robert's original French patent application. He returned to France in order to have more detailed drawings made and to arrange for the transfer of Robert's original working model to England. Soon after the grant of the English patent two London stationers, Henry and Sealy Fourdrinier, who already operated hand-made paper mills, bought a one-third share in the rights to the new machine, so beginning their long and complex involvement in the development of the machine that

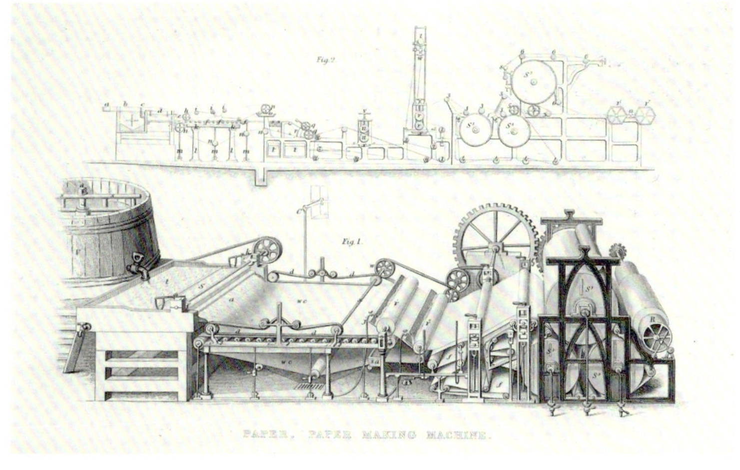

fig 20. Papermaking Machine, Steel Engraving, showing two different types of machine. The pulp is transferred from the vat 'V' onto the sluice, under a slice 't' which distributes the pulp evenly onto the wire cover 'wc'. The newly formed sheet passes through a set of press rolls and then through steam heated drying cylinders 'S' before being reeled up 'R'. This illustration must date from after 1820 and Thomas Crompton's invention of the drying cylinder. Until that date all machine-made paper was dried like hand-made paper in lofts.

would eventually be known world-wide as the Fourdrinier: about all they would gain from the venture which, despite its success, would eventually bankrupt them. The first working production machine was built for them by Bryan Donkin at Two Waters Mill in Hertfordshire in 1804.

Many English papermakers were interested in the new machine. They were familiar with Bryan Donkin through his engineering work and through the company that made papermaking moulds (see cat.no.1). Some, like Elliott (see cat.nos.55 and 56) and the Kent makers Phipps and Buttanshaw,[3] saw the enormous potential of the machine very early on and quickly converted their mills. Others, like William Balston, thought long and hard about it before deciding to continue making paper by hand, because they did not believe that the machine, despite the quantity of it could produce, would ever make paper of sufficient quality. Balston was visiting the Fourdriniers at one of their mills at St Neots in the course of his deliberations, when his wife wrote to him:

> It appears to me, that going to Two Waters must lengthen your journey . . . should you afterwards adopt this machine, it may be advantageous to yourself to have seen them all – I shall like much to go with you to Dover and I think you will there have an opportunity of seeing how far Mr Phipps finds it possible to realise the advantage that Fourdrinier states, and consequently, of determining better whether it will be desirable for your own purpose.[4]

It was in fact not until 1932 that Springfield Mill had a paper machine installed, though the Balstons had bought a paper machine before. In 1899 they had acquired Medway Mill, half a mile down-river from Springfield, which produced brown paper on a machine. But the machine was stripped-out and replaced by three vats for making hand-made paper. R.J. Balston had bought the mill primarily because the smoke from its boiler chimney constantly drifted across his garden. Buying the mill enabled him to shut the boiler down.[5]

Given the extraordinary working partnership between Turner and Whatman papers, a partnership that lasted some sixty years, to the great credit of them both, it is perhaps fortunate that William Balston decided against installing a machine in 1808. Turner appears to have had no fondness for machine-made papers. At this date, being made primarily as low grade printing papers, they were quite simply incapable of providing him with the surfaces, strengths and freedom to work, at least in colour, in his inimitable way. But as the pencil drawings on the torn down sheets, (referred to in cat.nos.55 and 56 footnote 4) show, they were increasingly capable of taking pencil.

The growing demand on papermakers for both volume and quality and the commercial pressures exerted by the new machines on the hand-made papermakers, led to very definite changes in both the production and design of hand-made papers. Bleaching and additives were increasingly used in an attempt to turn inferior fibre into 'quality' papers. There was a discernible lessening in the quality of all papers throughout Europe in the period following the Napoleonic Wars though some of the best mills strove to turn out the finest product possible, with little thought of compromise. The quality of paper generally would deteriorate even further in the following decades, so much so that Henry Allnutt of Ivy Mill, Maidstone, remarked in 1848 that 'a pure paper has not been made these past twenty years.' The claim that no one has made a decent paper in twenty years appears to be one that has echoed down the generations.[6]

1 Clapperton, 1967, p.16.

2 Patent No.2487. 'An Invention of making paper in Single Sheets without seams or joining, from one to 12 feet and upwards wide & from one to 45 feet and upwards in Length.'

3 There are hand-made papers by both these makers in the Bequest, but no papers made by machine:

TB LXXXIV, *Academies* sketchbook. In use 1804.
Super Royal 32mo
Page size: 73 × 111 ($2\frac{7}{8} \times 4\frac{9}{16}$)
White wove
Watermarked: I BUTTW / 1798
Shadows present: single faced mould.
Made by John Buttenshaw, Hamptons Mill West Peckham, Kent.

TB CX, *Cockermouth* sketchbook. In use 1809.
Paper bound sketchbook
184 × 114 × 7 ($7\frac{1}{4} \times 4\frac{1}{2} \times \frac{5}{16}$)
Page size: 182 × 113 ($7\frac{3}{16} \times 4\frac{7}{16}$)
Demy Octavo
White laid writing paper
Chain lines: 27–28mm (approx $1\frac{1}{8}$ in) apart variable.
Laid line frequency: 8 per cm (20 per in)
Watermarked: Fleur-de-Lys / 1802 (part mark only)
Countermarked: W PHI . . . (part mark only)
Made by William Phipps at Crabble Mill, River, Kent.

TB CCX, *Academy Auditing* sketchbook. In use 1824.
Paper bound sketchbook
184 × 114 × 7 ($7\frac{1}{4} \times 4\frac{1}{2} \times \frac{5}{16}$)
Page size: 182 × 113 ($7\frac{3}{16} \times 4\frac{7}{16}$)
Demy Octavo
White laid writing paper
Chain lines: 27–28 mm (approx $1\frac{1}{8}$ in) apart, variable.
Laid line frequency: 8 per cm (20 per in)
Watermarked: Fleur-de-Lys (part mark only)
Countermarked: . . . PPS (part mark only)
Made by William Phipps at Crabble Mill, River, Kent.
In spite of the 15 years between their use, and in the case of TB CCX the 22 years between production and use, these two sketchbooks contain sheets of the same paper.

4 Catharine Balston to William Balston, 16th March 1808. Balston and Whatman Archive, Kent County Archives. U 2161/Z1/2.

5 Hugh Balston, 'The Role of the Small Specialist in the Modern Environment', in *Paper*, 10th May 1982, p.35

6 Letter from T.A. Malone to W.H. Fox Talbot, 23rd April 1848, discussing the making of a very pure base paper for Fox Talbot's photography. The letter reads:

> I have seen the process for making paper at Whatmans and at Allnutts – both of Maidstone in Kent. Mr Hollingworth [the writer had visited Turkey Mill, rather than Springfield] the proprietor of 'Whatman's Mill' advised me to go to his friend Mr Allnutt, as he is fond of trying experiments.
>
> Mr Allnutt will try flax if we particularly wish it but would rather try linen rags foreign linen is free from cotton he would make it without chlorine and would take every precaution to keep out pins and buttons which often escape the sorter's eye and become ground and diffused throughout the pulp.

55 Landscape with Trees; stormy effect

298×495 ($11\frac{3}{4} \times 19\frac{1}{2}$)

Sheet and a half Post Folio

255×406 ($10\frac{1}{16} \times 16$)

White wove printing paper
Watermarked: none visible[1]
Inscribed 'Elliott's paper
Made by Richard Elliott, Chesham Bois Mill, Buckinghamshire[2]

Watercolour

Turner Bequest: CCLXIII 14
D25136

56 The Crimson Clouds

298×495 ($11\frac{3}{4} \times 19\frac{1}{2}$)

White wove printing paper
Watermarked: none visible[1]
Inscribed 'Elliott's paper'
Made by Richard Elliott, Chesham Bois Mill, Buckinghamshire[2]
Watercolour

Turner Bequest: CCLXIII 170
D25292

56A Raking light detail of wire texture, surface and paint film. × 7 magnification.

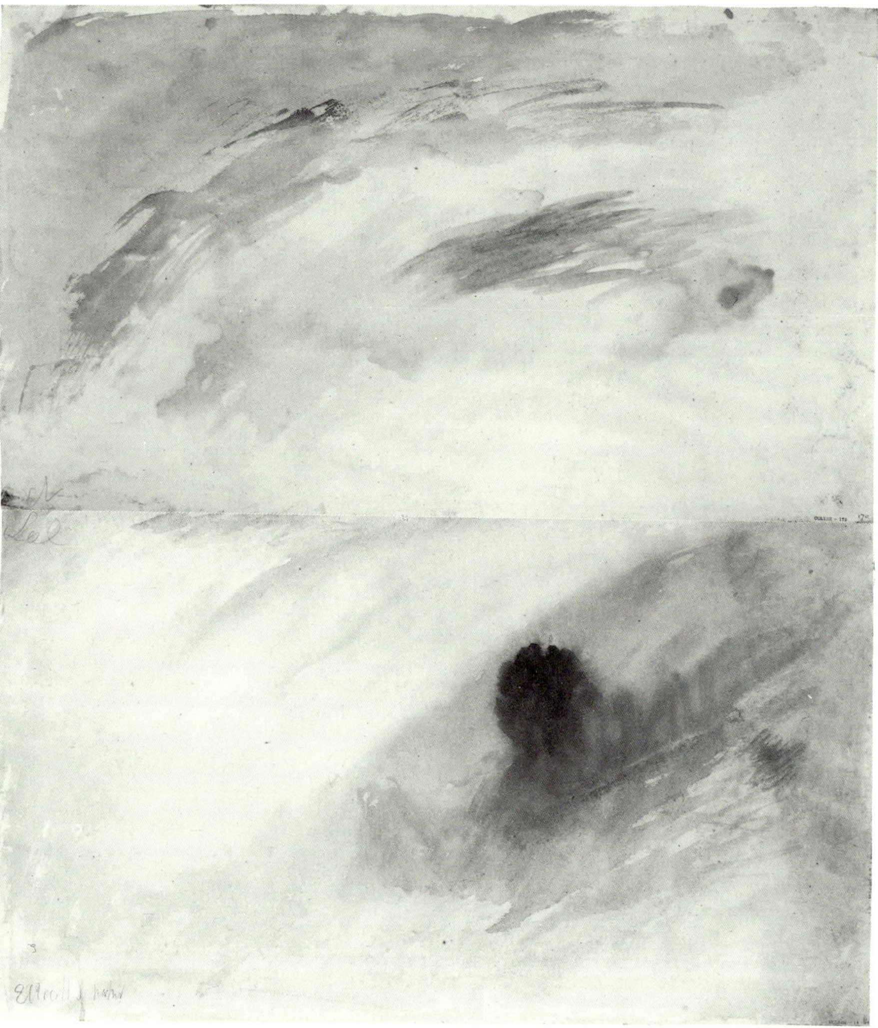

55&56

These two sheets, each with three cut edges and one torn edge, are the two halves of a single sheet. The sheet has not been trimmed by Turner, but is how the paper left the mill, for this is a machine-made paper. It was made as a continuous sheet and then trimmed before being packed, the sheet in this case being 'Sheet and a half Post' 596×495 ($23\frac{1}{2} \times 19\frac{1}{2}$), a printing size. The majority of early machine-made papers were made for printing rather than any other use. One wonders if the unsuitability of such printing papers for watercolour work was what prejudiced Turner against machine-made papers. One would not expect any of the machine-made papers at this date to possess the subtle character and qualities necessary to meet and challenge the demands made on them by the watercolour artists: qualities that have always characterised the best hand-made artists paper.

Andrew Wilton dates this drawing, with its companion to the early 1830s and relates it to the watercolour 'LLanthony Abbey, Monmouthshire'.[3] I have chosen to end this exhibition with these two works, despite the fact that they were worked on after the period dealt with in this exhibition, because they are the only two examples so far identified of early machine-made papers worked on by Turner. The internal evidence of the sheets and the details of the probable maker's history would suggest a manufacturing date of somewhere around 1810, which puts it with a very few years of the introduction of the first machine-made production papers.

Other machine-made papers have been identified among Turner's later work: sketches on small sheets torn down from larger pieces, many of them from various continental tours, suggesting that he was in these cases using papers that were to hand rather than chosen specifically for the purpose.[4]

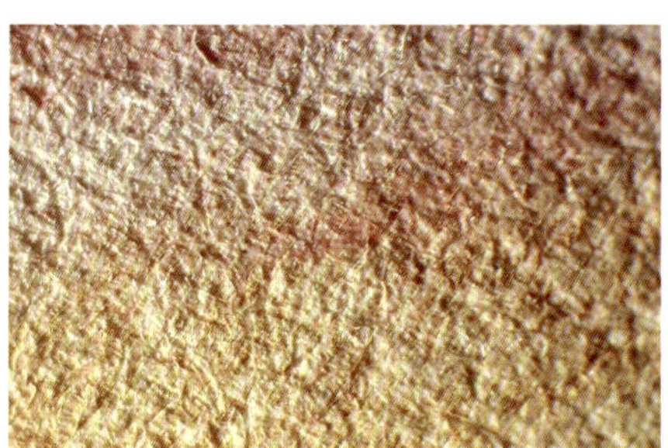

56A

In the Bequest as a whole, there are very few annotations relating to the origin of the paper being worked on. Another pair of machine-made half sheets bear the inscription 'Willow paper'.[5] It has so far proved impossible to determine quite what this annotation means. There appears to be no record, in all the usual sources, of either a papermill, or a papermaker, by the name of Willow. One other possibility is that the annotation refers to the fibre the paper was made from. Because of the increasing difficulty in obtaining consistent quantities and qualities of rags, papermakers had been researching alternatives to rags since the mid-eighteenth century. Willow bark had been tried as a papermaking fibre as early as 1787, when Mr Thomas Greaves, of Warrington was awarded a silver medal and ten guineas by the Society for the Encouragement of Arts, Manufactures and Commerce, for making 'the greatest quantity, not less than ten reams, of the best and most useful papers from vegetable substances not previously used.' Turner's 'Willow paper' does not seem to be Mr Greaves' paper. It is made from a blend of bleached cotton and linen. Perhaps the answer is simply: that Turner was given the sheet by a Mr Willow.[6]

1 Until 1839 the only machine-made papers which carried watermarks were various unsuccessful trial sheets. William Joynson patented the first successful watermarking process for machine-made papers on February 21 1839. Patent no.7977.

2 Richard Elliott was granted a licence to erect a Fourdrinier paper machine at Chesham Bois Mill, on July 1st 1807. Up to that time he had been operating two vats for making hand-made paper. *Evidence to the Fourdrinier Committee*, 1837.

3 In conversation.

4 The bulk of the papers catalogued by Finberg as TB CCCXLI, CCCXLII, CCCXLIII, and CCCXLIV have been torn or folded down from larger sheets. It has been possible in many cases to reassemble the original sheets of paper. Amongst them are some machine-made papers, most probably of European rather than English manufacture:

(a) part of a Grey-green wove. TB CCCXLI – 361, 436, 439–42.
(b) White wove, Imperial. Heavily flecked with process dirt and shives. This whole sheet can be reconstructed from TB CCCXLIV 21–22, 54–55, 116–123, 137–142, 348–349.
(c) Buff wove, Imperial. Another whole sheet made up from TB CCCXLIV 17–19, 40–42, 86–91, 187–188, 192–93, 254–255, 354.
(d) White wove letter paper. TB CCCXLIV 214–226, 217 shows the marks where the machine wire has been joined together.
(e) White wove letter paper. Stamped SIHD, probably a continental paper maker, as yet unidentified. TB CCCXLIV – 183–186, 202–205, 271–289, 322.
(f) Cream wove. TB CCCXLIV 355, 356

5 TB CCLXIII 32, 125. These two works are the torn-down halves of a single, lightweight wove small Imperial sheet 736 × 552 (29 × 21$\frac{3}{4}$). Small Imperials were usually made as wrapping papers.

6 Hunter, 1974, p.329.

Glossary

These definitions apply to paper usage during Turner's lifetime. In some cases these definitions would not apply to modern hand-made, or machine-made papers.

ALUM: Traditionally, potash alum, but superseded, later in the nineteenth century by aluminium sulphate. Added to *gelatine* in the *sizing* of paper, to stabilise the gelatine and aid its bite into the surface of the sheet.

ASS: Curved wooden post on the corner of the *vat*, where the *mould* is rested after the sheet has been formed.

BACK: The mark left in the centre of a hand-made sheet of paper when dried over ropes.

BEATER: machine invented in Holland, in the seventeenth century, for the preparation of *pulp*, consisting of a heavy *beater roll* rotating above a *bedplate*, placed midway down one side of an oval trough.

BEATER ROLL: Barred roll used to crush, cut and *fibrillate* the *fibre* as it passes round the *beater*.

BEDPLATE: a barred plate, situated in the base of the beater and over which the roll passes.

BROKE: flawed paper that is not of sufficient quality to sell, usually repulped.

CHAIN LINES: Lines visible in a *laid paper* when it is held up to the light. Caused by the wires used to hold the *laid wires* together.

COUCH: the action of transferring the newly formed wet sheet from the *mould* to the *felt*, hence *coucher*.

COVER: old name for the forming surface of the *mould*.

CURING: Allowing the paper to mature for a time before packing and sale.

DECKLE: a removable frame which fits on and around the working surface of the *mould*, retaining the *pulp* on it's surface, during the formation of the sheet.

DECKLE EDGE: the slightly ragged edge to the sheet found in hand-made paper, and caused by small amounts of pulp seeping under the *deckle* during formation.

DOUBLE FACED MOULD: mould with a secondary supporting wire layer underneath the formation surface. Developed at the very end of the eighteenth century.

DRY PRESS: The various pressing sequences given to the sheets after drying.

DUSTER: a wire mesh drum used to shake loose dirt out of rags.

ENGINE: see *beater*.

FELTS: woven woollen blankets used in the transfer of the wet sheets off the *mould* and during the first *wet press*.

FELT SIDE: the side of the paper which first comes into contact with the *felt* after formation. Opposite to *wire side*.

FERMENTATION: old method of preparing rags for the *beater*, which involved letting piles of wet rags heat up and begin to rot.

FIBRE: plant based cellulose used in making paper. During Turner's lifetime the paper industry changed its raw material use from fibre obtained from linen rags and old ropes, sailcloth etc, to cotton rags and wood based fibres.

FIBRILLATION: the action of breaking up the surface of the individual cellulose *fibres* used to make the paper. It takes place during beating.

FINISH: used when describing the nature of the surface of the sheet.

FORM: The action of making a sheet of paper. Also the old name for the *mould*.

FURNISH: the various raw materials used in making paper. Particularly used for the *fibre* or blend of fibres used.

GELATINE: A type of *size* added as a coating to the dry sheet, to prevent ink and paints bleeding across the surface. Has the added effect of increasing the surface strength of the sheet. Gelatine is made from animal products, hides, hooves, bones etc.

GLAZING: the degree of smoothness or polish of a paper surface.

HALF STUFF: partially beaten *fibre*.

HOLLANDER: see *beater*.

HOG: a wooden paddle used to keep the *fibre* in suspension in the *vat*. Later replaced by a mechanical paddle fitted in the base of the vat.

HOT-PRESSED (OR HP): One of the three traditional *finishes* of hand-made paper. Originally produced by pressing the paper between hot metal plates, this finish is now approximated by passing the metal plates and paper between glazing rollers.

HYDRATION: a process taking place during *beating* whereby the fibres, through crushing and *fibrillation*, take up water.

INSIDES: Used to describe the best paper, used as the 'inside' *quires* of a *ream*, when paper was packed with the best paper protected by lower quality paper, placed top and bottom of the ream, see *outsides*.

LAID LINES: tightly spaced parallel lines seen in *laid paper* when it is held up to the light, see *chain lines*.

LAID PAPER: Paper made on a laid *mould*.

LAYER: The worker who separates the *felts* and wet sheets of paper after pressing.

LOADING: non-cellulose material added to the pulp: eg 'smalts' finely powdered cobalt blue glass added to rags to make them appear whiter. Or China clay added to bulk up the fibre and act as an aid to ink retention.

LOOK-THROUGH: the internal structure of the sheet of paper when looked at with transmitted light.

MATURING: see *curing*.

MOULD: a rectangular wooden frame covered with a sieve-like *laid* or *wove wire* surface, used for forming sheets of paper by hand. The mould is dipped into the *pulp* in the *vat* and lifted out. The excess water drains away through the *mould cover*, leaving the *pulp* as a thin flat sheet on the surface of the *mould*.

NOT: A traditional paper *finish*, slightly rough and unglazed, produced by pressing wet paper against itself, after the first *wet press*.

OUTSIDES: second quality papers, used top and bottom of the *ream*, to protect the good sheets, see *insides*.

PACK: pile of wet sheets, after separation from the *felts*, after the first press. Or small stack of paper prepared for *glazing*.

PLATE GLAZING: method of producing sheets of smooth paper by interleaving the sheets with metal plates and passing the whole *pack* through glazing rollers.

PLATE PAPER: paper designed for copperplate engraving.

PRINTINGS: Papers designed for letterpress printing.

POST: the pile of newly formed sheets and *couching felts*, ready for pressing.

PULP: the cellulose *fibre*, held in solution, from which paper is made.

QUIRE: During Turner's lifetime, 24 sheets of paper. Now, more usually 25 sheets.

RAGS: formerly the principal raw material for hand-made paper made in the European tradition. Generally linen for the finest papers, but increasingly after the end of the eighteenth century, from cotton goods. By association also used for old hemp rope, sailcloth, etc.

REAM: Traditionally 480 sheets (20 *quires*, each of 24 sheets), though this varied, depending on the use the paper was to be put to: eg a printers ream was 516 sheets. Now counted as 500 sheets.

RETREE: sheets with minor faults. Usually sold 10% cheaper.

RETTING: the rotting down of flax to begin the break up of the stems. Sometimes applied to a similar process used with rags. see *fermentation*.

RIBS: thin wooden struts fixed into the frame of the *mould* to support the *wire mould* cover.

ROUGH: Traditional paper surface, formed by the *weave* of the *felts* during the first *wet press*.

SALLE: the room in the mill where the sorting, *curing* and packing of paper took place.

SHADOWS: thicker areas in the sheet, formed either side of the *ribs* on a *single faced mould*, as the water draining through the wire is drawn to the *ribs*.

SHAKE: the *vatman's* action of dipping, shaking and forming the sheet.

SHIVES: (sometimes SHEAVES) specks visible in the finished paper, caused by impurities in the raw materials used.

SINGLE-FACED MOULD: a mould on which the wire surface sits directly on the supporting *ribs*.

SIZE: originally a solution of *gelatine*, gum or starch, used to make the paper water resistant. Now any chemical which has the same effect, whether by coating the finished sheet, or by addition to the *pulp* before formation.

SPUR: group of sheets dried together as a wad.

STAMPER: early machine for making *pulp*, consisting of several sets of large wooden hammers, driven by a waterwheel, falling into mortars, filled with rag. Superseded by the *beater*.

STATIONER: takes his name from his *station* or shop: the name was used to distinguish himself from itinerent street vendors.

STOCK: see *pulp*.

STUFF: *pulp* ready for making into paper.

STUFF CHEST: storage vat for *pulp*.

TEXTURE: the actual surface of the sheet, can be altered at various stages of the process.

TREBLES, or TRIBBLES: racks of drying ropes.

TUB-SIZING: the addition of *size* after the sheet has been formed, pressed, dried and allowed to *cure*.

VAT: contains the *pulp* from which the paper is formed.

VATMAN: person who works at the *vat* forming the sheets.

WATERLEAF: unsized paper.

WATERMARK: an image in the sheet, formed by varying the density of the *pulp* at certain points in the sheet, by raising or lowering the surface of the *mould* at selected places. Usually done by attaching a design in wire to the working surface of the *mould*.

WET PRESS: the first pressing received by the newly formed sheets.

WILD: used to describe the *look-through* of a poorly formed sheet.

WIRE MARK: more accurate term for a *watermark*.

WIRE PROFILE: the wire design used to form the *watermark*.

WIRE SIDE: the side of the paper next to the wire during the formation of the sheet. Opposite to *felt side*.

WRAPPINGS: low grade coloured papers, destined for wrapping various articles, but often, because of their strengths, colour, tones etc used by artists for both chalk, pencil and colour.

WRITINGS: papers designed for the quill or the steel nib.

WOVE MOULD: *mould* whose cover is made from woven wire, rather than *laid* and *chain* wires.

WOVE PAPER: paper made on a *wove mould*.

Bibliography

All books published in London unless otherwise stated.

UNPUBLISHED SOURCES

Various archives and unpublished sources have been consulted in the course of this research. These include:

The Archives of the National Paper Museum, Greater Manchester Museum of Science and Industry, Manchester.

The unpublished transcription of *The Journal of Joshua Gilpin*, by A.P. Woolrich.

The Simmons Collection of data on the Watermills of England, Science Museum Library Archives, London.

The Whatman and Balston Archives, Kent County Archives, Maidstone.

Wilton, A., *The Revised Catalogue of the Drawings in the Turner Bequest*, In preparation.

Winsor & Newton Archives, Harrow, Middlesex.

TURNER

Bacharach, A.G.H. *Turner and Rotterdam*, 1974

Butlin, M. & E. Joll, *The Paintings of J.M.W. Turner*, 2 vols, 1984 (revised edition)

Chumbley, A. & Ian Warrell, *Turner and the Human Figure*, exhibition catalogue, 1989

Cormack, M., *J.M.W. Turner, R.A. 1775–1851. A catalogue of Drawings and Watercolours in the Fitzwilliam Museum*, Cambridge, 1975

Farington, J., *The Diary of Joseph Farington*, Yale 1979.

Finberg, A.J., *A Complete Inventory of the Drawings of the Turner Bequest . . .*, 2 vols, 1909

Finberg, A.J., *The History of Turner's 'Liber Studiorum'*, 1924

Finberg, A.J., *The Life of J.M.W. Turner*, 1961

Fitzwilliam Museum, Cambridge, *Gilpin to Ruskin: Drawing Masters and their Manuals, 1800–1860*, exhibition catalogue, 1988

Gage, J., *Colour in Turner: Poetry and Truth*, 1969

Gage, J., *J.M.W. Turner: 'A Wonderful Range of Mind'*, 1987

Gage, J., *George Field and His Circle*, exhibition catalogue, Cambridge, 1989

Hartley, C., *Turner Watercolours in the Whitworth Art Gallery*, Manchester, 1984

Herrmann, L., *Ruskin and Turner*, 1968

Herrmann, L., *Turner: Paintings, Watercolours, Prints and Drawings*, 1986

Hill, D., *In Turner's Footsteps*, 1984

Leitch, W.L., 'The Early History of Turner's Yorkshire Drawings', *Atheneum*, 1894

Lloyd, M., 'A Memoir of J.M.W. Turner, R.A. by "M.L."', reprinted in *Turner Studies*, 1984 Vol.4, no.1, p.22

Lyles, A., *Young Turner: Early Work to 1800*, exhibition catalogue, 1989

Lyles, A. & D. Perkins, *Colour into Line*, exhibition catalogue, 1989

Manchester City Art Gallery, *Turner at Manchester*, 1982

'M.I.H.', 'The Use of Indigo. Turner's Drawings', reprinted in *Turner Studies*, 1985, Vol.5, no.1, pp.25–26

Perkins, D., *Turner: The Third Decade*, exhibition catalogue, 1990

Powell, C., *Turner in the South*, 1987

Powell, C., 'Turner's Travelling Companion of 1802; A Mystery Resolved?', *Turner Society News*, 1990, no.54, pp.12–15

Rawlinson, W.G., *The Engraved Work of J.M.W. Turner, R.A.*, 2 vols. 1908–1913

Roget, J.L., *History of the Old Watercolour Society*, 1891

Shanes, E., *J.M.W. Turner: the Foundations of Genius*, exhibition catalogue, Taft Museum, Cincinatti, 1986

Smiles, S., 'The Devonshire Oil Sketches of 1813', *Turner Studies*, 1989, Vol.9, no.1, pp.10–26

Thornbury, W., *The Life of J.M.W. Turner R.A.*, 2 vols. 1862

Upstone, R., *Turner: The Second Decade*, exhibition catalogue, 1989

Upstone, R., 'Lyons: Picture Notes', *Turner Studies*, 1988, Vol.8. no.2, p.58

Wilkinson, G., *Early Sketchbooks: Drawings in England, Wales and Scotland*, 1972

Wilkinson, G., *The Sketches of Turner R.A.*, 1974

Wilton, A. and J. Russell, *Turner in Switzerland*, Zurich, 1976

Wilton, A., *The Life and Work of J.M.W. Turner*, 1979

Wilton, A., *Turner and the Sublime*, exhibition catalogue, 1980

Wilton, A., *Turner in Wales*, exhibition catalogue, 1984

Wilton, A., *Turner in his Time*, 1987

Wilton, A., *J.M.W. Turner: the 'Wilson' Sketchbook*, 1988

Wilton, A., 'A Rediscovered Turner Sketchbook', *Turner Studies*, 1986, Vol.6, no.2, pp.9–23

Wilton, A., 'Turner and the Iconography of Landscape', *Turner Society News*, 1988, no.49, pp.5–1

PAPER AND MATERIALS

'A Series of Articles on Writing Materials originally published in the *Saturday Magazine*, 1838–9, reprinted 1984

Balston, H., 'The Role of the Small Specialist in The Modern Environment', *Paper*, 10th May 1982

Balston, T., *James Whatman, Father & Son*, 1957

Balston, T., *William Balston, Paper Maker, 1759–1849*, 1954

Bath Chronicle, 29th July 1809

Boithias, J-L. and C. Mondin, *Les Moulins à Papier at les Anciens Papetiers d'Auvergne*, Nonette, 1981

Bolam, F., (ed), *Papermaking*, 1965

Bolam, F., (ed), *Stuff Preparation for Paper and Paperboard Making*, 1965

Bower, P.A.H., *Basic Principles of Papermaking*, 1980

Bower, P.A.H., 'Paper' from *The Calligrapher's Handbook*, 1985

Bower, P.A.H., 'J.M.W. Turner's use of paper: The first Swiss Tour, 1802. *The Quarterly*, 1989

Campbell, H., 'Remarks on the Present State of Papermaking in England and France' published in Nicholson's *Journal of Natural Philosophy*, Vol.2, 1802

Camus, A.G., 'Histoire et procédés du Polytypage', Paris 1802 republished in George A. Kubler, *Historical Treatises, Abstracts and Papers on Stereotyping*, New York, 1941

Chater, M., *Family Business: A History of Grosvenor Chater 1690–1977*, 1977

Churchill, W.A., *Watermarks in Paper*, Amsterdam, 1935

Clapperton, R.H., *The Papermaking Machine*, 1967

Cohen, C., *The James Mcbey Collection of Watermarked Paper*, Cambridge, Massachusetts, 1981

Cohen, C. and G. Wakeman, (eds), *The Art of Making Paper*, 1978

Coleman, D.C., *The British Paper Industry, 1495–1860*, 1958

Collinson, The Reverend J., *The History and Antiquities of the County of Somerset*, 1791

Dawe, E.A., *Paper and its Uses*, 2 vols. 1939

Evans, J., *The Endless Web: 1804–1954*, 1955

Evidence to the Fourdrinier Committee, 1837

Finlay, M., *Western Writing Implements*, 1990

Henry Cooke – Papermaker 1773–1973, 1973

Heawood, E., *Watermarks mainly of the 17th and 18th centuries*, Hilversum, 1986

Hickey, W., *Memoirs*

Hills, R.L., *Papermaking in Britain, 1488–1988*, 1988

Hunter, D., *Papermaking*, 1974

Juries of The Royal Commission for the Exhibition of The Works of Industry of All Nations, *Report on Paper*, 1851

Kälin-Sautter, Hans B., 'Wappen in Schweizer Wasserzeichen', *I P H Yearbook 1986*

Krill, J., *English Artists Paper*, 1987

Labarre, E.J., *Dictionary and Encyclopaedia of paper and paper-making*, Amsterdam, Second edition 1952

Lafaurie, J., *Les Assignats et les papiers-monnaies émis par l'état au XVIIIe siècle*, Paris, 1981

Le Français de la Lande, J.J., *L'Art de Faire le Papier*, 1761

Les Papeteries Johannot à Annonay, Lyon, 1935

Loeber, E.G., *Supplement to E.J. Labarre's Dictionary and Encyclopaedia of Paper and Paper-making*, Amsterdam, 1967

Loeber, E.G., *Paper Mould and Mouldmaker*, Amsterdam, 1982

Lyddon, D. and P. Marshall, *Paper in Bolton, A Papermakers Tale*, 1975.

London Gazette, May 1–5 1804

Mayer, R. *The Artists Handbook of Materials and Techniques*, 1987

Murray, J., *Observations and Experiments on the Bad Composition of Modern Paper*, 1824

Osborne, R., *Lights and Pigments*, 1980

'Paper' from *The Cyclopaedia or Universal Dictionary*, 1819

'Paper' from *The Encyclopaedia Brittanica*, 1797

'Paper' from *The Engineers and Mechanics Encyclopaedia*, 1836

Portal, Sir Francis, Bt., *Portals*, Oxford, 1962

Proceedings at the Old Bailey, 1770–1, No.VII, case 610 on the Trial of Edward Burch and Mathew Martin

Reynaud, Marie-Hélène, *Les Moulins à Papier d'Annonay à l'ére préindustrielle*, Annonay, 1985

Shorter, A.H., *Paper Making in the British Isles*, 1971

Shorter, A.H., *Paper Mills and Papermakers in England, 1495–1800*, Hilversum, 1957

Staples, P.J., *The Artists' Colourmen's Story*, 1984

Thomson, A.G., *The Paper Industry in Scotland, 1590–1861*, 1974

Index

Abbreviations: pm = papermaker.
Paper mills are listed alphabetically and grouped under Paper Mills.
All watermarks and countermarks (indicated by +) are listed under Watermarks, and in the form that they appear in the sheet. / indicates a change of line within the watermark.